Cambridge IGCSE®
Literature in English

STUDENT'S BOOK

Also for Cambridge IGCSE (9-1), Cambridge O Level
and Cambridge IGCSE World Literature

Mike Gould, Chris Green,
Kurt A. Johnson, Alexandra Melville
Series Editor: Anna Gregory

William Collins' dream of knowledge for all began with the publication of his first book in 1819.

A self-educated mill worker, he not only enriched millions of lives, but also founded a flourishing publishing house. Today, staying true to this spirit, Collins books are packed with inspiration, innovation and practical expertise. They place you at the centre of a world of possibility and give you exactly what you need to explore it.

Collins. Freedom to teach.

Published by Collins

An imprint of HarperCollins*Publishers*
The News Building
1 London Bridge Street
London
SE1 9GF

Browse the complete Collins catalogue at
www.collins.co.uk

© HarperCollins*Publishers* Limited 2018

10 9 8 7 6 5 4 3 2 1

ISBN 978-0-00-826203-7

All rights reserved. No part of this publication may be reproduced, stored in a retrieval system, or transmitted in any form by any means, electronic, mechanical, photocopying, recording or otherwise, without the prior written permission of the Publisher or a licence permitting restricted copying in the United Kingdom issued by the Copyright Licensing Agency Ltd., Barnard's Inn, 86 Fetter Lane, London, EC4A 1EN.

British Library Cataloguing in Publication Data

A catalogue record for this publication is available from the British Library.

Authors: Mike Gould, Chris Green, Kurt A. Johnson, Alexandra Melville
Development editor: Judith Walters
Series editor: Anna Gregory
Commissioning editor: Catherine Martin
In-house editor: Alexander Rutherford
Copyeditor: Catherine Dakin
Proofreader: Claire Throp
Photo researcher: Alexandra Wells
Cover designers: Kevin Robbins and Gordan MacGlip
Cover illustrator: Maria Herbert-Liew
Typesetter: Jouve India
Production controller: Tina Paul
Printed and bound by: Grafica Veneta SpA

®IGCSE is a registered trademark

All exam-style questions, sample answers and commentary in this title were written by the authors. In examinations, the way marks are awarded may be different.

MIX
Paper from
responsible sources
FSC® C007454

This book is produced from independently certified FSC paper to ensure responsible forest management.

For more information visit:
www.harpercollins.co.uk/green

We would like to thank the following international teachers for reviewing chapters of the book:

Marina Spyrou, Head of Languages Department, Pascal English School, Lefkosia, Cyprus;

Hannah Beeson, English Teacher, King's College Panama, The British School of Panama, Panama City, Panama; Stephen Partington, Principal and English and Literature Teacher, Lukenya Academy, Kenya; Matthew Pim, Head of Faculty for English and Humanities, GEMS Cambridge International School, Kampala, Uganda; Okan Önder, English Teacher, Bilkent Erzurum Laboratory School, Çat yolu üzeri Yıldızkent, Erzurum, Turkey; Rachel Evans, Principal, Nova School, Málaga, Spain; Naghma Shaikh, JBCN International, Borivali, Mumbai, India

Contents

Introduction: How to use this book v

Chapter 1 • Key concepts — 7

- 1.1 Understanding writers' use of language
- 1.2 Exploring character and characterisation
- 1.3 Introducing theme
- 1.4 Exploring settings
- 1.5 Understanding how form works
- 1.6 Understanding genre
- 1.7 Understanding structure
- 1.8 Exploring viewpoint and narration

Chapter 2 • Key skills — 33

- 2.1 Approaching a text
- 2.2 Referring to the text and selecting quotations
- 2.3 Exploring ideas and attitudes in texts
- 2.4 Exploring implied meaning
- 2.5 Exploring writers' methods
- 2.6 Communicating a personal response
- 2.7 Exploring alternative interpretations

Chapter 3 • Studying prose — 55

- 3.1 Approaching prose genres
- 3.2 Understanding plot
- 3.3 Exploring structure
- 3.4 Tackling themes
- 3.5 Exploring setting
- 3.6 Exploring character
- 3.7 Extension: Exploring character in depth
- 3.8 Viewpoint and narrative perspective
- 3.9 Extension: Exploring narrative style
- 3.10 Exploring language
- 3.11 Extension: Exploring symbolism
- 3.12 Viewing through context
- 3.13 Making interpretations
- 3.14 Planning and writing a critical essay
- 3.15 Evaluating your critical essay
- 3.16 Planning and writing a passage-based essay
- 3.17 Evaluating your passage-based essay
- 3.18 Planning and writing a critical commentary on unseen prose (IGCSE only)
- 3.19 Evaluating your critical commentary on unseen prose (IGCSE only)

Chapter 4 • Studying poetry — 125

- 4.1 What to expect when you read a poem
- 4.2 Exploring themes and ideas
- 4.3 Exploring language
- 4.4 Exploring form, sound, rhyme and rhythm
- 4.5 Exploring structure in poetry
- 4.6 Exploring setting in poetry
- 4.7 Viewpoint and perspective
- 4.8 Exploring speaker, voice and character in poetry
- 4.9 Understanding context in poetry
- 4.10 Making different interpretations
- 4.11 Planning and writing a critical essay
- 4.12 Evaluating your critical essay

4.13 Extension: Developing an overview
4.14 Evaluating your work
4.15 Planning and writing a critical commentary on an unseen poem (IGCSE only)
4.16 Evaluating your critical commentary on an unseen poem (IGCSE only)

Chapter 5 • Studying drama — 187

5.1 Approaching drama
5.2 Exploring dramatic genres
5.3 Exploring writers' use of dramatic structure
5.4 Understanding dramatic language
5.5 Understanding character in drama
5.6 Understanding dramatic characterisation
5.7 Exploring themes in drama
5.8 Analysing setting and staging
5.9 Evaluating the dramatic effectiveness of plays
5.10 Extension: Evaluating key points and moments
5.11 Planning and writing a critical essay
5.12 Evaluating your critical essay
5.13 Planning and writing a passage-based essay
5.14 Evaluating your passage-based essay

Chapter 6 • Preparing for coursework (optional in some Cambridge IGCSE courses) — 245

6.1 Preparing for a critical coursework essay
6.2 Planning a critical coursework essay
6.3 Writing a critical coursework essay
6.4 Planning and preparing an empathic response
6.5 Writing an empathic response
6.6 Evaluating your work: coursework-style responses

Glossary of key terms — 277
Acknowledgements — 279

Introduction

Collins *Cambridge IGCSE® Literature in English Student's Book*: introduction

The Collins *Cambridge IGCSE® Literature in English Student's Book* offers a skills-building approach to the Cambridge IGCSE®, IGCSE (9–1) and O Level Literature in English syllabuses and the IGCSE World Literature syllabus. It is designed to help you develop the skills you need to be successful in the study of literature, to explore your set texts in depth and tackle examinations with confidence.

In every chapter, you will read an exciting range of texts from different eras and cultures, chosen to expand your experience and enjoyment of literature in English.

How the book is structured

Chapters 1 and 2

Chapters 1 and 2 introduce the concepts, terminology and skills which underpin the Cambridge syllabuses. These chapters could be used as part of your transition from lower secondary, to recap and reinforce your existing knowledge.

Chapter 1 introduces you to the key concepts of literary study, from characterisation to form and structure. It is designed to help you begin to talk about the effects of writers' choices and to give you a vocabulary with which to do so.

Chapter 2 introduces you to the key skills you need to develop as a student of English Literature. These range from demonstrating your understanding of literary texts, to analysing language in depth, to responding in personal and original ways.

The focus here is on your own analytical writing: how you can write convincingly about the effects of writers' choices and begin to construct your own interpretations of texts.

Chapters 3, 4 and 5

Chapters 3, 4 and 5 provide a starting point from which to explore each of the major forms you will study in your course. The key concepts from Chapter 1 will be revisited in the context of poetry, prose or drama to help you appreciate what is unique about each form and the different methods poets, novelists and dramatists have at their disposal.

Your analysis and writing skills will be developed throughout. At the end of each chapter, you will be given the opportunity to apply your skills to a range of exam-style tasks, writing a critical essay, a response to a passage from a longer text and, in Chapters 3 and 4, a response to an unseen poem or prose passage.

These chapters can be used as a way into each of your set play(s), novel and poems or they can be dipped into throughout the course, in particular to hone your ability to respond to unfamiliar texts.

Extension lessons in these chapters ask you to take your thinking further by exploring a more challenging text or concept or by taking a more sophisticated approach to your own writing.

Chapter 6 (optional in some Cambridge IGCSE courses)

If your school is following the coursework route, Chapter 6 shows you how the skills and understanding developed in the rest of the book can be used to best effect in your critical or empathic coursework task.

How each lesson is structured

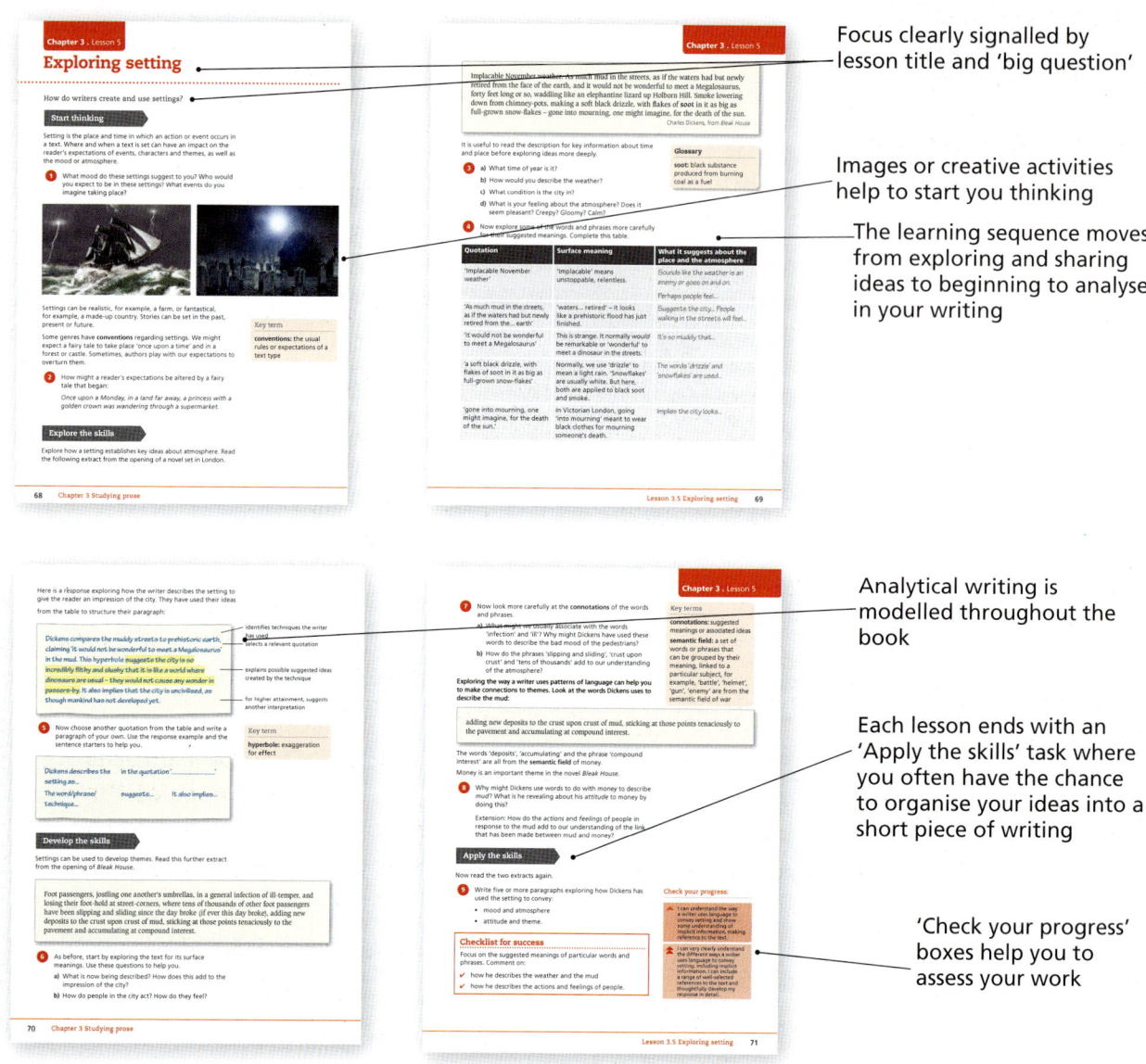

Checking your progress

Tasks are included throughout the book which could be used as assessment opportunities to help you gauge progress. The longer exam-style tasks are supported by sample responses at different levels to help you understand how you can improve your work. These sample tasks, responses and all commentary on the responses have been written by our author team, not by Cambridge International.

We hope our skills-building approach helps you to unlock the fundamentals of your Cambridge International Literature in English course and encourages you to read and enjoy a wide range of literary texts.

Anna Gregory
Series Editor

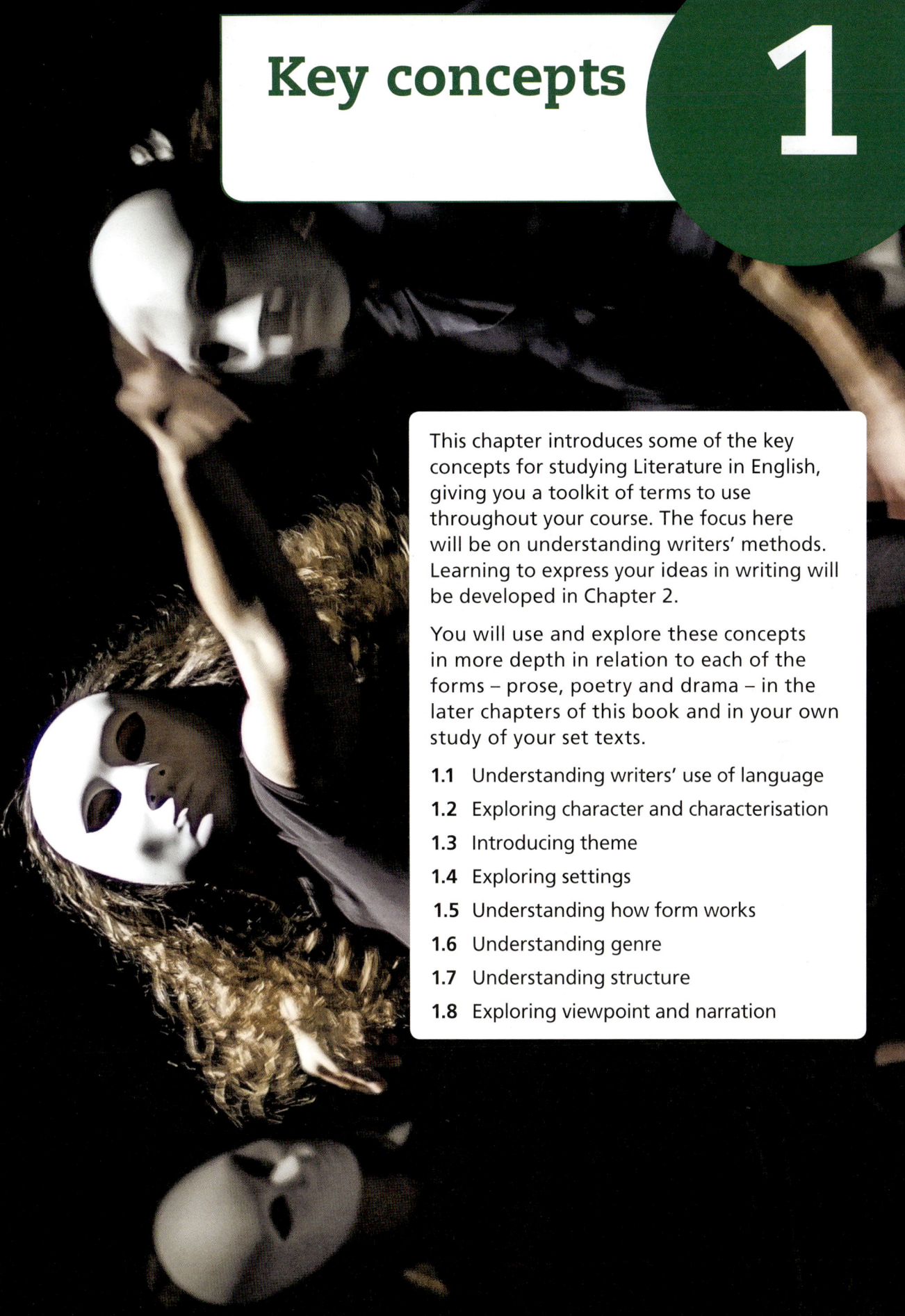

Key concepts 1

This chapter introduces some of the key concepts for studying Literature in English, giving you a toolkit of terms to use throughout your course. The focus here will be on understanding writers' methods. Learning to express your ideas in writing will be developed in Chapter 2.

You will use and explore these concepts in more depth in relation to each of the forms – prose, poetry and drama – in the later chapters of this book and in your own study of your set texts.

1.1 Understanding writers' use of language

1.2 Exploring character and characterisation

1.3 Introducing theme

1.4 Exploring settings

1.5 Understanding how form works

1.6 Understanding genre

1.7 Understanding structure

1.8 Exploring viewpoint and narration

Chapter 1 . Lesson 1

Understanding writers' use of language

How do writers use language to create different effects?

Start thinking

Even simple word choices can create very different meanings. For example, imagine you are describing a tree. You could write:

> *tall, emerald tree*

But just think of how many other descriptions you could create by simply replacing the two **adjectives**.

1 Write five further descriptions using this structure:

………. [*adjective*] …………..[*adjective*] tree

Think of adjectives to do with shape, colour, movement – or anything else. Make them as different as possible!

Key term

adjectives: words that describe a noun

Explore the skills

As you look closely at language, you should ask:

- What particular language choices has the writer made?
- How do these choices make me – and perhaps other readers – feel, or what do they make me think?
- What is the writer trying to express or make me imagine?

Read one poet's description about a place:

> By a dim road, o'ergrown with dry thin grass,
>
> Mary Coleridge, from 'Cut it down'

2 What two things has the writer chosen to describe?

3 What adjectives has she used in each case?

4 What feelings do these descriptions immediately evoke? Think of their **connotations**. Use the nouns from this word bank.

| wildness | richness | joy | loneliness | secrecy |
| well-being | isolation | bleakness | neglect | |

Key term

connotations: ideas or associations brought to mind beyond the literal or surface meaning

8 Chapter 1 Key concepts

Chapter 1 . Lesson 1

Now read the rest of the opening to the poem.

> By a dim road, o'ergrown with dry thin grass,
>   A little straggling, wild, wind-beaten tree,
> Stood, like a sentry, where no feet might pass,
>   And storm-swept by the sea.

 a) What do you imagine and feel when you read the verse? You could copy the lines on to a sheet of paper and write as many reactions as you can to individual words or phrases.

Look at the spider diagram below:

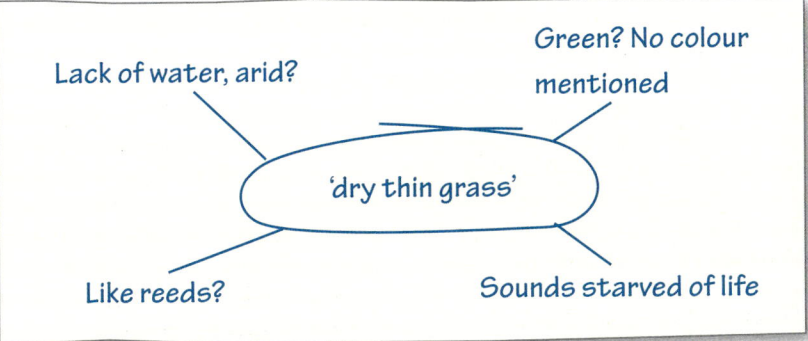

b) Complete the diagram for the rest of the poem, focusing on the adjectives in particular.

Imagery

Writers also use **imagery** to create effects. But what is imagery?

Key term

imagery: vivid pictures created by words and phrases

Device	Example	Effect
simile: comparison made between two different objects, people, and so on, using the word 'like' or 'as'	'a wind-beaten tree… <u>like a sentry</u>'	The comparison suggests the tree is watching over or guarding something – unwelcoming!
metaphor: a stronger form of comparison that states that something really *is* something else	Mary Coleridge could have written, 'a wind-beaten tree, *a sentry*, where no feet might pass…'	This stronger comparison stresses the impression that the tree is protecting or blocking out all humanity.
extended metaphor: takes a central comparison and revisits it in different ways through a text or extract	Mary Coleridge could have added: 'It stands guard along the road, warning us to keep away While armies of clouds gather in battle lines above…'	

Lesson 1.1 Understanding writers' use of language

6 How is the metaphor developed or extended in the third example? Which words link to the idea of conflict – and what impression is given of nature as a whole?

Sense effects

Writers often choose words that appeal to the senses.

7 a) Which of the five senses (sight, sound, touch, taste and smell) are evoked by the opening verse of this poem?

> The wind one morning sprang up from sleep,
> Saying, "Now for a frolic! now for a leap!
> Now for a mad-cap, galloping chase!
> I'll make a commotion in every place!"
> So it swept with a bustle right through a great town,
> Creaking the signs, and scattering down
> Shutters; and whisking, with merciless squalls,
> Old women's bonnets and gingerbread stalls.
> There never was heard a much lustier shout,
> As the apples and oranges trundled about;
> And the urchins, that stood with their thievish eyes
> Forever on watch, ran off each with a prize.
>
> William Howitt, from 'The Wind in a Frolic'

b) The highlighted parts in the poem create sound effects. Match the techniques to the highlighted sections.

Technique	Definition	Example
assonance	the repetition of vowel sounds in a sequence of words with different consonant beginnings	'rustling, bustling sound of her large wedding dress'
onomatopoeia	the sound of the word matches its meaning	'The car hit the wall with a *bang*, followed by the loud *hiss* as the tyre burst and air rushed out.'
repetition	repeated words or phrases for impact or rhythmic effect	'*Out, out*, brief candle!' (Shakespeare)
alliteration	repeated consonant sounds at the start of a sequence of words	'His *s*oul *s*wooned *s*lowly…' (James Joyce)

8 What overall effect about the wind is created by these uses of sound? Think about: pace and rhythm, mood and atmosphere.

Chapter 1 . Lesson 1

Develop the skills

Sentence structure and variety

Writers also choose the shape, type and length of sentences carefully to create effects.

The following extract is from a novel about Claire, a piano teacher in Hong Kong in the 1940s.

> **9** What different sentence lengths and styles do you notice here? Look for:
> - short or simple **statements**
> - **exclamations** or **minor sentences**
> - longer sentences developing thoughts or ideas.

Key terms

statements: sentences in which a main idea or event is declared

exclamations: phrases or sentences which indicate surprise, shock or anger

minor sentences: phrases that stand for a whole sentence but omit an element, such as the subject

> It started as an accident. The small **Herend** rabbit had fallen into Claire's handbag. It had been on the piano and she had been gathering up the sheet music at the end of the lesson when she knocked it off. It fell off the doily (a doily! On the **Steinway**!) and into her large leather bag. What had happened after that was perplexing, even to her. Locket had been staring down at the keyboard, and hadn't noticed. And then, Claire had just… left. It wasn't until she was downstairs and waiting for the bus that she grasped what she had done. And then it had been too late. She went home and buried the expensive porcelain figurine under her sweaters.
>
> Janice Y. K. Lee, from *The Piano Teacher*

Glossary

Herend: a type of luxury, hand-painted porcelain

Steinway: a very expensive type of piano

> **10** Why do you think the writer has used a range of sentence types and styles? Read the text aloud, listening for the changes in pace and tone, and then consider:
> - how the writer arouses our curiosity
> - how the writer emphasises points for emotional power or surprise
> - how the writer explains things the character does.

Apply the skills

> What overall impression do you get of Claire and her thoughts from this paragraph, based on the points you have considered above?

Check your progress:

 I can recognise the language choices writers make.

 I can explain the effects of these choices.

Lesson 1.1 Understanding writers' use of language   **11**

Chapter 1 . Lesson 2

Exploring character and characterisation

What are 'characters' and how do writers create them?

Start thinking

Most successful stories involve a central **character** – a person who you would say the story is about.

1 a) As a game, in one minute, write down as many names of main characters as you can think of – and the story or tale each character comes from. For example:

Mowgli – *The Jungle Book*

Dracula – *Dracula* (!)

b) Spend a minute or two thinking or discussing what it is about these characters that makes them so memorable. How do they influence the plot?

Explore the skills

The process of creating characters is called **characterisation**. The methods writers use to make their inventions come to life include:

- describing their appearance and clothing
- showing how they speak and what they say
- showing how they move (gestures and actions) and behave
- showing how others speak or react towards them.

2 Look at this image of a well-known character from a Charles Dickens novel. How do you imagine he would move and speak, based on his appearance?

12 Chapter 1 Key concepts

Setting is also part of characterisation: the place a character lives or spends time in can give an insight into what they are like.

3 For example, imagine each of these was a stage design for a play. What sort of character might be found in:

- a modern grey-walled apartment, functional with no artwork or books, plain sofa and hard metal chairs
- a dusty sitting room with battered old leather sofa, shelves of old books, and an oak desk looking out onto a sunny orchard
- a narrow alleyway with grimy water running down the middle and shadows cast by a flickering iron lamp high up on a window-ledge?

Use your imagination! You could add a sentence introducing your character to each description. You could start: *Enter a ……….*

Characters are sometimes categorised. This can help writers and readers to understand their function – what they are *for* in a story. For example:

the protagonist	The main character whose actions we follow – and is the main 'driver' in the plot; he or she is aiming to do something, get somewhere, learn something.
the antagonist	Often an equally important character, but in the story is the one who causes problems or is an obstacle to the protagonist.
minor character	A character who may influence the story but is not the main focus.
'flat' character	Minor characters may be – though not always – straightforward and 'flat' in that the reader never really gets to see their thought processes or **empathises** with them in the same way as a main character.
'rounded' or multi-dimensional characters	'Rounded' characters are characters we learn a lot about and whose feelings and motives are explained. Multi-dimensional characters are those who have a range of aspects to them – perhaps surprising ones (for example, an apparent villain who we learn is a carer for his old mother).

> **Key terms**
>
> **empathises:** able to put yourself in the shoes of someone else and understand their situation
>
> **narration:** the telling, or manner of telling, of a story

You can usually tell who the protagonist of a story is from the **narration**. If the story is told in the first person ('I') then it is likely that this person is the protagonist – the reader is following their experiences.

Lesson 1.2 Exploring character and characterisation   13

Read this extract about a young girl called Lu Si-yan and then answer the questions that follow.

My mother stood in the shadows of our kitchen, but she didn't look at me and she didn't say a word. Uncle took me tightly by the wrist. As he led me from the house, my mother reached out her hand towards me and clawed the air as though trying to pull me back. Then she picked up my little brother and hid behind the door, but I saw her face wither with pain and, in that moment, fear gripped my heart.

'Where are you taking me, Uncle Ba?' I cried.

'It's for the best,' he replied, his mouth set grimly.

'You're hurting my arm,' I cried.

Sally Grindley, from *Spilled Water*

4 How does the writer present the three characters in this extract?

   a) Who might be the protagonist and the antagonist?

   b) Are there any 'flat' characters here?

5 Consider the characterisation of each of the three people mentioned in the extract. Copy and complete this table, filling in any information that is given in the text.

Character	Appearance	Speech and actions	How others react	Overall impression?
Lu Si-yan	n/a	Asks questions; 'cried' out; watches her mother closely.	Uncle holds her wrist 'tightly', and hurts her arm. Mother can't look at her or speak.	Innocent girl who doesn't understand what's happening. Makes us feel sorry for her.
Uncle				
Mother				

Develop the skills

A key aspect of characterisation is change: the 'journey' a character goes on. Sometimes this is a real one, or it could also be an emotional one.

Chapter 1 . Lesson 2

Read this further extract from *Spilled Water*. It comes from the end of the book after Lu Si-yan has been sold as a servant, but has finally escaped. In doing so, she has been taken ill, but her Uncle Ba has found her.

> 'I have travelled a thousand miles to find you, Si-yan. I had all but given up when the hospital made contact.'
>
> 'Why so much effort, Uncle Ba?' I turned towards him. He looked shrunken somehow, and haggard. He avoided my gaze and sat back down in the chair. Then he leant forward and tried to take my hand. I pulled it away sharply. How dared he?

6 How have both characters changed from the earlier extract? Think about the methods writers use to convey character: their appearance, speech, movement, actions and reactions.

A character's 'journey' can take many forms.

Key terms

Bildungsroman: German term meaning 'education or growth novel'

adversary: enemy or rival

A character:

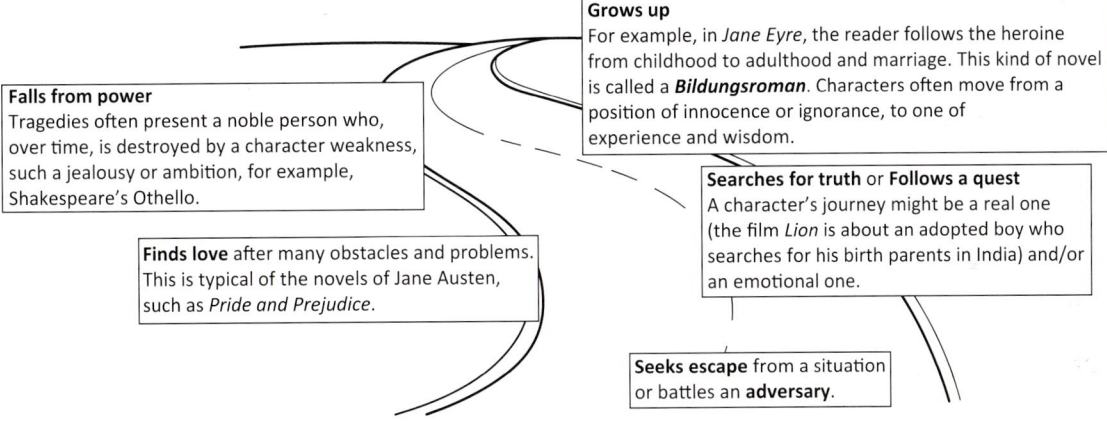

Grows up
For example, in *Jane Eyre*, the reader follows the heroine from childhood to adulthood and marriage. This kind of novel is called a ***Bildungsroman***. Characters often move from a position of innocence or ignorance, to one of experience and wisdom.

Falls from power
Tragedies often present a noble person who, over time, is destroyed by a character weakness, such as jealousy or ambition, for example, Shakespeare's *Othello*.

Searches for truth or **Follows a quest**
A character's journey might be a real one (the film *Lion* is about an adopted boy who searches for his birth parents in India) and/or an emotional one.

Finds love after many obstacles and problems. This is typical of the novels of Jane Austen, such as *Pride and Prejudice*.

Seeks escape from a situation or battles an **adversary**.

Of course, many stories combine these elements too.

Apply the skills

7 Thinking of your set texts, or any stories you know, are there any examples where a character goes on a journey – either an emotional one or a real one (or both)?

a) What are they like at the beginning?

b) How does what they experience change them?

c) What are they like at the end of the story?

Check your progress:

▲ I can understand the different sorts of characters which can be found in texts.

▲ I can explain the techniques writers use to develop characters.

Lesson 1.2 Exploring character and characterisation   15

Chapter 1 . Lesson 3

Introducing theme

What are themes and how can I identify them in texts?

Start thinking

In very simple terms, there are three ways to approach a text:

- The first is to explore *what* story it tells: what happens when, where and to whom.
- The second is to consider *how* it is told – for example, the writer's structural or language choices.
- The third is: *why* it is told. Does the writer, or the text, have something more to say or show readers than a set of interesting events or vivid descriptions? What larger issues or experiences does the text make readers think about?

This third approach relates to the **themes** of the text – the *ideas* that arise or are explored by the writer through the *what* and the *how*. These are often expressed in **abstract** nouns or phrases such as 'Ambition', 'Conflict' or 'Growing up'.

> **Key terms**
>
> **themes:** key ideas running through a text
>
> **abstract:** the opposite of concrete; something that cannot be seen, like an emotion

1 Here are the blurbs from two well-known stories/films. Can you identify the words or phrases from the blurbs that suggest what the themes are?

Two young lovers from rival families in Verona fall in love. Can they escape the violent conflict between their families, or the hand of Fate? Or will their hopes and dreams end in tragedy?

An actress and a jazz pianist in Los Angeles are unsure whether to follow their dreams and ambitions, or stay together for love. Whatever path they choose, someone will get hurt...

16   Chapter 1 Key concepts

Chapter 1 . Lesson 3

Explore the skills

2 Think of any recent film or story that you have seen or read.

  a) Briefly jot down the events: the *what*, *who*, *where* and *when*.

  b) Then, look at some of these 'theme words'. Which, if any, fit the film/story you're thinking of? Can you think of others?

  > loneliness   regret   love   loss   family   change
  > memory   childhood   poverty   fate

Often, it is useful to describe themes in more specific ways.

For example:

- *How* ambition can destroy a reputation
- Conflict *between* old and young
- Growing up *in* the 1960s

But how do you identify the core idea or theme?

Read the following verse from a poem about a successful farmer called Yusman Ali.

> His life fell and broke like a brown jug on a stone
> In middle age his four sons drowned in one boat up a pleasant river,
> The wife's heart cracked and Yusman Ali was alone, alone, alone.
> Madness howled in his head. His green fields died.
> He burns the wild wood in his barren yard alone…
>
> Ian Macdonald, from 'Yusman Ali, Charcoal Seller'

3 What are the bare facts of the story? Do they tell you anything? (For example, are they happy, sad, funny or weird?)

4 How does the language make you feel? Does it create a particular mood? Copy and complete the table below.

Word or phrase	Meaning	Mood or emotion suggested
'His life *fell and broke* like a *brown jug on a stone*' And 'Wife's heart *cracked*…'	His life as he knew it ended. His wife died or was heartbroken. Both were like ornaments that were broken and couldn't be mended.	Tragic – it is so sudden Sad – he loses everything
'*alone, alone, alone*…' and 'in his *barren* yard *alone*'		
'Madness *howled*…'		
'*Green* fields *died*…'		

Lesson 1.3 Introducing theme   17

From this sort of analysis, you can start to deduce the theme(s). Read two students' explanations of this part of the poem:

Jed:

The poem is incredibly sad; you can't help but feel sorry for Ali who is left totally 'alone' after the tragic accident. He even loses his business – it seems like everything is against him. Even his 'green fields' die.

Nadja:

The poem explores loss and the effect it has on people. The simile of the broken jug and the linked metaphor of the 'cracked' heart show how deep the suffering is. Another key idea is isolation – how a sudden tragic event can leave you totally alone in the world.

5 Which of these two responses focuses more on the *themes* of the poem? Write down any 'theme words' used by Jed or Nadja that suggest this.

Develop the skills

Another key skill you will need to develop is being able to trace themes across a text. This might be through the different verses of a poem – or in different chapters of a book, or acts of a play. The way a writer treats or explores a theme may change, or the theme may be broken up into different sub-themes. For example:

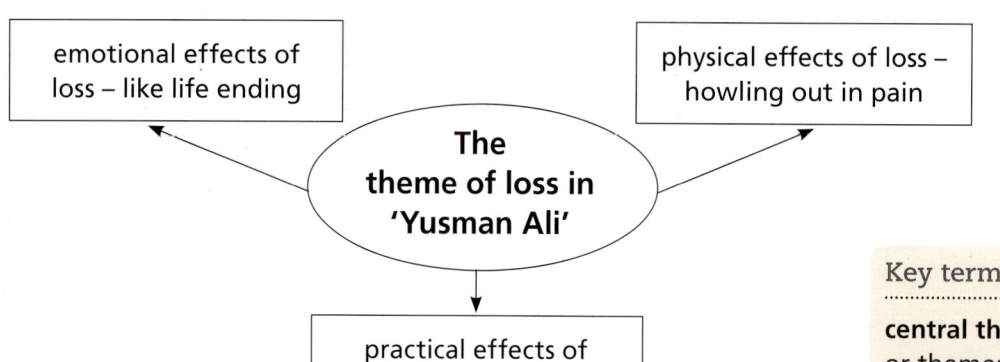

Key terms

central themes: key ideas or themes that occur throughout a text

secondary theme: a less important theme or idea that is either explored in less depth, or is only relevant to certain parts of the text

The main theme is loss, but each line from the poem deals with a different aspect of it.

Equally, writers often explore more than one theme in a text. Some of these will be **central themes**, others **secondary** or less important themes or ones that are especially relevant to a particular part of the text.

Chapter 1 . Lesson 3

Read this summary of Laila Lalami's short story, 'The Homecoming'.

> Aziz has been away working in Spain for five years sending money back to his wife in Morocco. Finally, he returns for two weeks but his time away has changed him, and Morocco has changed too. He finds it difficult to fit back into life, is bored and struggles to connect with his wife, even though he still finds her 'beautiful'. When she realises he is not coming home for good, she decides to join him in Madrid, but he tells her he hasn't earned enough for her papers and leaves.

6 Based on this summary, what do you think the themes of the story are? Consider:
- the main or central themes
- the secondary themes.

For example, would 'how Morocco has changed' be a central or secondary theme?

Apply the skills

Now read this short extract from the end of 'The Homecoming' and answer the questions that follow. Aziz is about to leave Morocco to return to Madrid.

> 'When are you sending me the papers?' she asked, at last.
>
> 'I don't know,' he replied.
>
> Zohra started crying. Aziz tapped her shoulder in an awkward attempt at consolation. He couldn't imagine her with him in Madrid. She was used to the neighbours' kid pushing the door open and coming in. She was used to the outdoor market, where she could haggle over everything. She was used to having her relatives drop by without notice. He couldn't think of her alone in an apartment, with no one to talk to, while he was at work. And he, too, had his own habits now. He closed his suitcase and lifted it off the bed. It felt lighter than when he had arrived.
>
> Laila Lalami, from 'The Homecoming'

7 How is the theme of separation explored in this extract? Think about:

a) how Zohra responds to Aziz

b) what Aziz thinks about Zohra coming to Madrid

c) what he says about himself.

8 Are any other secondary themes touched upon in this extract? If so, which?

9 Why does the writer choose to end with the image of the suitcase? Think about what Aziz says about its weight at the start and end of his stay.

Check your progress:

▲ I understand what themes are and can identify them in some texts.

▲ I understand and can explain some of the different ways themes are explored by writers.

Lesson 1.3 Introducing theme   19

Chapter 1. Lesson 4

Exploring settings

How does understanding a writer's use of setting help me understand the text as a whole?

Start thinking

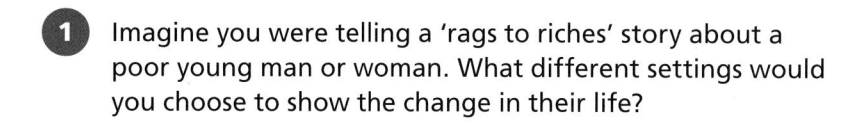

1 Imagine you were telling a 'rags to riches' story about a poor young man or woman. What different settings would you choose to show the change in their life?

Explore the skills

Writers often convey important ideas or plot development through settings, but the term can mean different things.

For example, it can refer to:

- a specific physical place – a hallway, a building or a lake
- a more general place, such as a city or country
- an event or occasion, such as a football match or a wedding.

2 Which kind of setting is being described in each of these examples?

a) It is a northern country; they have cold weather, they have cold hearts.

Cold; tempest; wild beasts in the forest. It is a hard life.

Angela Carter, from 'The Werewolf'

b) Bolted and locked since the war by long-dead hands,
Next to the shadowy church, the closed school stands.

Raymond Wilson, from 'The Closed School'

c) She clutched her fan, and, gazing at the gleaming, golden floor, the azaleas, the lanterns, the stage at one end with its red carpet and gilt chairs and the band in a corner, she thought breathlessly, "How heavenly; how simply heavenly!"

Katherine Mansfield, from 'Her First Ball'

Chapter 1 Key concepts

Chapter 1 . Lesson 4

3 How would you describe the mood created by each of the descriptions above? Focus on particular words or phrases and what they reveal as you explain your answer.

Select a sentence or phrase and annotate it with your ideas.

For example:

> … they have **cold** weather, they have **cold** hearts.
>
> Cold; **tempest;** wild beasts in the forest. It is a hard life.

- 'cold' here means bad weather – which links to the storm
- 'cold' in this case means unfriendly, or emotionless

How do the other descriptions add to the unwelcoming mood?

4 Which of the descriptions of setting provides an insight into a character's feelings? What particular features of the setting tell us this?

Develop the skills

Now read this longer extract from 'The Homecoming' by Laila Lalami. Aziz has returned, after some years, to his home town. He is on a bus.

> Aziz sat by a window and looked at the streets passing by. New buildings had sprung up everywhere, squat apartments with tiny windows that had been outlined with Mediterranean tiles, in a futile attempt to make them more appealing. Internet cafes were now interspersed with tailor shops and hairdressers. He was startled away from the window when a bus coming in the other direction passed by, only inches away.
>
> Laila Lalami, from 'The Homecoming'

5 What do the highlighted sections tell us about the city, as Aziz experiences it? Make notes on:
- how the city has changed
- what the traffic is like.

6 What do these descriptions suggest about Aziz himself?

Apply the skills

7 Write a paragraph about 'The Homecoming', explaining how the setting reveals Aziz's state of mind.

Check your progress:

▲ I can recognise the way settings are used by writers for different effects.

▲ I can explain how particular words and phrases related to setting create meaning and impact.

Lesson 1.4 Exploring settings   21

Chapter 1 . Lesson 5

Understanding how form works

How can I recognise aspects of form in texts?

Start thinking

Look at the short text below:

> 'Twas on the shores that round our coast
>   From Deal to Ramsgate span.
> That I found alone on a piece of stone
>   An elderly naval man.
> His hair was weedy, his beard was long,
>   And weedy and long was he,
> And I heard this **wight** on the shore recite,
>   In a singular minor key: [...]
>
> W. S. Gilbert, from 'The Yarn of the Nancy Bell'

1 What *sort* of text is this? *(a poem? a novel? a play?)*

2 What clues tell you this?

Glossary

wight: creature

Explore the skills

Each **form** has its own conventions or patterns, and by paying attention to these, you can explore the effects created.

Key term

form: a set of agreed conventions or rules which give an identifiable shape to a piece of literary writing

3 Read the following descriptions of different **forms**. Which one describes:

- novels
- poetry
- drama (plays)?

a.	Has a series of events, uses descriptive detail, characters, and takes the reader on a journey towards a conclusion. Usually split into chapters.
b.	Presents a story, using mostly dialogue and movement to show events and characters to the reader/audience. Often divided into scenes or acts.
c.	Condenses ideas, using the ideas behind the words, sounds of the words (sometimes in rhyme or through rhythms), and ways they are organised to tell a story or describe a feeling or an idea.

Chapter 1 Key concepts

Chapter 1 . Lesson 5

Develop the skills

Certain forms suit particular stories or ideas. Oscar Wilde's plays depend on social interaction and witty use of speech – perfectly suited to drama. Read the opening to *The Importance of Being Earnest*.

Morning-room in Algernon's flat in Half-Moon Street. The room is luxuriously and artistically furnished. The sound of a piano is heard in the adjoining room.

[Lane is arranging afternoon tea on the table, and after the music has ceased, Algernon enters.]

ALGERNON   Did you hear what I was playing, Lane?

LANE   I didn't think it polite to listen, sir.

ALGERNON   I'm sorry for that, for your sake. I don't play accurately—any one can play accurately—but I play with wonderful expression. As far as the piano is concerned, sentiment is my **forte**. I keep science for Life.

Oscar Wilde, from *The Importance of Being Earnest*

Glossary

forte: strength

4 What do you notice about the form? Look closely at:
- the layout: where the names are, how speech is shown
- the language: how movement or style of speaking is shown; the tense used for actions.

5 How well suited is the form to its story, in your opinion? Would it work as well as a poem?

Now read the following extract.

"There never is anyone in the mill, surely!" exclaimed Mary, as the sea of upward-turned faces moved with one accord to the eastern end, looking into Dunham Street, the narrow back lane already mentioned.

The western end of the mill, whither the raging flames were driven by the wind, was crowned and turreted with triumphant fire. It sent forth its infernal tongues from every window hole, licking the black walls with amorous fierceness; it was swayed or fell before the mighty gale, only to rise higher and yet higher, to ravage and roar yet more wildly.

Elizabeth Gaskell, from *Mary Barton*

---

6 Which literary form (play, poem or story) does this passage belong to? What conventions does it use?

7 What would you need to do to turn it into a piece of drama? What challenges would you face?

Check your progress:

▲ I can recognise how the form of plays, poems and stories differ.

▲ I can recognise different forms of writing and understand how these can influence their impact or meaning.

Apply the skills

8 Rewrite part or all of the passage above as a poem using what you know of poetic form. Once you have finished, consider what has been gained or lost.

Lesson 1.5 Understanding how form works   23

Chapter 1 . Lesson 6

Understanding genre

Why is it important to know about different styles and types of text?

Start thinking

1 Look at these four covers of plays or novels. Can you tell what genre of text each one is? Which would appeal to you the most?

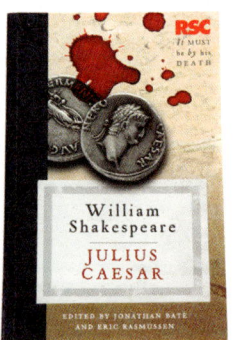 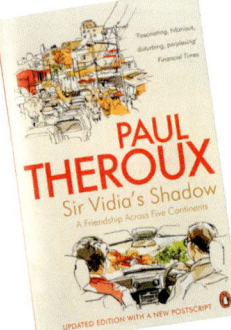 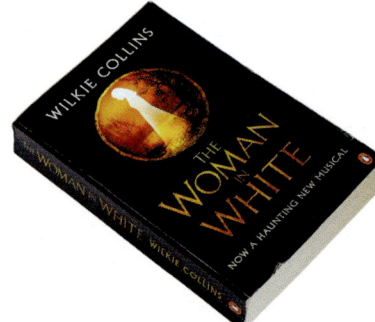 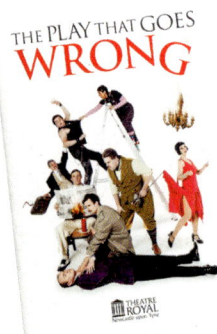

Explore the skills

The term **genre** means 'group' or 'type'. Each of the texts above belongs to a particular genre. This means that the text shares features with other similar texts.

For example:

> **Key terms**
>
> **flaw:** a character weakness, such as pride
>
> **pastoral:** of the countryside

Genre	Comedy	Tragedy
plot	A misunderstanding, disguises, someone trying to fool another person, people falling in or out of love. Often ends in marriage or reconciled rivals.	A noble or important person who suffers a fall from grace due to some sort of character **flaw**. Has powerful emotions and may include violent or dramatic events. Usually ends in death or suicide for the hero or main character/s.
setting or background	Often, but not always, homely settings such as family houses, streets, **pastoral** scenes.	Wartime or tribal/political conflict; battlefields, castles or government buildings.
characters	Young lovers, but sometimes older people as figures of fun.	Royalty or important/respected people.

Chapter 1 Key concepts

Chapter 1 . Lesson 6

2 In what way does the following play description fit one of the two genres above?

> A young prince believes his father, the King, was murdered by his Uncle. He contemplates revenge but makes the mistake of thinking too much about the situation, thus causing a chain of events which leads to the death of others and, ultimately, himself.

The other two genres represented by the covers opposite are 'the Gothic' and the non-fiction 'travel writing'.

3 a) What would you expect the main **conventions** of travel writing to be?

b) Have you heard of **Gothic literature**? Can you think of any typical gothic tales?

Develop the skills

Language can also give a clue to a text's genre. Silly **puns** and other forms of word-play are common in comedies, whilst heightened language (exaggerated or powerful descriptions of setting or behaviour) is a key feature of tragedy or gothic stories.

For example:

> He looked ==wildly== round him, expecting that some ==dreadful== apparition would meet his eyes, the sight of which would ==drive him mad==. A cold shivering ==seized== his body, and he ==sank== upon one knee.
>
> Matthew Lewis, from *The Monk*

Key terms

conventions: typical features of a text

Gothic literature: a popular form of storytelling which came to prominence in the 17th century. It is a very broad genre but often includes supernatural or dream-like happenings; a villain who seeks to destroy or corrupt an innocent, younger person; gloomy, remote settings such as castles or ruins in mountainous areas or forests

puns: usually playing on two meanings of the same word or two words with the same sound to create humour. For example: 'I know the best *plaice* to buy fish'

4 Replace the highlighted words and phrases with the following. How do they change the effect? Do they make it less gothic?

| uncertainly | nasty | disturb him a bit | got hold of | went down |

Apply the skills

Texts do not always belong to just one genre. Often they will combine elements of different genres.

5 Consider any of the plays, poems or novels you are studying. Write a paragraph explaining:
- what genre or genres you believe they are influenced by
- any reasons why this might be the case.

Check your progress:

▲ I can identify some basic conventions of well-known genres.

▲ I can explain how texts can be a mix of different genres.

Lesson 1.6 Understanding genre   25

Chapter 1 . Lesson 7

Understanding structure

What is structure and why is it important?

Start thinking

1. Imagine you are writing an **autobiography** of your life so far.
   - Where would you begin? (With your birth? Or would you choose a different focus, such as your family's background?)
   - How would you divide it up? (Would you have chapters for every year you have lived – or separate it in a different way?)
   - What would you include? (Everything? Or particular key moments?)

These kinds of decisions would help to shape the **structure** of your story. This is a vital element of any text, and affects the way the reader responds.

Across a whole text, structure can refer to the following:

- the plot: the order or sequence in which events or information is revealed to the reader (for example, whether it is **chronological** or involves **flashbacks**, what tense/s are used)
- how a text is divided up (for example, through verses or paragraphs and what is included or left out of them)
- repeating patterns (for example, some old stories involve a traveller meeting three different people or facing three challenges during a **quest**)
- how a text begins and ends (for example, whether the ending returns to the start).

2. Think of a well-known folk or fairy tale from your own culture or which you heard as a child. Make brief notes on its structure. (What order is it told in? Are there any repeated patterns or links?)

> **Key term**
>
> **autobiography:** someone's life story told from their own point of view

> **Key terms**
>
> **chronological:** told in the order in which things actually happened
>
> **flashbacks:** when a character suddenly goes back in time to earlier events
>
> **quest:** a journey in search of something or someone

26   Chapter 1 Key concepts

Chapter 1 . Lesson 7

Explore the skills

One way of describing structure in stories is through a five-stage pyramid which shows how the plot or action develops.

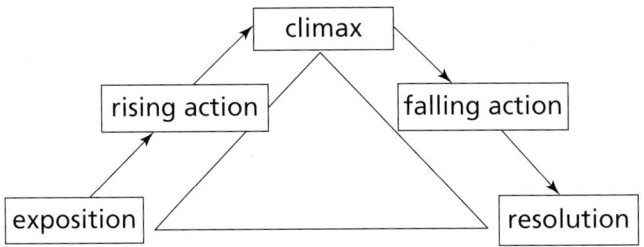

exposition	the beginning – the way things are before the 'real action' begins
rising action	the hero faces problems or obstacles that must be overcome
climax	the turning point or most dramatic moment
falling action	the events that follow on from the climax
resolution	the end of the main character's story/tying up of any loose ends for good or bad

3 Read this summary of one version of the Chinese tale 'Mulan'. Can you re-sequence the events and match each section to the stages in the pyramid?

a) Mulan's father is old and has no sons. She is washing clothes when she finds out that the army is recruiting new soldiers.

b) There is a terrible battle and Mulan fights heroically. The emperor wants to reward her, but is astonished to discover she is female!

c) Mulan asks for nothing but a horse to ride home.

d) Her father is too old and unwell to fight, so she decides to join the army as his 'son' and disguises herself as a man. She leaves carrying the sword inherited from the ancestors of the family. She fights bravely for over a decade.

e) She returns to her home town but sadly discovers that her father has passed away.

Lesson 1.7 Understanding structure 27

Of course, structure is equally – perhaps even more – important in poetry. Poets make a range of choices about structure to create impact or recount an experience. For example:

Structural devices	Choices poets have to make
dividing up the text as a whole	Should I keep it as one continuous 'block' of words or separate it into verses? If so, what will each line or verse focus on?
line or verse patterns	Should any of my lines or verses be repeated? If so, which and why?
sound, rhyme or rhythm patterns	Should I use a particular rhyme pattern? Should there be a regular rhythm or beat to each line, or should it change?
the overall shape	Should I create a link in language, sound or ideas between the start and end of the poem?
time	Will my poem shift in time between the present, the past and the future – or simply stick to one time or moment? If so, how will this be shown?
voice	Will the voice or perspective stay the same throughout – or will it shift to a new person, place, and so on?

Read the first two verses of Emily Brontë's poem, 'Remembrance'.

> Cold in the earth—and the deep snow piled above thee,
> Far, far removed, cold in the dreary grave!
> Have I forgot, my only Love, to love thee,
> **Severed** at last by Time's all-severing wave?
>
> Now, when alone, do my thoughts no longer hover
> Over the mountains, on that northern shore,
> Resting their wings where heath and fern-leaves cover
> Thy noble heart forever, ever more?
>
> Emily Brontë, from 'Remembrance'

4 How many structural devices can you identify here? For example, think about:
- the repetition of particular words or phrases
- the use of rhyme
- anything else you notice.

Glossary

Severed: cut in two with a sharp blade

5 Poets' use of structure is very deliberate, so you need to think about what response it creates in you. For example, the following words all appear twice in the first verse: 'cold', 'far', 'love', 'thee', 'severed/severing'. What mood or feel do these words create?

6 Both verses contain questions. What do you think the speaker is asking? What do you call this structural feature and how does it contribute to the text's effect?

Develop the skills

You have seen from the poem that structure is not just about the whole text. For example, the second line of the poem is:

'Far, far removed, cold in the dreary grave!'

The repetition of 'far' emphasises how distant and deep the burial of the loved one is. But the line could also have been structured:

'Cold in the dreary grave, far, far removed!'

7 How would this change have affected the emphasis or the power of the line?

As this shows, structure also involves word, sentence or paragraph order. Now read this opening to a novel:

> Why at the beginning of things is there always light? Dorrigo Evans' earliest memories were of sun flooding a church hall in which he sat with his mother and grandmother. A wooden church hall. Blinding light and him toddling back and forth, in and out of its transcendent welcome, into the arms of women. Women who loved him. Like entering the sea and returning to the beach. Over and over.
>
> Bless you, his mother says as she holds him and lets him go. Bless you, boy.
>
> Richard Flanagan, from *The Narrow Road to the Deep North*

— this question is a general observation

— this sentence shifts from the general to the specific – who, where and when

8 How do the remaining sentences of the first paragraph build on, or develop, the opening two sentences?

9 What else do you notice? Think about:
- the length and variety of sentences – why does the writer use short or minor sentences? What is their effect?
- any echoes or links between words and phrases in the text.

Apply the skills

10 Print out a copy of the poem 'Remembrance'. Using a range of coloured pens or highlighters, create a visual exploration of the structure of the text, perhaps using the same colour for linked words or phrases, or drawing arrows between similar ideas.

Check your progress:

▲ I can recognise aspects of structure in whole texts and within lines or sentences.

▲ I can identify a range of structures and comment on their effects.

Chapter 1 . Lesson 8

Exploring viewpoint and narration

What different types of narrator do writers use?

Start thinking

Writers use a range of narrative **viewpoints** or **narrators**:

- the **first person**: stories told from the 'I' point of view:
  '**I** stepped onto the stage, **my** hands shaking.'
- the **third person**: stories told from the 'he/she' point of view:
  '**She** (or '**The girl**') stepped onto the stage, **her** hands shaking'.

The second person is used rarely in prose but often in poetry:
'**You** stepped onto the stage, **your** hands shaking'.

> **Key terms**
>
> **viewpoints:** the positions from which stories are told
>
> **narrators:** people telling stories

1 Think of any poem or novel you have read recently.
- What person is it in?
- Does it stay the same or change at any point?

Explore the skills

Here is the opening line to a short story.

> In the silence of the room the woman sat, looking across the lawn at empty windows, horizon below the sky.
>
> Maureen Ismay, from *The Bed Sitting Room*

As a reader, you may feel you are watching the woman from a distance.

Now look at these two other versions.

> In the silence of the room I sat, looking across the lawn at empty windows, horizon below the sky.

> In the silence of the room you sat, looking across the lawn at empty windows, horizon below the sky.

2 What changes have been made?

3 How does the mood or tone change in each case?

Chapter 1 . Lesson 8

Develop the skills

What other types of narration are there? Have you come across any of these forms of narration in any stories you have read?

Type	Meaning	Example	Effect
omniscient narrator	All-seeing – the narrator knows everything about the character and the story.	'Let us picture him in his new car, shiny and expensive. How cruel Fate is! Little does he know the nasty surprise awaiting him at the office, those simple words – "You're fired!"'	The narrator is an observer who talks to the reader, watching and commenting – rather like a chess-player, moving the pieces around.
multiple narrators	many	**Chapter 1: Tony's story** Let me describe the day when I left her, and why… **Chapter 2: Fiorella** The sun was gone when I met him in the Plaza San Marco…	Provides a range of perspectives on the same event, perhaps helping the reader see that things are not always straightforward.
unreliable narrator	What is said cannot always be trusted or believed.	'You think I'm mad? Well, I can tell you I'm not. I'm as sane as you…'	Can create drama or tension as secrets are revealed, or allow the reader to get inside the head of someone evil or cunning.

4 Which would you choose if you were telling a story about a childhood friendship that falls apart in adulthood?

Apply the skills

Read this extract from a story.

> For fifteen years I'd been a gardener in New York City. A gardener in Manhattan? I hear you say. **Cushy** *number.* So some people have no ambition, so what? I liked regularity. One year's experience fifteen times. When I did change jobs it was to a garden centre. Something more stable. Out of the rain.
>
> Russell Celyn Jones, from *The Coalminer's Scarf*

Glossary

Cushy: an informal word meaning 'easy' or 'comfortable'

Check your progress:

▲ I can understand what narration is and can identify some different styles of narration.

▲ I can comment on some of the effects of a range of narrative styles.

5 Write a paragraph about the style of narration here. You could think about:
- the use of the first person and what it adds
- how close or distant the narrator sounds to the reader
- anything else that stands out.

Lesson 1.8 Exploring viewpoint and narration

Check your progress

- I can recognise language devices writers use.
- I can understand the different sorts of characters which can be found in texts.
- I can understand what 'themes' are and can identify them in some texts.
- I can recognise the way settings are used by writers for different effects.
- I can recognise how the form of plays, poems and stories differ.
- I can identify some basic conventions of well-known genres.
- I can recognise aspects of structure in whole texts and within lines or sentences.
- I can understand what narration is and can identify some different styles of narration.

- I can explain the effects of writers' language choices.
- I can explain the techniques writers use to develop characters.
- I can understand some of the different ways themes are explored by writers.
- I can explain how particular words and phrases related to setting create meaning and impact.
- I can recognise different forms of writing and understand how these can influence a text's impact or meaning.
- I can explain how different genres have different conventions and how texts can be a mix of different genres.
- I can identify a range of structures and structural features and can comment on their effects.
- I can comment on some of the effects of a range of narrative styles.

Key skills 2

Chapter 2 helps you to build on the understanding that you have developed in Chapter 1 about writers and their methods.

In Chapter 2, we will examine the key skills you need to develop to be successful in your Literature in English course and what they mean for your writing. You will learn how to express your ideas clearly in writing.

- **2.1** Approaching a text
- **2.2** Referring to the text and selecting quotations
- **2.3** Exploring ideas and attitudes in texts
- **2.4** Exploring implied meaning
- **2.5** Exploring writers' methods
- **2.6** Communicating a personal response
- **2.7** Exploring alternative interpretations

Chapter 2 . Lesson 1

Approaching a text

How do you study and understand the content of a text?

Start thinking

When you are writing about a poem, story, novel or play, you will need to demonstrate your detailed knowledge of the text.

To develop a more detailed, fuller understanding, you should:

- read the text thoroughly and deliberately
- highlight and underline key words and phrases as you read to pick out key events, ideas and language
- ensure you understand the language that is used
- break the text into sections and summarise what happens in your own words.

1 Can you think of any other ways that could help you get to know a text well?

Explore the skills

Read the excerpt from 'The Tell-Tale Heart' (1843) by Edgar Allan Poe. In the story, the narrator describes how he commits the murder of an old man in the dead of night. At this point in the story, the old man is terrified by the sound of the intruder (the narrator) in his bedroom.

Glossary

tattoo: rhythmic tapping or drumming

> Meantime the hellish **tattoo** of the heart increased. It grew quicker and quicker, and louder and louder every instant. The old man's terror *must* have been extreme! It grew louder, I say, louder every moment! – do you mark me well? I have told you that I am nervous: so I am. And now at the dead hour of the night, amid the dreadful silence of that old house, so strange a noise as this excited me to uncontrollable terror. Yet, for some minutes longer I refrained and stood still. But the beating grew louder, louder! I thought the heart must burst. And now a new anxiety seized me – the sound would be heard by a neighbour! The old man's hour had come! With a loud yell, I threw open the lantern and leaped into the room. He shrieked once – once only. In an instant I dragged him to the floor, and pulled the heavy bed over him. I then smiled gaily, to find the deed so far done. But, for many minutes, the heart beat on with a muffled sound. This, however, did not vex me; it would not be heard through the wall. At length it ceased. The old man was dead. I removed the bed and examined the corpse. Yes, he was stone, stone dead. I placed my hand upon the heart and held it there many minutes. There was no pulsation. He was stone dead. His eye would trouble me no more.
>
> Edgar Allan Poe, from 'The Tell-Tale Heart'

— Chunk 1
— Chunk 2
— Chunk 3
— Chunk 4
— Chunk 5
— Chunk 6

34 Chapter 2 Key skills

Chapter 2 . Lesson 1

2. Read carefully and thoroughly through the text again.

3. Highlight key words or phrases that help you understand what happens.

4. Highlight and look up the meaning of any words you don't know.

Develop the skills

5. Next, break the text into sections and summarise each section. You will see that one student has decided on six chunks for this text.

Apply the skills

6. Practise applying the reading stages again, this time with a section of the story from later that night.

> When I had made an end of these labours, it was four o'clock – still dark as midnight. As the bell sounded the hour, there came a knocking at the street door. I went down to open it with a light heart, – for what had I *now* to fear? There entered three men, who introduced themselves, with perfect suavity, as officers of the police. A shriek had been heard by a neighbour during the night; suspicion of foul play had been aroused; information had been lodged at the police office, and they (the officers) had been deputed to search the premises.

Check your progress:

▲ I can understand how to approach reading a new text.

▲ I can use key strategies for reading and understanding a text thoroughly.

Lesson 2.1 Approaching a text   35

Chapter 2 . Lesson 2

Referring to the text and selecting quotations

How do you choose the best references and quotations?

Start thinking

As you write about the text, you will need to make reference to it to support your ideas and demonstrate your detailed knowledge.

Reference to the text includes:

- the use of quotations
- a reference to key events or features from a text.

1 Which of these examples uses quotation and which refers to the text without quotation?

> The author also writes that when the pipe bursts, 'silver crashes to the ground / and the flow has found / a roar of tongues.' This shows how valuable the water was.

> The story is narrated from the perspective of the young girl, so we are unable to see or understand what she doesn't see.

Every point you make should be supported by one of the two types of reference.

Explore the skills

As you explore a text, you will need to gather quotations that develop your understanding of the author's tools: plot, theme, character, setting, language and structure.

Read the passage on the following page. Here, a 16-year-old named Frank describes his father's strange behaviour.

36 Chapter 2 Key skills

Chapter 2 . Lesson 2

> My father once **had me believing** that the earth was a **Mobius strip**, not a sphere. He still maintains that he believes this, and makes a great show of sending off a manuscript to publishers down in London, trying to get them to publish a book expounding this view, but I know he's just mischief-making again, and gets most of his pleasure from his acts of stunned disbelief and then righteous indignation when the manuscript is eventually returned. This occurs about every three months, and I doubt that life would be half as much fun for him without this sort of ritual.
>
> Iain Banks, from *The Wasp Factory*

Let's say you are answering the question: 'How does the author portray Frank's father?'

Glossary

Mobius strip: a geometric surface which only has one side and one edge

2 a) Read through the text and highlight or pick out anything that reveals the father's character.

For example:

> 'had me believing' – makes it sound like his dad liked to trick him, or else that his dad just had odd ideas

b) Make a note each time of what your quote shows about Frank's father.

3 In answering the question above, you may decide to make the point that the author portrays Frank's father as unusual, even bizarre.

a) Rank the following quotations in order, from the most relevant (1) to least relevant (6) to support this point.

b) Why have you decided to order them in this way?

- 'had me believing'
- 'still maintains he believes this'
- 'sending off a manuscript'
- 'pleasure from… stunned disbelief and righteous indignation'
- 'mischief-making again'
- 'every three months'

Read the following response:

> The author portrays Frank's father as an unusual individual. For example, the author writes how he has 'this sort of ritual' of sending off a manuscript to a London publisher 'every three months' in order to 'expound' his belief that the world is shaped something other than 'a sphere'.

Lesson 2.2 Referring to the text and selecting quotations

4 **a)** What do you notice about how the quotation fits into the flow of the sentence. (See the highlighted section.)

  b) Identify other examples where the quotation fits into the flow of the sentence.

The response continues:

> Frank realises that the belief itself is 'mischief-making' – just some 'fun'. However, the idea that this is a 'ritual', or something he does again and again, as if it is a compulsion – or worse, an action that has deeper, perhaps religious, significance – ==suggests the strange, deluded, even dangerous mental state of his father.==

5 **a)** Where do you see the writer of the response quoting from the text and where are they referring to it?

  b) Look at the highlighted text. How is the writer of the response using the quotation here?

6 Use a similar approach to write a sentence integrating the quotation 'had me believing that the earth was a Mobius strip' and analysing what it might suggest about Frank's father:

> The narrator explains that his father............... This suggests that..........

7 Now write a sentence about Frank's father that integrates and analyses another quotation.

Develop the skills

Read the passage below, again from *The Wasp Factory*. In this excerpt, Frank returns to his home, which is on an island, at night and looks at his house.

> I got to the island eventually. The house was dark. I stood looking at it in the darkness, just aware of its bulk in the feeble light of a broken moon, and I thought it looked even bigger than it really was, like a stone-giant's head, a huge moonlit skull full of shapes and memories, staring out to sea and attached to a vast, powerful body buried in the rock and sand beneath, ready to shrug itself free and disinter itself on some unknowable command or cue.

Chapter 2 . Lesson 2

8. Look up the word 'disinter'. What does it mean? If this is a story about dark secrets coming to the surface, why might this be an appropriate choice of word?

> **Key term**
>
> **connotations:** ideas or associations brought to mind beyond the literal or surface meaning

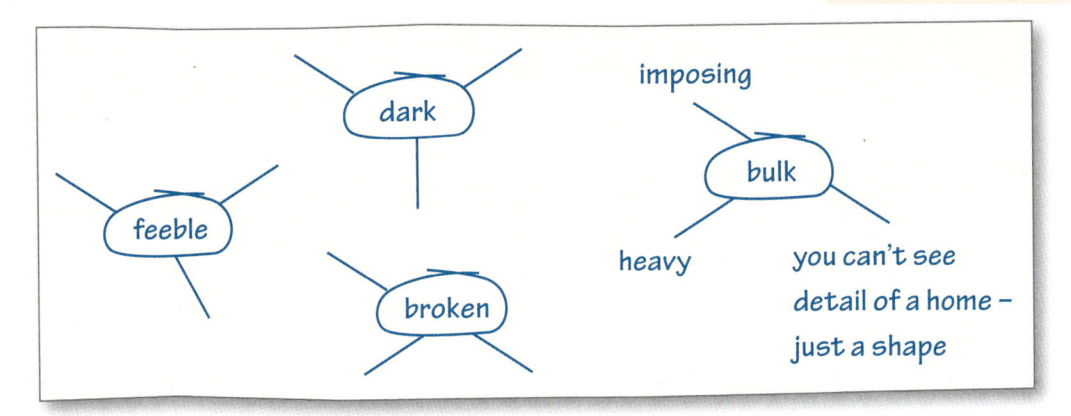

9. Consider the quotations: 'The house was dark' and 'its bulk in the feeble light of a broken moon'. Use the mind-maps below to map out their key meanings and **connotations**:

- dark
- feeble
- broken
- bulk — imposing, heavy, you can't see detail of a home – just a shape

10. Choose quotations from the text that make the house seem ominous. Make notes about the effect of each.

Apply the skills

11. Write a paragraph to answer the question: 'How does the author make the narrator's house seem ominous?'

Checklist for success
✔ Include integrated quotations.
✔ Explain what each quotation suggests about the house.

Check your progress:

▲ I can choose appropriate textual references and quotations.

▲ I can identify and employ key strategies for making references to the text and analysing their effects in writing.

Lesson 2.2 Referring to the text and selecting quotations

Chapter 2 . Lesson 3

Exploring ideas and attitudes in texts

How are ideas and attitudes developed within a text?

Start thinking

As you explore a text, you will need to look beyond the surface and show your understanding of the themes, feelings, ideas and attitudes which are expressed through the plot, characters, setting, structure and language used.

You are about to read part of a short story entitled 'Everyday Use'.

1 What does the phrase 'everyday use' make you think of? Does it have positive or negative **connotations**?

> **Key term**
>
> **connotations:** the associations brought to mind by a word or phrase

Explore the skills

Read the following extract. The narrator is a black woman with two daughters: Dee, who has adopted the African name Wangero while doing African Studies at university, and Maggie, a young teenager who still lives in their poor, rural home. Here, Dee visits her home.

> After dinner **Dee (Wangero)** went to the trunk at the foot of my bed and started **rifling** through it. [...] Out came Wangero with two quilts. They had been pieced by Grandma Dee and then Big Dee and me had hung them on the quilt frames on the front porch and quilted them [...] In both of them were scraps of dresses Grandma Dee had worn fifty and more years ago. Bits and pieces of Grandpa Jarrell's Paisley shirts. And one teeny faded blue piece, about the size of a penny matchbox, that was from Great Grandpa Ezra's uniform that he wore in the Civil War.
>
> "Mama," Wangero said **sweet as a bird**. "Can I have these old quilts?"
>
> [...]
>
> "Why don't you take one or two of the others?" I asked.
>
> "**No**," said Wangero. "I **don't** want those. They are stitched around the borders by machine."
>
> "That'll make them last better," I said.
>
> "That's not the point," said Wangero. "These are all pieces of dresses Grandma used to wear. She did all this stitching by hand..."

— Dee has changed her name; is she authentic or insincere?
— a careless, inconsiderate action; doesn't care about anything else

— again, simile to suggest insincerity; is this an act?

— generally negative, selfish attitude

Chapter 2 Key skills

Chapter 2 . Lesson 3

"Some of the pieces, like those lavender ones, come from old clothes her mother handed down to her," I said, moving up to touch the quilts. Dee (Wangero) **moved back** just enough so that I **couldn't reach the quilts. They already belonged to her.** "**Imagine!**" she **breathed** again, clutching them **closely to her bosom.**

— greedy, covetous actions

— sincere? Like she just heard this for the first time

"The truth is," I said, "I promised to give them quilts to Maggie, for when she marries John Thomas."

She gasped like a bee had stung her.

"Maggie can't appreciate these quilts!" she said. "She'd probably be backward enough to put them to everyday use."

"I reckon she would," I said. "God knows I been saving 'em for long enough with nobody using 'em. I hope she will!" I didn't want to bring up how I had offered Dee (Wangero) a quilt when she went away to college. Then she had told me they were old-fashioned, out of style.

"But they're *priceless*!" she was saying now, furiously[…]

"She can have them, Mama," [Maggie] said, like somebody used to never winning anything, or having anything reserved for her. "I can 'member Grandma Dee without the quilts."

Alice Walker, from 'Everyday Use'

2 Read the student annotations. What do we learn about Wangero in the extract? Do you agree with her actions? Explain your answer, drawing on evidence from the text.

Develop the skills

Without directly making judgements, Alice Walker guides our reactions to each character through the way she presents them.

3 How does Walker make us feel about the character of Maggie? Annotate a copy of the text, highlighting and commenting on details that lead you to this conclusion.

Apply the skills

4 Using your annotations and notes from Questions 2 and 3, write a paragraph to answer this question:

Which character does Alice Walker make us sympathise with in this passage, and how?

Check your progress:

▲ I can identify and infer the key attitudes within a text.

▲ I can analyse ideas and attitudes with reference to the text.

Lesson 2.3 Exploring ideas and attitudes in texts

Chapter 2 . Lesson 4

Exploring implied meaning

What is 'implied meaning'?

Start thinking

Read this conversation between two friends:

Milo: How much do I owe you for lunch?

Racheal (waving her hand): Oh, forget it; it's nothing.

1
   a) Write out the dictionary definitions for 'forget' and 'nothing'. Do the dictionary definitions make sense in this context?

   b) What does Racheal mean, then, when she says, 'forget it; it's nothing'? How do you know?

   c) What is implied by Racheal 'waving her hand'?

Explore the skills

When you write about a literary text, you need to show you not only understand the explicit meanings of literary texts, but are able to delve more deeply, looking for implicit meanings. Read the poem below.

Nettles

My son aged three fell in the **nettle** bed.
'Bed' seemed a curious name for those green spears,
That regiment of spite behind the shed:
It was no place for rest. With sobs and tears
The boy came seeking comfort and I saw
White blisters beaded on his tender skin.
We soothed him till his pain was not so raw.
At last he offered us a watery grin,
And then I took my hook and honed the blade
And went outside and slashed in fury with it
Till not a nettle in that fierce parade
Stood upright any more. Next task: I lit
A funeral pyre to burn the fallen dead.
But in two weeks the busy sun and rain
Had called up tall recruits behind the shed:
My son would often feel sharp wounds again.

Vernon Scannell

Glossary

nettle: plant native to the UK which causes a searing rash if in contact with skin

Chapter 2 Key skills

2 a) What do you think the poet means when he says that 'Bed' is a 'curious name' for the grouping of nettles?

b) What words and phrases does the poet use to show us that his son felt pain?

c) What words and images does the poet use to imply the cruel intent of the nettles?

Develop the skills

3 What are the literal and implied meanings for these key words?

Key word or phrase	Literal meaning	Implied meaning in the poem
'spears'	long, sharp, knife-like weapons	The nettles are like weapons used to jab, pierce and injure people.
'White blisters'		White suggests…
'tender skin'		Tender suggests…
'pyre'		
'recruits'		

4 How does the father react to his son's pain? Why do you think he does this?

5 What do you think are the implications of the final line? Does Scannell mean his son will literally fall into the nettle bed again? Or does he mean something else?

Apply the skills

The poem is entitled 'Nettles'; however, an argument can be made that this poem isn't about nettles at all.

6 Write a paragraph explaining why this poem *is not* actually about nettles. What, then, is it implicitly about? You could use this writing frame to help you.

> On the surface, 'Nettles' seems to be about ………. However, on another level it seems that the poem is about more than this. Several words have implied meanings, for example…… suggests….., and ……suggests……. Perhaps the poem's implicit meaning is that ……

Check your progress:

▲ I can understand the difference between literal and implied meaning.

▲ I can analyse language and texts beyond the surface meaning.

Lesson 2.4 Exploring implied meaning

Chapter 2 . Lesson 5

Exploring writers' methods

How do authors shape meaning?

Start thinking

Read the stanza below, from Simon Armitage's poem, 'The Manhunt':

> only then would he let me trace
> the frozen river which ran through his face,
>
> Simon Armitage, from 'The Manhunt'

1 Consider what you have learned previously about a writer's use of language, rhythm, rhyme, form, structure and perspective.

   a) Which literary techniques can you find in these lines?

   b) What do you think are the key words in these lines? Why?

   c) What sense of the rhythm, rhyme or structure do you get from this stanza?

   d) From whose perspective do you get this description?

Explore the skills

To write about literature successfully, you need to explain how and why authors use various linguistic, structural and literary techniques in their text, and what their effects are.

However, you will need to do more than just 'feature spot' – that is, just identify the author's use of similes, metaphors or rhyme scheme.

Once you identify the technique, you then need to explain its relevance to the context and discuss its effects.

Try always to answer the questions of **why** the author uses this technique and **how** it is effective: what does it make you feel, think or imagine?

44   Chapter 2 Key skills

Chapter 2 . Lesson 5

2 Read the two responses below. Which do you think only 'feature spots' and which one discusses the *how* and *why*?

A

> In 'The Manhunt', Armitage uses the metaphor 'the frozen river which ran through his face' to describe a soldier's war injuries. The image creates an ironic contrast of physical pain that is 'frozen' or still on the surface, but emotionally still raging and rapid underneath. The metaphor clearly suggests how the physical scarring and his stony exterior masks deep emotional distress.

B

> In the poem 'The Manhunt', Armitage uses a metaphor to describe the man's face. This is effective because it is comparing the man's face with a river. This is also imagery, because the reader can clearly see the picture in their mind. 'Frozen' and 'river' are opposites which shows that the man is in pain because of his injuries.

Now read the whole poem.

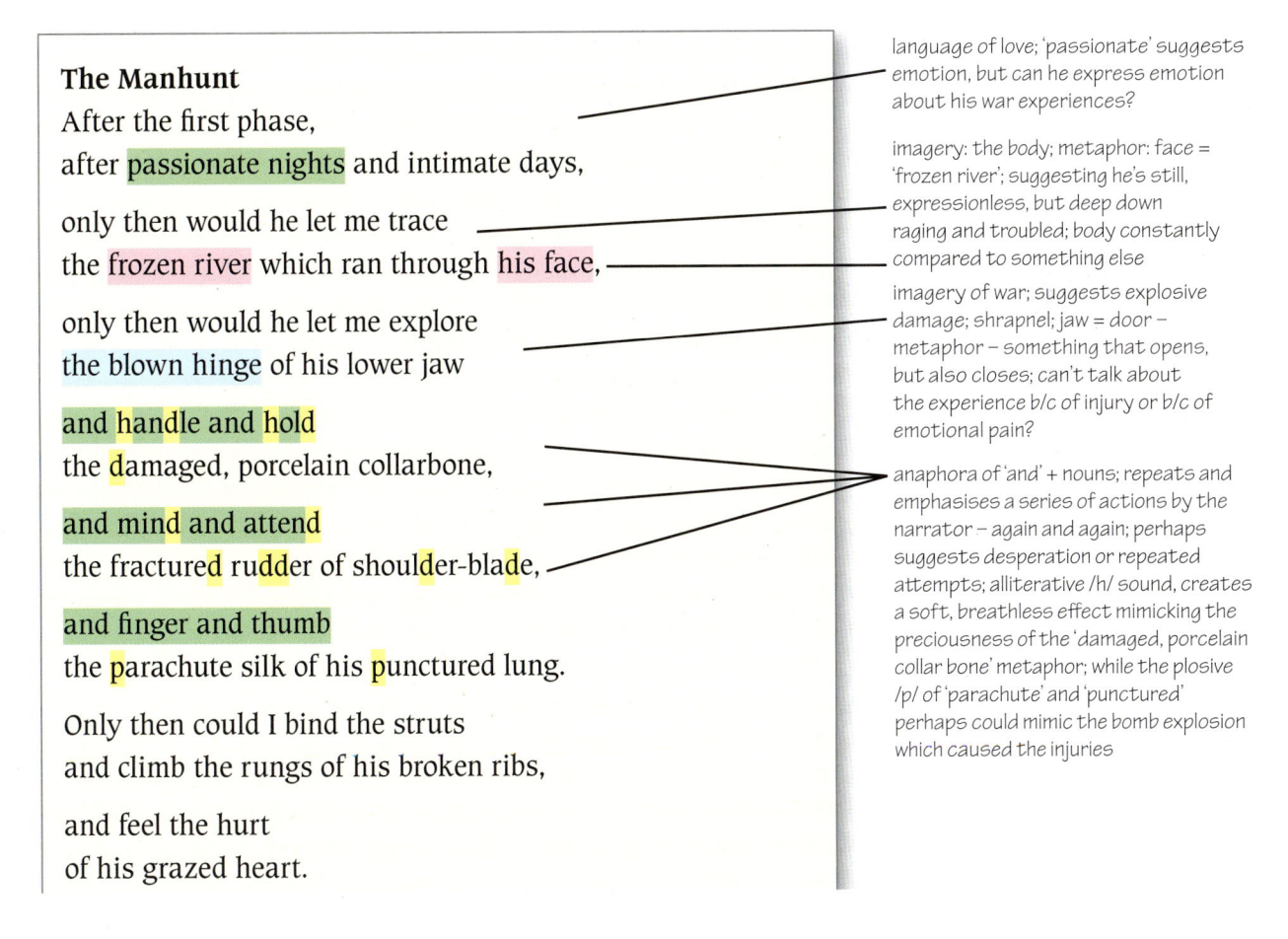

The Manhunt
After the first phase,
after passionate nights and intimate days,

only then would he let me trace
the frozen river which ran through his face,

only then would he let me explore
the blown hinge of his lower jaw

and handle and hold
the damaged, porcelain collarbone,

and mind and attend
the fractured rudder of shoulder-blade,

and finger and thumb
the parachute silk of his punctured lung.

Only then could I bind the struts
and climb the rungs of his broken ribs,

and feel the hurt
of his grazed heart.

---

language of love; 'passionate' suggests emotion, but can he express emotion about his war experiences?

imagery: the body; metaphor: face = 'frozen river'; suggesting he's still, expressionless, but deep down raging and troubled; body constantly compared to something else

imagery of war; suggests explosive damage; shrapnel; jaw = door – metaphor – something that opens, but also closes; can't talk about the experience b/c of injury or b/c of emotional pain?

anaphora of 'and' + nouns; repeats and emphasises a series of actions by the narrator – again and again; perhaps suggests desperation or repeated attempts; alliterative /h/ sound, creates a soft, breathless effect mimicking the preciousness of the 'damaged, porcelain collar bone' metaphor; while the plosive /p/ of 'parachute' and 'punctured' perhaps could mimic the bomb explosion which caused the injuries

Lesson 2.5 Exploring writers' methods   45

> Skirting along,
> only then could I picture the scan,
>
> the foetus of metal beneath his chest
> where the bullet had finally come to rest.
>
> Then I widened the search,
> traced the scarring back to its source
>
> to a sweating, unexploded mine
> buried deep in his mind, around which
>
> every nerve in his body had tightened and closed.
> Then, and only then, did I come close.
>
> Simon Armitage

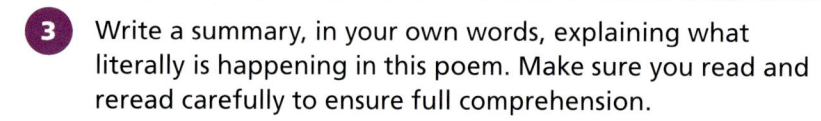

3 Write a summary, in your own words, explaining what literally is happening in this poem. Make sure you read and reread carefully to ensure full comprehension.

4 Now read the student's annotations, then continue to annotate your own copy of the poem, picking out language and imagery that you notice, and thinking about the effect on you.

5 Use your annotations to look for patterns of word usage. Create a table like the one below to catalogue language linked to a specific **theme** or **semantic field**.

War	Love	The body
'blown hinge'	'passionate nights'	'face'

Key terms

theme: an idea running through a text

semantic field: a set of words or phrases that can be grouped by their meaning, linked to a particular subject: for example, 'battle', 'helmet', 'gun', 'enemy' are from the semantic field of war

Develop the skills

6 Consider all the war imagery. What does this semantic field tell you about the person being described?

7 The poet writes about 'a sweating, unexploded mine / buried deep in his mind, around which every nerve in his body had tightened and closed.' What do you think this image means literally? What does it suggest metaphorically?

8 Explore the metaphor 'foetus of metal beneath his chest'. What ideas and themes does foetus suggest? What does the metaphor 'foetus of metal' foreshadow? How does this metaphor link to the line 'a sweating, unexploded mine / buried deep in his mind'?

Now read the following definitions of poetic techniques.

Feature	Meaning	Frequent effect
plosive	repetition or grouping of /b/ /p/ /t/ /d/ sounds	Creates an abrupt, sharp, sometimes shocking effect.
repetition		Creates rhythm and a sense of significance in repeated word or image; could suggest multiple meanings of the same thing.
enjambment	a continuation of a phrase beyond the end of a line of poetry	Breaks off a sentence into two or more lines; creates friction, discord, a 'broken' structure; could offer two meanings.
anaphora	the repetition of a phrase often at the beginning of a stanza in poetry	Creates a grammatical repetition to emphasise key points.

9 Consider the phrase 'attend / the fractured rudder of shoulder-blade'. The repetition of the /t/ and /d/ sound are examples of **plosives**. What effect do they have here? How do the sounds of the poem help us understand the image? What is a 'rudder' and what happens if it's broken?

10 Consider the structure of the poem, looking at the length of the stanzas, the use of repetition, enjambment and anaphora, as well as the way the narrative unfolds. How does the way the author shapes the text reflect the key ideas within the text?

11 Who is the narrator of this poem? How do you know that?

Apply the skills

12 Choose three different poetic techniques and write a paragraph to show how Simon Armitage uses these techniques to create meaning in 'The Manhunt'. You can use this frame to help you.

> In 'Manhunt', Simon Armitage uses a number of techniques to communicate how war has affected the man described in the poem. He uses………..'…………...'. This suggests….

Check your progress:

- I can identify key techniques and structural features within a text.
- I can analyse key techniques and features and explain their effects.

Chapter 2 . Lesson 6

Communicating a personal response

How do you organise your written response to a question?

Start thinking

1 Read the following response to the poem 'The Manhunt', which you read in Lesson 2.5.

> In the poem 'The Manhunt,' the poet talks about an injured solider. 'Frozen river which ran through his face.' This shows that he was injured. The author uses a metaphor. This shows that there wasn't literally a frozen river in his face.

a) What do you think of this response?

b) What does this do well?

c) What three suggestions for improvement might you give the writer of the response?

Explore the skills

Communicating a personal response to a text involves planning, organising and writing your own ideas in a way that is clear, cohesive and even sophisticated. In doing so, you need to incorporate all the skills you have been introduced to in this chapter.

So, what should a good piece of writing about literature include?

> I. A clearly stated **point** or argument linked to the question.
>
> II. **Evidence** from the text, introduced and/or embedded.
>
> III. **Explanation** of key words from the quotation, as well as any relevant techniques.
>
> IV. **Links** back to the question and consideration of **effects on the reader** – your personal response.

Chapter 2 . Lesson 6

A paragraph which follows those guidelines may look something like this, in response to the following question:

'How does Armitage create a sense of the damaging effects of war in 'The Manhunt'?'

> In 'Manhunt', Simon Armitage uses a number of techniques to communicate how war has affected the man described in the poem. He uses a metaphor to describe the scars on the man's face as 'a frozen river', which suggests that the man seems still, expressionless, and cold, but that deep down he is raging and troubled. This sense of how war has damaged the man builds as Armitage uses a listed series of metaphors with the semantic field of military equipment to describe the man's other shocking injuries. He has, for example, 'the fractured rudder of a shoulder blade' and 'the parachute silk of his punctured lung.' Here the repeated 'd', 'p' and 'f' sounds add to the sense of harsh brutality.

- key point identified – linked to question
- relevant techniques identified
- embedded quotations
- clear explanations of effect on reader

2 Read the following responses to the question: 'How does the author powerfully portray the man in the poem?'

First, decide which of these **points** best addresses the question.

3 Why did you choose the point you did? What was missing from the other responses?

A
> The author shows he's injured when he says 'damaged, porcelain collarbone'.

B
> The author shows that the narrator clearly loves the man when he writes how the narrator is allowed to 'feel the hurt / of his grazed heart.'

C
> The author powerfully portrays the man in the poem as injured physically, mentally and emotionally.

Lesson 2.6 Communicating a personal response   49

4 Now read the supporting evidence from the text below. Which evidence would support the best point from Question 3?

a.
> 'finger and thumb / the parachute silk of his punctured lung.'

b.
> For example, the author uses a metaphor to show his physical and emotional pain in the middle of the poem when he writes about the 'fractured rudder of shoulder-blade'.

c.
> The author writes how 'Only then could I bind the struts' and 'Skirting along', using imagery to show how the narrator reacts to the man.

5 Again, why did you choose the evidence sentence you did? What was ineffective about the others?

Develop the skills

6 Now read the beginning of the paragraph, which combines the best point with the best evidence. Annotate the sentences with the features of an effective personal response. Some have already been done for you.

> The **author powerfully portrays the man in the poem** as injured physically, mentally and emotionally. For example, the author uses a metaphor to show his physical and emotional pain in the **middle of the poem** when he writes about the 'fractured rudder of shoulder-blade'.

— words from question in opening sentence

— quotation 'embedded' in the text

~~Words from the question in the opening sentence~~	The key point	Relevant technique identified
Introduced quotation	~~Quotation 'located' in the text~~	Appropriate quotation from text selected to support point

50 Chapter 2 Key skills

Chapter 2 . Lesson 6

Notice that the analysis of the effect of the quotation has not yet been developed in this paragraph. Consider the quotation: 'fractured rudder of shoulder-blade'. 'Fractured', along with 'shoulder-blade', clearly link to the idea in the **point** about 'physical pain' but the student's introduction to the quotation also suggests that this metaphor shows emotional pain.

7 Look at the word 'rudder'. Use the exercises below to explore how 'rudder' might show emotional pain.

   a) Define 'rudder'. Where would you find one and what is its purpose?

   b) Now think about a 'fractured rudder'; how would a fracture affect a rudder?

   c) Finally, how might this **image** link to emotional pain and the man's ability to deal with the world?

   d) What effect does this **image** and **metaphor** have on the reader?

8 You are now going to complete the paragraph with an analysis of the effect of the quotation. You can use these prompts if you find them helpful.

> - The adjective 'fractured' literally means to be broken and usually broken beyond use, whereas 'rudder' refers to...
> - The combined imaged of a 'fractured rudder' suggests... [explain the image and then link it to physical and emotional pain]
> - This image makes the reader think/feel...

Apply the skills

9 Improve this paragraph on 'The Manhunt' from the 'Start thinking' section by re-writing it, using the structure suggested above.

> In the poem 'The Manhunt,' the poet talks about an injured solider. 'Frozen river which ran through his face.' This shows that he was injured. The author uses a metaphor. This shows that there wasn't literally a frozen river in his face.

Check your progress:

▲ I can recognise the structural features of a clearly expressed response.

▲ I can employ those structural features in my own response.

Lesson 2.6 Communicating a personal response

Chapter 2 . Lesson 7
Exploring alternative interpretations

Is there only one way to read a text?

Start thinking

1. When you look at this picture, what do you see? You will probably see one image right away, but will then see another image if you keep looking. Once you can see the two images, it is very difficult to 'unsee' either image again.

Explore the skills

Read this poem.

Between Walls

the back wings
of the

hospital where
nothing

will grow lie
cinders

in which shine
the broken

pieces of a green
bottle

William Carlos Williams

On its surface, the poem is clearly an image; however, it is rather **ambiguous**.

2. a) Consider the title of the poem 'Between Walls'. What image does it create and what does it suggest?
   b) Make a list of words from the poem that may have negative **connotations**.

> **Key terms**
>
> **ambiguous:** open to more than one interpretation
> **connotations:** associations connected with a word

52 Chapter 2 Key skills

Chapter 2 . Lesson 7

3 a) Read this student response, which addresses the question: 'How does the writer create a powerful image in this poem?'

> The writer creates a powerful image in this poem by establishing a scene of desolation. For example, the title 'Between Walls' creates an image of being stuck or impeded by physical barriers, thereby creating a sense of isolation, even imprisonment. The scene takes place in the 'back wings' of the hospital, suggesting that this is a place where no one will – or even should – go, further developing that sense of isolation. Additionally, the fact that 'nothing / will grow' there shows that this is a dead place, unfit for the living. These images make the reader feel uncomfortable and uncertain.

b) What makes this response convincing and successful?

Develop the skills

4 Now make a list of words from the poem that have positive connotations. Consider words such as 'hospital', 'grow', 'shine' and 'green'.

Apply the skills

5 a) Read this second response to the same question.

> The writer creates a powerful image in this poem by establishing a scene of unconventional beauty. Initially, the title of the poem, 'Between Walls', creates the impression of a dark, lonely place – a place where nobody goes and where 'nothing will grow'. However, Williams juxtaposes this initial negativity with positive images. The fact that this scene takes place in a hospital – a place where people are made better – suggests a sense of optimism, recovery and rejuvenation. The 'green' colour of the bottle suggests ideas of plants and life, so that, even in this place where 'nothing / will grow', there is still a sense of vivacity and liveliness. The fact that the bottle 'shines' only heightens these themes of life, since the green glass is receiving its liveliness from the Sun and sunshine – just like a plant would. This verb develops the optimistic tone of the poem, in that this 'broken' bottle grows into an object of beauty and appreciation, thereby showing the reader how beauty can occur at any moment, in any place.

b) What makes this second response convincing?

The two responses interpret differently, but both are strong. As long as you have evidence and work from the text, your own personal response will be valid.

6 Which of the two responses do you agree with? Can you 'unsee' either of them?

Check your progress:

▲ I can understand that a text can be interpreted in different ways.

▲ I can understand that an interpretation is convincing when supported closely with textual evidence.

Lesson 2.7 Exploring alternative interpretations

Check your progress

- I can understand how to approach reading a new text.
- I can choose appropriate textual references and quotations.
- I can identify the key ideas within a text.
- I can understand the difference between literal and implied meaning.
- I can identify key techniques and structural features within a text.
- I can recognise the structural features of a clearly expressed response.
- I can understand that a text can be interpreted in different ways.

- I can use key strategies for reading and understanding a text thoroughly.
- I can identify and employ key strategies for making references to the text and analysing their effects in writing.
- I can analyse key ideas with reference to the text.
- I can analyse language and texts beyond the surface meaning.
- I can analyse key techniques and structural features in detail.
- I can employ the structural features of a clearly expressed response in my own writing.
- I can understand that an interpretation is convincing when supported closely with textual evidence.

Studying prose 3

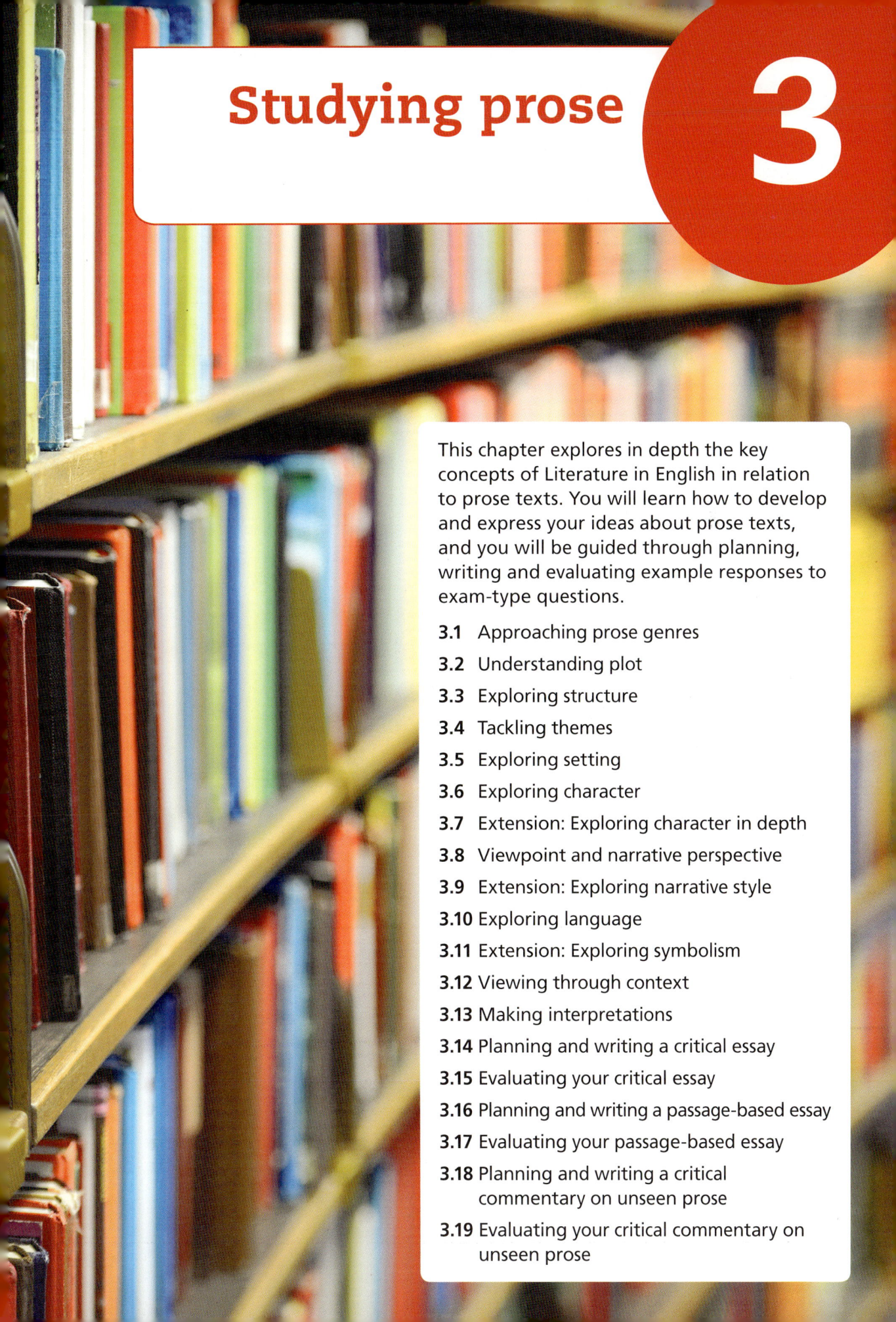

This chapter explores in depth the key concepts of Literature in English in relation to prose texts. You will learn how to develop and express your ideas about prose texts, and you will be guided through planning, writing and evaluating example responses to exam-type questions.

3.1 Approaching prose genres
3.2 Understanding plot
3.3 Exploring structure
3.4 Tackling themes
3.5 Exploring setting
3.6 Exploring character
3.7 Extension: Exploring character in depth
3.8 Viewpoint and narrative perspective
3.9 Extension: Exploring narrative style
3.10 Exploring language
3.11 Extension: Exploring symbolism
3.12 Viewing through context
3.13 Making interpretations
3.14 Planning and writing a critical essay
3.15 Evaluating your critical essay
3.16 Planning and writing a passage-based essay
3.17 Evaluating your passage-based essay
3.18 Planning and writing a critical commentary on unseen prose
3.19 Evaluating your critical commentary on unseen prose

Chapter 3 . Lesson 1

Approaching prose genres

How do writers use genre conventions?

Start thinking

There are many different prose genres, each with its own **conventions**. These conventions are made up of key elements such as plot, characters and setting.

1 a) Write a definition for five or more of the following genres, considering characters, events and setting.

For example:

> Travelogue: Non-fiction account of the writer's experience of a journey or places visited.

| a) Gothic | b) Autobiography | c) Science fiction | d) Thriller |
| e) Tragedy | f) Romance | g) Biography | h) Dystopian |

b) Extension: Which of these genres share elements?

Key term

conventions: the usual rules or expectations of a text type

Explore the skills

Authors may use conventions from more than one genre. This is known as a **hybrid** text. For example, a crime story set in the future would be a **hybrid** of crime fiction and sci-fi. Most prose set texts do not belong to one single genre, but contain elements of different genres which may affect your expectations of the text.

Genre can be implied through an author's language choices.

Key term

hybrid: a text combining conventions of two or more genres

2 What genres could the following words belong to?

> moon   blood   ethereal   haunted
> isolated   shadow

A writer may use genre conventions in unusual ways to play with readers' expectations.

3 a) Write a romantic description of a person, using the words above. For example:

> Her skin glowed like a full moon; I felt haunted by her radiant beauty...

b) How does using this vocabulary affect the romantic description?

56   Chapter 3 Studying prose

Chapter 3 . Lesson 1

Develop the skills

You are now going to explore genre conventions in an extract.

> The Hopi country is in Arizona, next to the Navajo country, and some seventy miles north of the Santa Fé railroad. [...] It consists of a square track of greyish, unappetising desert, out of which rise three tall arid mesas, broken off in ragged, pallid rock.
>
> D. H. Lawrence, from *Mornings in Mexico*

Read this student's notes on the text:

- describes place – place is real, not imaginary
- mainly factual – names, statistics 'seventy miles', 'three... mesas'
- present tense 'is in Arizona'
- gives sense of what you can see – adjectives 'greyish', 'ragged', 'pallid', 'arid'
- some opinions – 'unappetising' – finds place unpleasant

4 Write a paragraph identifying the possible genre of the text and the expectations this creates. Use the student's notes and these sentence starters to help you:

> The extract could belong to the genre... because it features conventions like... for example, '_____' I expect a text of this genre to...

Apply the skills

Now read the extract below.

> One of his eyes resembled that of a vulture – a pale blue eye, with a film over it. Whenever it fell upon me, my blood ran cold; and so by degrees – very gradually – I made up my mind to take the life of the old man, and thus rid myself of the eye forever.
>
> Edgar Allan Poe, from 'The Tell-Tale Heart'

5 Write a paragraph discussing the possible genres used and the expectations these set up. Consider characters, events and language

6 Read the first page of your prose set text. Identify any genre conventions and expectations set up.

Check your progress:

▲ I can understand and identify genre conventions.

▲ I very clearly explain how a writer uses genre conventions, carefully considering interpretations.

Chapter 3 . Lesson 2

Understanding plot

How do prose plots work?

Start thinking

For a story to have a plot, there must be a change or conflict to be solved. A plot often has a five-part structure:

1. **Exposition**
   We are introduced to the world of the story.
   For example: *Three bears live in a house in the wood.*

2. **Rising action**
   A conflict or change is introduced to the world of the story.
   For example: *A girl called Goldilocks enters their house while they are out. The girl eats their food, sits on their chairs and lies in their beds.*

3. **Climax**
   The conflict comes to a head.
   For example: *The bears return and find Goldilocks asleep.*

4. **Falling action**
   Events follow on from the climax.
   For example: *The bears roar. Goldilocks wakes up terrified.*

5. **Resolution**
   The disturbance is resolved in some way, happily or unhappily.
   For example: *Goldilocks screams and runs away.*

Alternatively, the story may be left unresolved, that is, a **cliffhanger**.

For example: *The bears find her and roar. She screams and...*

> **Key term**
>
> **cliffhanger:** an ending which leaves the reader in suspense

1 Following the above structure, invent the plot of a story using these pictures:

Explore the skills

A narrative can be complicated by adding further plot-twists, or a **sub-plot**. An example of **sub-plot** would be:

While Goldilocks is in the house, the bears climb trees looking for honey. They reach a beehive. But a bee stings the smallest bear. They quickly return home.

> **Key term**
>
> **sub-plot:** a secondary plot, running alongside the main plot

58 Chapter 3 Studying prose

Chapter 3 . Lesson 2

2 Add a sub-plot to your story.

Develop the skills

Stories are often told in **chronological** order (the order in which they happened). However, stories can also be **achronological** (events are told out of time order).

This may be done through a **flashback** (also called **analepsis**) or **flash-forward** (also called **prolepsis**).

Example of **analepsis** (flashback):

- *Goldilocks enters an empty house. She notices the bowls, chairs and beds are different sizes.*
- *The story cuts back to earlier in the morning, revealing three bears of different sizes waking and leaving the house.*
- *The story returns to the girl falling asleep. The bears arrive home. She flees.*

Example of **prolepsis** (flash-forward):

- *Goldilocks arrives at a house and pushes the door.*
- *The story cuts forward to her in the future, screaming in terror.*
- *The story returns to the girl exploring the empty house. She falls asleep. Three bears arrive home. She runs away, screaming.*

3 How does changing the **chronology** affect the reader's expectations in the story of Goldilocks?

4 What happens to your story if you alter the chronology?

Key terms

chronological: events are told in the order they occur in time

achronological: events are told in a different order from the order they occur in time

analepsis or **flashback:** the story cuts backwards in time to an event which happened earlier

prolepsis or **flash-forward:** the story cuts forward in time to an event which will happen later

Apply the skills

5 Read the first page of your set text. What, in the text, suggests this is the start of a story? Are there any clues that **foreshadow** later events?

Use these sentence starters to help:

> We can tell this is the start as… for example, '_____,'
> We could guess the next stage of the plot would…

Key term

foreshadow: hint at events which will come later in the plot

Check your progress:

▲ I can understand plot structure.

▲ I can very clearly understand how a writer uses plot, and how chronology and sub-plots may affect a reader's expectations.

Lesson 3.2 Understanding plot   59

Chapter 3 . Lesson 3
Exploring structure

How do writers use structural devices?

Start thinking

The structure of a text is the way it is put together: not just the plot, but the order of ideas and words which control how and when information is revealed, and the lengths of sentences and paragraphs. These can all influence the way a reader receives and responds to the text.

1 Read the sentence:

- *I knew he would get me into trouble.*

Now read the same sentence with altered **syntax**:

- *He, I knew, would get me into trouble.*

How does altering the **syntax** change the emphasis in the sentence?

2 Which of the following sentences creates more tension? Why?

a *Drops fell from the ceiling slowly, pooling in puddles the colour of blood.*

b *Drops fell from the ceiling, slowly pooling in puddles. The colour of blood.*

> **Key term**
>
> **syntax:** word order

60 Chapter 3 Studying prose

Chapter 3 . Lesson 3

Explore the skills

Authors carefully control the information they give readers (how much readers are allowed to know and when) through structural devices. These include:

Structural device	Example
juxtaposition: placing ideas next to each other, often highlighting differences	She turned from the warm, sunlit avenue, blossoming with the scent of summer, into a gloomy lane, chilly as a winter's night.
revealing or **withholding** information	Andre stared through the window. It couldn't be! Yet it was! He knew that face too well. With a gasp, he fainted.
lengths of sentences or paragraphs	Ali drew a sharp breath, glancing at the door handle; there was no doubt he'd heard a noise. Click.
altering the **focus** by zooming in or out, or panning across a scene	Across the hallway was a dark doorway and through the door stood a dark chair. There sat a man in darkness, one small eye blinking in his shadowy face, dark down to its pinpoint depths.

3 How do each of the devices in the table above help to create tension in the examples?

Read the following extract from the opening of a novel:

> Hale knew, before he had been in Brighton three hours, that they meant to murder him. With his inky fingers and his bitten nails, his manner cynical and nervous, anybody could tell he didn't belong – belong to the early summer sun, the cool **Whitsun** wind off the sea, the holiday crowd. They came in by train from Victoria every five minutes, rocked down Queen's Road standing on the tops of the little local trams, stepped off in bewildered multitudes into fresh and glittering air: the new silver paint sparkled on the piers, the cream houses ran away into the west like a pale Victorian water-colour; a race in miniature motors, a band playing, flower gardens in bloom below the front, an aeroplane advertising something for the health in pale vanishing clouds across the sky.
>
> It had seemed quite easy to Hale to be lost in Brighton.
>
> Graham Greene, from *Brighton Rock*

Glossary

Whitsun: holiday Sunday in spring

4 Start by thinking about what the writer focuses on in the extract.

  a) Put the following topics in order:
  - describes busy holiday crowd in the sun
  - returns to Hale
  - describes Hale's thoughts – he is nervous
  - describes his fingers and manner
  - describes bright, pale seafront and sky.

  b) Why would the author zoom out from the description of Hale and return to him later? What effect is created by shifting the focus from Hale to the scene beyond him and back again?

  c) What is emphasised by juxtaposing Hale and his 'bitten nails' with a description of 'the holiday crowd'?

Develop the skills

5 Explore the structure in depth:

a) The clause 'before he had been... three hours' is right in the middle of the first sentence. What information does it leave us waiting for? How would the sentence be different if that clause was at the end?

b) How do the lengths of the sentences about Hale compare to the third sentence, about the crowd and Brighton? Why might the author use these sentence lengths? What are we kept waiting for?

c) What is the impact of this punctuation and repetition: 'didn't belong – belong to the early summer sun'?

Apply the skills

6 How does the writer use structural devices to make this a memorable opening to the novel? In paragraphs, comment on:

- the order of topics
- sentence length
- syntax and punctuation.

Checklist for success

Follow these steps to structure your paragraphs:

✔ name the structural device

✔ clearly explain how it is used in the text

✔ discuss how it affects the reader's focus and responses to the text.

Check your progress:

▲ I can understand the way a writer uses structural devices, making reference to the text.

▲ I can very clearly understand the different ways a writer uses structural devices, thoughtfully developing my response in detail.

Chapter 3 . Lesson 4
Tackling themes

How do I gain a sense of key themes across a whole text?

Start thinking

A sense of overview is key to attaining high marks when analysing prose texts. A good way to explore how a text develops as a whole is by looking at how **themes** are portrayed across a text.

Authors may convey themes through a number of techniques, including:

- patterns of images
- characters
- settings
- events.

A repeated image can be used to develop a theme across a text.

1 What do you associate with volcanoes?

Read the following three extracts from across a novel about love.

> I remained sitting, looking up at him like a visit to a volcano, my Vesuvius, my Mauna Loa, spouting love

> This is love, moving to where the money is, and all the while a volcano or an ex-girlfriend might blow the whole thing to hell

> This was a San Francisco joke due to some rumors of a volcano lurking underneath the city [...] It was one of those news stories that made everyone giggle but might also be true. It was like love in that way
>
> Daniel Handler, from 'Adverbs'

2 a) The image of a volcano is explicitly connected to the theme of love. Why might the author repeatedly choose this image to explore love?

b) Explore how the recurring image is used to portray the theme of love. Complete the table on the following page.

64   Chapter 3 Studying prose

Chapter 3 . Lesson 4

Aspect of the volcano	What is implied about love
'looking up at him like a visit to a volcano... spouting love'	Suggests that when you are in love, your love interest seems to occupy your whole vision like an exciting landmark; it's as though you are covered and absorbed by love for them.
'a volcano or an ex-girlfriend might blow the whole thing to hell'	Suggests...
'a volcano lurking underneath the city'	The word 'lurking' could imply love...
'made everyone giggle but might also be true'	People giggle when they feel..... or... Suggesting love...

   c) Extension: How do the different ideas about the volcano come together to give an overall impression of love? Does the portrayal of love alter across the novel?

Explore the skills

You are now going to explore how a character can be used to develop a theme. Read this extract from near the start of a novel:

> She was a strong, agile girl, with stiff black hair [...] The first time you saw her take her hat off you got a surprise, for on her crown three white hairs glittered among the black ones like silver wires. It was typical of Rosemary that she never bothered to pull the white hairs out.
>
> George Orwell, from *Keep the Aspidistra Flying*

3 Explore what Rosemary's appearance reveals about the theme of social expectations:

   a) What do a few white hairs suggest about her age?
   b) Why do the white hairs cause 'surprise'?
   c) Why might a woman 'pull the white hairs out'?
   d) What does it suggest about Rosemary's attitude to social expectations that 'it was typical of Rosemary that she never bothered to pull the white hairs out'?

4 Now look more closely at the language used. The author tells us the hairs 'glittered' 'like silver wires'.

   a) What do you associate with glittering silver? Does this image seem positive or negative?
   b) What does it suggest about the author's attitude to Rosemary's aging hair?
   c) What could this imply about the author's view of social conformity?

Rosemary's character is described again towards the end of the novel, shortly after her marriage to the main character, Gordon:

> She had a touch of make-up on today, the first he had ever seen on her, and not too skilfully applied. [...] Rosemary looked twenty-eight, perhaps; Gordon looked at least thirty-five. But Rosemary had pulled the three white hairs out of her crown yesterday.

5 a) How has her appearance changed since the first extract?

b) What change must have taken place in her attitude to social expectations?

c) What does this change reveal about the theme of social conformity?

Develop the skills

Finally, several techniques can be combined to develop a theme across a short story. Read these extracts from across the short story 'The Flowers' by Alice Walker:

> Myop [...] felt light and good in the warm sun. She was ten, and nothing existed for her but her song, the stick clutched in her dark brown hand, and the tat-de-ta-ta-ta of accompaniment.
>
> [...] she made her own path, bouncing this way and that way, vaguely keeping an eye out for snakes. She found, in addition to various common but pretty ferns and leaves, an armful of strange blue flowers with velvety ridges [...].
>
> It was then she stepped smack into his eyes. Her heel became lodged in the broken ridge between brow and nose, and she reached down quickly, unafraid, to free herself. It was only when she saw his naked grin that she gave a little yelp of surprise.
>
> He had been a tall man. From feet to neck covered a long space. His head lay beside him [...]. Myop saw that he'd had large white teeth, all of them cracked or broken [...].
>
> Very near where she'd stepped into the head was a wild pink rose. As she picked it to add to her bundle she noticed a raised mound, a ring, around the rose's root. It was the rotted remains of a noose [...]. Myop laid down her flowers.
>
> And the summer was over.
>
> Alice Walker, from 'The Flowers'

6 a) The title of the story is 'The Flowers'. What do you associate with flowers?

b) 'Myopia' means short-sightedness. Why might the writer name the protagonist Myop? How is she literally or metaphorically short-sighted?

7 Complete the table to explore how the theme of lost innocence develops across the text.

Chapter 3 . Lesson 4

Technique	Quotations	What changes?	What could this suggest about the theme of lost innocence?
Setting			
• earlier	'warm sun'	The setting has become...	Myop's new knowledge takes the warmth and light out of her world
• later	'the summer was over'	as though the season...	
Image of flowers			
• earlier	'pretty ferns' 'strange blue flowers'	Myop collects flowers... By the end, she lays her flowers on a dead man.	The flowers change from... suggesting... to symbolising...
• later	'around the rose's root... remains of a noose' 'laid down her flowers'		
Character of Myop			
• earlier	'felt light and good... She was ten, and nothing existed for her' 'bouncing... vaguely keeping an eye out for snakes.'	Myop starts out feeling... and not really paying attention to danger. By the end...	Myop has become...
• later	'yelp of surprise' 'Myop saw... all of them cracked or broken'		

Apply the skills

8 How does the author portray the theme of lost innocence across the text? Use your notes from the table, and the example below, to write two or more paragraphs:
  - Name the technique and impression.
  - Give two quotations showing the change across the text.
  - Explain how the change connects to the theme.

Example:

> The author uses the setting to show a loss of innocence. At the start, Myop enjoys the 'warm sun' but by the end 'the summer was over' suggesting it has become cold and bleak. This implies that Myop's new knowledge of the world takes away her warm, light happiness, and makes her uncomfortable.

Check your progress:

▲ I can understand some of the ways themes are portrayed and start to explore meanings.

▲ I can very clearly understand the ways themes are portrayed and thoughtfully explore deeper implicit meanings in detail.

Lesson 3.4 Tackling themes

Chapter 3 . Lesson 5

Exploring setting

How do writers create and use settings?

Start thinking

Setting is the place and time in which an action or event occurs in a text. Where and when a text is set can have an impact on the reader's expectations of events, characters and themes, as well as the mood or atmosphere.

1 What mood do these settings suggest to you? Who would you expect to be in these settings? What events do you imagine taking place?

Settings can be realistic, for example, a farm, or fantastical, for example, a made-up country. Stories can be set in the past, present or future.

Some genres have **conventions** regarding settings. We might expect a fairy tale to take place 'once upon a time' and in a forest or castle. Sometimes, authors play with our expectations to overturn them.

> **Key term**
>
> **conventions:** the usual rules or expectations of a text type

2 How might a reader's expectations be altered by a fairy tale that began:

Once upon a Monday, in a land far away, a princess with a golden crown was wandering through a supermarket.

Explore the skills

Explore how a setting establishes key ideas about atmosphere. Read the following extract from the opening of a novel set in London.

Chapter 3 . Lesson 5

> Implacable November weather. As much mud in the streets, as if the waters had but newly retired from the face of the earth, and it would not be wonderful to meet a Megalosaurus, forty feet long or so, waddling like an elephantine lizard up Holborn Hill. Smoke lowering down from chimney-pots, making a soft black drizzle, with flakes of **soot** in it as big as full-grown snow-flakes – gone into mourning, one might imagine, for the death of the sun.
>
> Charles Dickens, from *Bleak House*

It is useful to read the description for key information about time and place before exploring ideas more deeply.

Glossary

soot: black substance produced from burning coal as a fuel

3
a) What time of year is it?
b) How would you describe the weather?
c) What condition is the city in?
d) What is your feeling about the atmosphere? Does it seem pleasant? Creepy? Gloomy? Calm?

4 Now explore some of the words and phrases more carefully for their suggested meanings. Complete this table.

Quotation	Surface meaning	What it suggests about the place and the atmosphere
'Implacable November weather'	'Implacable' means unstoppable, relentless.	Sounds like the weather is an enemy or goes on and on. Perhaps people feel…
'As much mud in the streets, as if the waters had but newly retired from the… earth'	'waters… retired' – it looks like a prehistoric flood has just finished.	Suggests the city… People walking in the streets will feel…
'it would not be wonderful to meet a Megalosaurus'	This is strange. It normally *would* be remarkable or 'wonderful' to meet a dinosaur in the streets.	It's so muddy that…
'a soft black drizzle, with flakes of soot in it as big as full-grown snow-flakes'	Normally, we use 'drizzle' to mean a light rain. 'Snowflakes' are usually white. But here, both are applied to black soot and smoke.	The words 'drizzle' and 'snowflakes' are used…
'gone into mourning, one might imagine, for the death of the sun.'	In Victorian London, going 'into mourning' meant to wear black clothes for mourning someone's death.	Implies the city looks…

Lesson 3.5 Exploring setting   69

Here is a response exploring how the writer describes the setting to give the reader an impression of the city. They have used their ideas from the table to structure their paragraph:

> Dickens compares the muddy streets to prehistoric earth, claiming 'it would not be wonderful to meet a Megalosaurus' in the mud. This hyperbole **suggests the city is so incredibly filthy and slushy that it is like a world where dinosaurs are usual – they would not cause any wonder in passers-by.** It also implies that the city is uncivilised, as though mankind has not developed yet.

- identifies techniques the writer has used
- selects a relevant quotation
- explains possible suggested ideas created by the technique
- for higher attainment, suggests another interpretation

5 Now choose another quotation from the table and write a paragraph of your own. Use the response example and the sentence starters to help you.

Key term

hyperbole: exaggeration for effect

> Dickens describes the setting as… in the quotation '_____'
>
> The word/phrase/technique… suggests… It also implies…

Develop the skills

Settings can be used to develop themes. Read this further extract from the opening of *Bleak House*.

> Foot passengers, jostling one another's umbrellas, in a general infection of ill-temper, and losing their foot-hold at street-corners, where tens of thousands of other foot passengers have been slipping and sliding since the day broke (if ever this day broke), adding new deposits to the crust upon crust of mud, sticking at those points tenaciously to the pavement and accumulating at compound interest.

6 As before, start by exploring the text for its surface meanings. Use these questions to help you.

   a) What is now being described? How does this add to the impression of the city?

   b) How do people in the city act? How do they feel?

Chapter 3 Studying prose

Chapter 3 . Lesson 5

7 Now look more carefully at the **connotations** of the words and phrases.

   a) What might we usually associate with the words 'infection' and 'ill'? Why might Dickens have used these words to describe the bad mood of the pedestrians?

   b) How do the phrases 'slipping and sliding', 'crust upon crust' and 'tens of thousands' add to our understanding of the atmosphere?

Exploring the way a writer uses patterns of language can help you to make connections to themes. Look at the words Dickens uses to describe the mud:

> adding new deposits to the crust upon crust of mud, sticking at those points tenaciously to the pavement and accumulating at compound interest.

The words 'deposits', 'accumulating' and the phrase 'compound interest' are all from the **semantic field** of money.

Money is an important theme in the novel *Bleak House*.

8 Why might Dickens use words to do with *money* to describe *mud*? What is he revealing about his *attitude* to money by doing this?

Extension: How do the *actions* and *feelings* of people in response to the mud add to our understanding of the link that has been made between mud and money?

> **Key terms**
>
> **connotations:** suggested meanings or associated ideas
>
> **semantic field:** a set of words or phrases that can be grouped by their meaning, linked to a particular subject, for example, 'battle', 'helmet', 'gun', 'enemy' are from the semantic field of war

Apply the skills

Now read the two extracts again.

9 Write five or more paragraphs exploring how Dickens has used the setting to convey:
   - mood and atmosphere
   - attitude and theme.

Checklist for success

Focus on the suggested meanings of particular words and phrases. Comment on:

✓ how he describes the weather and the mud
✓ how he describes the actions and feelings of people.

Check your progress:

▲ I can understand the way a writer uses language to convey setting and show some understanding of implicit information, making reference to the text.

▲ I can very clearly understand the different ways a writer uses language to convey setting, including implicit information. I can include a range of well-selected references to the text and thoughtfully develop my response in detail.

Lesson 3.5 Exploring setting   71

Chapter 3 . Lesson 6
Exploring character

How do writers create characters?

Start thinking

Characters are the people in a story. In some texts, characters may narrate the story or provide a viewpoint. Writers create characters through a number of techniques, including:

- descriptions and sometimes names
- dialogue and interactions with other characters
- actions and role in the narrative.

1 a) Practise inferring ideas about a character created through these techniques. What do you learn about this character?

Name:	Mr Grimroar
Description:	red-faced, as if a kettle was boiling inside his brain
Dialogue:	'Get back here!'
Actions:	Stamps out of the room, slamming the door.

b) Write your ideas as a paragraph, using these sentence starters:

The name 'Grimroar' suggests… The comparison to a boiling 'kettle' suggests he…

The imperative 'Get back here' sounds… His actions of 'slamming' and stamping imply he…

Explore the skills

Explore a character description from this opening of a novel:

> Jewel and I come up from the field, following the path in single file. Although I am fifteen feet ahead of him, anyone watching us from the cotton-house can see Jewel's frayed and broken straw hat a full head above my own […] Still staring straight ahead, his pale eyes like wood set into his wooden face, he crosses the floor in four strides
>
> William Faulkner, from *As I Lay Dying*

Chapter 3 Studying prose

Chapter 3 . Lesson 6

We can infer several impressions of Jewel from the extract.

2 Find relevant quotations to match these impressions:
- a) Jewel and the speaker have been working.
- b) Jewel and the speaker feel distant.
- c) Jewel is poor.
- d) Jewel may be older than the speaker.
- e) Jewel has fixed ideas and doesn't give much away.
- f) Jewel is confident.

3 What does the name 'Jewel' suggest?

Extension: What seems **ironic** about this name?

> **Key term**
>
> **ironic:** when words and their apparent meanings are deliberately the opposite of the situation or intended meaning

4 Explore the **language** used to convey the character of Jewel. Complete the table:

Technique/key words	Quotation	Impression of Jewel and *how* the impression was formed	Further interpretations
factual measurements: **fifteen feet**, **a full head**	'I am **fifteen feet** ahead of him' 'Jewel's... hat **a full head** above my own'	Jewel and the speaker are...	They may be...
adjectives: **frayed** and **broken**	'_____'	Jewel seems **poor** since his hat is '**frayed**', suggesting it's...	A hat shields from the sun – Jewel may work long hours in 'the field'
simile repetition	'eyes **like wood** set into his **wooden** face'	The repetition of '**wood**' make us think... Suggesting his face is...	The simile implies his eyes... He may feel...
verb: **strides**	'_____'	Makes Jewel seem...	The way he moves also implies...

Dialogue adds to our impressions of a character. Read the second extract, where Jewel keeps falling asleep at his jobs:

> "If you ain't sick, what's the matter with you?"
> "Nothing," Jewel said. "I'm all right."
> "All right?" pa said. "You're asleep on your feet this minute."
> "No," Jewel said. "I'm all right."
> "I want him to stay at home to-day," ma said.
> "I'll need him," pa said. "It's tight enough, with all of us to do it."

Lesson 3.6 Exploring character 73

5 Add to your table about Jewel:

Technique	Quotation and key words	Impression of Jewel and *how* the impression was formed	Further interpretations
dialogue, repetition	'_____'	Jewel repeatedly insists... Suggesting...	He may not want the others to feel... Because Pa says 'it's tight' suggesting...

Here is a response, exploring how the writer creates an impression of Jewel. They used their notes from the table to structure their paragraph:

> Faulkner's description of Jewel's 'frayed and broken straw hat' implies that he is poor, since the adjectives 'frayed' and 'broken' suggest the hat is worn out, so he is unlikely to wear it unless he can't afford a new one.

- identifies techniques
- selects a relevant, focused quotation
- gives an impression
- explains how the impression was created

6 The writer of the response could add other interpretations to develop this answer further. Use the table and these sentence starters to add another interpretation to their paragraph:

> We also know Jewel comes 'from the field' so maybe he wears the 'straw hat' to... suggesting...

7 Using your table and the example to help you, write three or more paragraphs of your own. Comment on the writer's use of **description** and **dialogue**.

Follow these steps to build your paragraphs:

- What has the writer used to give you an impression?
- Give a focused quotation, picking out key words and techniques.
- What impression did this give?
- How did you arrive at this impression?
- Are there other interpretations?

Develop the skills

Read the following extract from a novel. Claudia describes the arrival of a lodger, Mr Henry, at her parents' house.

74   Chapter 3 Studying prose

Chapter 3 . Lesson 6

Annotations (left side):
- What does the trick suggest about Mr Henry? What is the effect on the children?
- What does this phrase reveal about Mr Henry?
- What does this short sentence emphasise about the impact he has made?
- How does this clause affect our view of what has come previously? What do you now feel about Mr Henry?

Extract:

So when Mr Henry arrived on a Saturday night, we smelled him. He smelled wonderful. Like trees and lemon **vanishing cream**, and Nu Nile Hair oil and flecks of **Sen-Sen**.

He smiled a lot, showing small, even teeth with a friendly gap in the middle. Frieda and I were not introduced to him – merely pointed out. [...] To our surprise, he spoke to us.

"Hello there. You must be **Greta Garbo**, and you must be **Ginger Rogers**."

We giggled. Even my father was startled into a smile.

"Want a penny?" He held out a shiny coin to us. Frieda lowered her head, too pleased to answer. I reached for it. He snapped his thumb and forefinger, and the penny disappeared. Our shock was laced with delight. We searched all over him, poking our fingers into his socks, looking up the inside back of his coat [...]

We loved him. Even after what came later, there was no bitterness in our memory of him.

Toni Morrison, from *The Bluest Eye*

Annotations (right side):
- What does this short sentence suggest about the first impression Mr Henry makes on the children?
- What does this list suggest about Mr Henry's attitude to his personal appearance?
- What impression does this give of him?
- What do you feel about his teeth? How do they connect to your ideas about his breath mints and hair oil?
- What does the adjective 'friendly' imply about his personality?
- What is unusual about him, compared to the children's usual experience with adults?
- Why does he pretend they are film stars? What does this dialogue suggest about his personality?
- What is the reaction of the children? And their father?
- What impact has he had on Frieda?

8 Answer the questions in the annotations to explore how Mr Henry is portrayed.

Apply the skills

9 Write an analysis of the character of Mr Henry, using quotations and your ideas from the previous task. Explore the impressions you get of his:
- appearance
- personality
- effect on other characters.

Comment on the writer's use of techniques, including **description** and **dialogue**.

Glossary
- **vanishing cream:** moisturiser
- **Sen-Sen:** breath mints
- **Greta Garbo, Ginger Rogers:** Hollywood film stars

Check your progress:

▲ I can understand how a writer conveys ideas about a character, making relevant inferences.

▲ I can very clearly understand different methods a writer uses to convey ideas about a character, and thoughtfully analyse relevant and detailed interpretations.

Lesson 3.6 Exploring character

Chapter 3 . Lesson 7

Extension: Exploring character in depth

How does a writer use the way a character speaks and what they say to reveal their personality?

Start thinking

A character's personality can be conveyed through the way they tell the story and what they say.

Read the extracts below taken from a novel, *Wuthering Heights*, by Emily Brontë. Extract A is narrated by Lockwood. Extract B is narrated by Nelly Dean.

A: Lockwood

> Wuthering Heights is the name of Mr Heathcliff's dwelling. 'Wuthering' being a significant provincial adjective, descriptive of the atmospheric tumult [...] in stormy weather.

B: Nelly Dean

> I was almost always at Wuthering Heights [...] I ran errands too and helped to make hay, and hung about the farm

1. What differences do you notice between the two characters' language? Think about their use of: a) vocabulary b) the types of sentence they use.
2. Which one do you think is of higher social status? What about their language tells you this?
3. Which one is a visitor and which is local to the countryside? How can you tell?

Explore the skills

A writer can make a character reveal things about themselves through what they say about other characters. Lockwood chooses to tell us about his first impression of Heathcliff but actually reveals more about Lockwood's *own* character.

> He is [...] rather slovenly, perhaps, yet [...] he has an erect and handsome figure; and rather morose. Possibly, some people might suspect him of a degree of under-bred pride; I have a sympathetic chord within that tells me it is nothing of the sort; I know, by instinct, his reserve springs from an aversion to showy displays of feeling [...] He'll love and hate, equally under cover [...] – I bestow my own attributes over-liberally on him.
>
> Emily Brontë, from *Wuthering Heights*

Chapter 3 Studying prose

Chapter 3 . Lesson 7

4 First, what judgements does Lockwood make about Heathcliff in each of the highlighted descriptions?

Now think about how the way Lockwood talks about Heathcliff actually reveals something about himself:

5 Lockwood says: 'I bestow my own attributes over-liberally on him'. Which of Heathcliff's supposed qualities does he believe are really his own?

6 Lockwood uses several qualifiers: 'some', 'might', 'perhaps', 'possibly'. Which of Heathcliff's qualities does Lockwood seem to dismiss? Why might Lockwood do this?

7 Lockwood claims he has a 'sympathetic chord' and 'instinct' which reveal Heathcliff's personality to him. What does this suggest about Lockwood's *own* personality?

8 Lockwood asserts Heathcliff will 'love and hate equally'. Yet this is their very first meeting. What does this judgement reveal about Lockwood?

Develop the skills

Now read Lockwood's statements about himself and Heathcliff, who lives isolated on a windswept moor near Lockwood's lonely rented house.

> 'In all England, I do not believe that I could have fixed on a situation so completely removed from the stir of society. A perfect **misanthropist's** Heaven – and Mr Heathcliff and I are such a suitable pair to divide the desolation between us.'

> 'I felt interested in a man who seemed more exaggeratedly reserved than myself.'

Now read Lockwood's dialogue with Nelly:

> 'Mrs Dean [...] tell me something of my neighbours – I feel I shall not rest, if I go to bed; so, be good enough to sit and chat an hour'

9 Does your impression of Lockwood from his dialogue and his attitude towards Heathcliff match his portrayal of himself as a 'reserved' 'misanthropist'?

10 Is Lockwood a good judge of himself? Summarise your ideas in a couple of sentences.

Glossary

misanthropist: someone who dislikes people and human company

Check your progress:

- I can comment on effects of dialogue and narrative voice, referring appropriately to the text.
- I can confidently explore how dialogue and narrative create character, integrating many well-chosen textual references.

Apply the skills

11 What impression does Brontë create of Lockwood? Using your responses to the previous sections to help you, write three or more paragraphs considering: his language and dialogue; what he says about himself; what he says about others.

Lesson 3.7 Extension: Exploring character in depth

Chapter 3 . Lesson 8
Viewpoint and narrative perspective

How does viewpoint affect a reader's understanding of a text?

Start thinking

Narrative viewpoint is the perspective from which a story is told. Some genres have conventions regarding narrative viewpoint, for example, an autobiography is told in the first **person**.

In prose, there are several possible narrative viewpoints or **persons**.

> **Key term**
>
> **person:** point of view from which communication is delivered

1 Match the correct example on the right to the viewpoint on the left:

Viewpoint		Example
first person	**'I', 'me':** The narrator is within the story, giving their own point of view.	We saw Kelvin beside the road.
third person omniscient	**'he' 'she':** The narrator is outside the story. They seem omniscient (all-knowing), observing multiple characters and events.	You watched Kelvin dart into the road. You didn't move.
third person limited	**'he' 'she':** Again, the narrator is outside the story. However, their scope is more limited, following just one character.	I saw Kelvin dart into the road. I screamed.
second person	**'you':** Often found in advertising and poetry, this directly addresses the reader.	Frank rounded the corner as Kelvin ran for it. Sonny screamed.
first person plural	**'we', 'us':** Voicing the collective thoughts of several narrators.	Kelvin knew he had to run. He saw Frank approaching. He heard a scream.

2 Tell a partner about your day, using the first person.

3 Now get your partner to narrate your day, using the third person. How does this affect the telling?

Each narrative viewpoint creates different effects.

4 Complete the table, filling in the appropriate viewpoint to match the effect of writing from that perspective. The first row is done for you.

78 Chapter 3 Studying prose

Chapter 3 . Lesson 8

Narrative viewpoint	Effect of the viewpoint
first person	Creates a **subjective** and **biased** view of the story. Limits the narrative to events the speaker was aware of, but allows the reader to empathise with a character and understand their thoughts.
_____ person	Lets the reader follow a character's personal journey, but with more distance than first person. Lets the writer have range across the narrative, but less so than a fully omniscient speaker.
_____ person	Readers feel like they have been assigned the role of a character. Feels like the writer is addressing them directly.
_____ person	Allows the writer maximum range to describe events. Readers may know more than characters, helping to create suspense. Readers may relate less closely to characters, however.

Key terms

subjective: a personal view
biased: taking a particular side

Explore the skills

5 Read the following three extracts. For each one, discuss:

a) what person it is told in

b) what you feel is the effect of this on you as the reader.

> They asked where you learned to speak English and if you had real houses back in Africa and if you'd seen a car before you came to America. They gawped at your hair. Does it stand up or fall down when you take out the braids? They wanted to know. All of it stands up? How? Why? Do you use a comb? You smiled tightly when they asked those questions.
>
> Chimamanda Ngozi Adichie, from *The Thing Around Your Neck*

> He didn't have a suitcase or even a jacket, but I knew.
>
> My mouth opened and a roar started but it never came. And a pain in my chest, and I could hear my heart pumping the blood to the rest of me. I was supposed to cry; I thought I was. I sobbed once and that was all.
>
> Roddy Doyle, from *Paddy Clarke Ha Ha Ha*

Lesson 3.8 Viewpoint and narrative perspective

> Unoka was, of course, a debtor, and he owed every neighbour some money, from a few cowries to quite substantial amounts.
>
> He was tall but very thin and had a slight stoop. He wore a haggard and mournful look except when he was drinking or playing on his flute. He was very good on his flute...
>
> Chinua Achebe, from *Things Fall Apart*

6 Explore the effects of these narrative choices.

a) Re-write the first extract in the **first person**. How does this alter the way you feel about the narrator's feelings?

b) The second extract is a child's response to his father leaving for good. Re-write the extract in the **third person**, using the speaker's name, Paddy. How does this alter the way you relate to the character? Is there anything he says about himself which you would not include in a third person perspective? Why?

c) Re-write the second extract as if it was a **first person adult** perspective, recalling the event when he is grown up. What do you choose to alter?

d) The third extract describes Unoka. How might he describe himself in the **first person**? What information do you think he would alter or leave out from his own perspective?

Develop the skills

Some writers use multiple narrators. Read these extracts from *The Poisonwood Bible* by Barbara Kingsolver, describing Nathan Price, a missionary who takes his family to the Congo. It is written from the perspective of his wife Orleanna and two of his daughters, Leah and Rachel.

Leah

> This is what I most admire about Father: no matter how bad things might get, he eventually will find the grace to compose himself. Some people find him overly stern and frightening, but that is only because he was gifted with such keen judgement and purity of heart. [...] Being always the first to spot flaws and transgressions, it falls upon Father to deliver penance. [...] I know that someday, when I've grown large enough in the Holy Spirit, I will have his wholehearted approval.

Orleanna

> My steadfast husband tore his hair in private [...]. I held him in my arms at night and saw parts of his soul turn to ash. Then I saw him reborn, with a stone in place of his heart. Nathan would accept no more compromises [...]. He noticed the children less and less.

Chapter 3 . Lesson 8

Rachel

> It was Mother who decided to contribute most of the flock for feeding the village [...]. Yet, for all her slaving over a hot stove, Father hardly noticed how she'd won over the crowd. [...] I was sore at Father all right, for us having to be there in the first place. [...] When he gets his mind set on something you'd just as well prepare to see it through.
>
> Barbara Kingsolver, from *The Poisonwood Bible*

7 Explore the effects of the multiple narrative:

a) What details about Nathan's personality do the three narrators comment on? What is implied about his character by details mentioned by more than one narrator?

b) What do Leah and Orleanna say about Nathan Price's heart? What does this reveal about their different experiences of him?

c) What does Leah focus on when describing her relationship with her father? What does this imply about her?

d) How are Rachel's feelings about her father different from her sister Leah's? What might affect her viewpoint as the elder sister?

e) Leah says Nathan has 'keen judgement' and 'purity'. What evidence is there from her own and the other narratives to support or contradict this opinion?

Apply the skills

8 Why might the author choose to give us three different perspectives of Nathan Price? What effects have been created?

Use your ideas from the previous task to write three or more paragraphs discussing:

- what is revealed about Nathan Price
- similarities and differences between the narrators' views
- what can be inferred about the different narrators' concerns.

Checklist for success

Include:
- ✔ relevant quotations
- ✔ exploration of the possible effects on a reader.

Check your progress:

▲ I can identify narrative viewpoint and make inferences about the impact on a reader.

▲ I can very clearly and thoughtfully explore several interpretations of a writer's choice of narrative perspective.

Lesson 3.8 Viewpoint and narrative perspective

Chapter 3 . Lesson 9

Extension: Exploring narrative style

How do I explore an ambiguous narrative?

Start thinking

Some authors make their narratives deliberately **ambiguous**.

1 Why might an author want to create an ambiguous narrative? What experience will this give the reader?

One way of creating ambiguity is through an untrustworthy first person narrator, giving us a biased view. Another is through multiple narrators, providing different viewpoints. More unusual and complex is the use of **free indirect style**.

> **Key terms**
>
> **ambiguous:** suggesting more than one interpretation
>
> **free indirect style:** a third person narrative where the narrator adopts the voice of a character, seeming to merge first person subjectivity with third person narration

Explore the skills

Free indirect style allows a writer to merge the voice of a character with a third person narrative. It is easiest to understand through an example.

Read this extract from *Emma* by Jane Austen. Emma was trying to set up her friend Harriet with someone they both knew. Unfortunately, he thought Emma was interested in him instead.

> The hair was curled, and the maid sent away, and Emma sat down to think and be miserable. – It was a wretched business indeed! Such an overthrow of every thing she had been wishing for! – Such a development of every thing most unwelcome! – Such a blow for Harriet! [...]
>
> "If I had not persuaded Harriet into liking the man, I could have born any thing."
>
> Jane Austen, from *Emma*

2 Reread the highlighted section:
   a) Are these Emma's thoughts or the narrator's? Where does the narrator's voice begin and end?
   b) How is this narrative different from straightforward third person narrative?

82   Chapter 3 Studying prose

Chapter 3 . Lesson 9

Free indirect style has some advantages for an author.
- It creates ambiguity in the narrative.
- It can 'trick' us into accepting a character's subjective views as reality, so later events are more surprising.
- It can create irony or humour, as the third person presentation of a character's own voice gives us distance to be more judgmental about their words than a first person narrative.

3 What effects are created in the extract above? Irony? Humour? Tension? How do you think the writer wants us to feel about Emma's thoughts?

Develop the skills

Read the following extract, also by Austen. Isabella and her friend Catherine have been riding in separate carriages and have just returned to Catherine's home.

> the astonishment of Isabella was hardly to be expressed, on finding that it was too late in the day for them to attend her friend into the house:—
>
> "Past three o'clock!" it was inconceivable, incredible, impossible! and she would neither believe her own watch, nor her brother's nor the servant's [...] It was ages since she had had a moment's conversation with her dearest Catherine [...] with smiles of most exquisite misery, and the laughing eye of utter despondency, she bade her friend adieu...
>
> Jane Austen, from *Northanger Abbey*

4 Highlight words which seem to be Isabella's in one colour, and those which seem to be the narrator's in another. What do you notice?

5 By delivering Isabella's own words in the third person, we have more distance from them. Does this make her words more or less believable in your view?

6 Underline the **hyperbole** and **superlatives**. Do you think Isabella is sincere in her disappointment at running out of time? Why?

7 What do the **oxymorons** *'smiles of... misery'* and *'laughing... despondency'* imply about Isabella? What are her actions in these quotations? How do her actions compare to the way they are described?

Key terms

hyperbole: exaggeration

superlatives: adjectives expressing the highest degree, for example, *best, most*

oxymorons: combination of opposing ideas, for example, *white blackness*

Check your progress:

▲ I can recognise effects of ambiguity in a narrative, making appropriate reference to the text.

▲ I can confidently explore how narrative style creates multiple meanings, integrating many well-chosen and detailed textual references.

Apply the skills

8 In paragraphs, explain how Austen has created an ironic and revealing character portrayal in the above narrative. Consider:
- narrative ambiguity and use of the free indirect style
- other language techniques.

Lesson 3.9 Extension: Exploring narrative style

Chapter 3 . Lesson 10

Exploring language

How do writers use language techniques in prose?

Start thinking

Writers use language techniques to build readers' impressions of characters, settings and events.

1 Match the technique to the most appropriate example.

Technique	Example
A. interesting verbs	Z) Delicately, she brushed her glamorous, radiant hair.
B. interesting adverbs and adjectives	Y) The rollercoaster was a roaring giant, his breath in our hair.
C. metaphor	X) The room was as dirty as a slime-filled pond.
D. extended metaphor	W) I couldn't know. No-one could know.
E. repetition	V) The room was a slimy pond.
F. personification	U) She was greedy and mean; her brother was kind.
G. simile	T) The room was a slime-filled pond, clothes scattered like weed; the damp air felt like a clammy fish.
H. listing	S) She slouched in. Scurrying away, the cat mewled. She scowled.
I. contrast	R) There were dirty cups, plates, toys, shoes and socks.

Other techniques include oxymoron, onomatopoeia, alliteration and assonance.

Extension: Use these techniques to describe a playground at break time.

A prose writer uses several techniques to build an overall impression, often in combination with structural devices, such as juxtaposition and sentence length.

2 Writers also use a range of sentence types. Write an example for each of the following. The first has been done for you.

- **minor:** sentence without a main verb, used for effect, for example, *The car in the road*.
- **declarative:** statement sentence, ending with '.'
- **interrogative:** question sentence, ending with '?'
- **exclamatory:** exclamation sentence, ending with '!'
- **imperative:** command sentence, an instruction

Chapter 3. Lesson 10

Explore the skills

You are now going to look more closely at a writer's use of language in an extract from a short story.

> With ==despair – cold, sharp despair – buried== deep in her heart like a wicked knife, Miss Meadows, in cap and gown and carrying a little baton, trod the cold corridors that led to the music hall. Girls of all ages, rosy from the air, and bubbling over with that gleeful excitement that comes from running to school on a fine autumn morning, hurried, skipped, fluttered by; from the hollow class-rooms came a quick drumming of voices; a bell rang, a voice like a bird cried, 'Muriel.'
>
> Katherine Mansfield, from 'The Singing Lesson'

When you read a text for the first time, note down key information about character and setting before exploring language more deeply.

3 a) What building are we in?

b) What time of year is it?

c) Where is Miss Meadows going? What is she carrying? What do you infer about her role?

d) How would you describe her mood?

e) What is the mood of the girls?

4 Now explore Mansfield's language techniques more closely.

a) How does the punctuation in the highlighted part of the text emphasise the meaning?

b) What words are repeated in the extract? Why might the author repeat these words?

c) What simile in the first sentence describes how Miss Meadows is feeling? What does this simile imply about her pain?

d) What adjectives in the first sentence add to our impression of her mood?

e) What verb is used to describe how Miss Meadows moves down the corridors? What list of verbs describes the pupils' movements? What contrast is created?

f) What adjective describes the classrooms? How does this reflect Miss Meadows' mood?

g) The short story is called 'The Singing Lesson'. What sounds do we hear? How do they compare with Miss Meadows' mood?

Lesson 3.10 Exploring language   85

h) How does the final simile echo a verb describing the girls earlier? What does this language pattern emphasise about the girls? How do they compare with Miss Meadows?

i) We might expect the author to use exclamatory sentences when conveying such intense emotions. What do you make of the fact that the passage is two long declarative sentences?

Looking for patterns of language is a good way to gain a sense of overview.

5 Complete the table to explore how the writer creates links and contrasts between Miss Meadows and her surroundings:

Mood of Miss Meadows		Atmosphere of surroundings	
Technique and quotation	**What is implied**	**Technique and quotation**	**Implied link or contrast with Miss Meadows?**
verb 'trod'	Implies Miss Meadows feels…	list of verbs: _____	Girls' movements seem… Contrasting with… who…
adjective 'cold'	Miss Meadows…	adjectives 'cold' and '_____'	Classrooms seem…
simile '_____'	Her pain feels…. And the word 'wicked'…	simile '_____' and verb 'fluttered'	Girls are compared to…
_____ 'buried', 'deep'	Her feelings are…	adjectives, noun phrases 'gleeful _____', 'bubbling', 'rosy', '_____ drumming'	Girls are described… In comparison, Miss Meadows…

Here is a response, exploring how the writer uses language to convey an impression of Miss Meadows and her surroundings. They used ideas from the second and fourth rows of the table to structure their paragraph, drawing quotations together in a pattern:

> Mansfield juxtaposes Miss Meadows' despair with her surroundings. The adjective 'cold' describes her despair, implying isolation and discomfort; it is then also used to describe the school: 'cold classrooms'. Her misery seems reflected in the chilly building. This is in contrast to the happy school girls – they are 'rosy' – an adjective implying warmth, or happy blushes, while Miss Meadows is 'cold' and miserable. The comparison emphasises her despair and pain – like the freezing classrooms, her cold misery is at odds with the youthful liveliness of the students.

- selects a relevant pattern of quotations
- gives an overall impression created by the pattern of language
- identifies techniques the writer has used
- explains possible ideas suggested by the technique
- for higher attainment, draws ideas together in an overview

6 Choose another pattern of language and write a paragraph of your own. Use the example above, and the following sentence starters to help you.

86   Chapter 3 Studying prose

Chapter 3 . Lesson 10

Mansfield contrasts _____ through the use of _____ in the quotations '_____' and '_____'. Together, these suggest _____ and _____ while the girls are '_____'. The use of _____ implies they _____ compared to Miss Meadows _____

Develop the skills

A writer may build on images to create a *motif*. Read this further extract from 'The Singing Lesson'.

Key term

motif: recurring image or idea

> The Science Mistress stopped Miss Meadows.
>
> 'Good mor-ning,' she cried, in her sweet, affected drawl. 'Isn't it cold? It might be win-ter.'
>
> Miss Meadows, hugging the knife, stared in hatred at the Science Mistress [...]
>
> 'It is rather sharp,' said Miss Meadows, grimly.
>
> The other smiled her sugary smile.
>
> 'You look fro-zen,' said she [...] (Had she noticed anything?)

7 Look at the three patterns developed.

a) Despair:
- What image from the first extract has become an extended metaphor? What does it imply about Miss Meadows?
- What other idea first linked with her despair has been continued from previously?
- In two colours, highlight vocabulary associated with each of these two motifs. What do you notice?

c) Distrust:
- What punctuation emphasises the Science Mistress' way of talking?
- What phrase implies this is fake?
- What sentence type and punctuation imply Miss Meadows' paranoia?

b) Ironic contrast:
- What adjectives create a contrast between the Science Mistress and Miss Meadows?
- What is the purpose of the Science Mistress' interrogative? How is her purpose at odds with Miss Meadows' mood?
- What is ironic about the dialogue 'It is rather sharp' and 'You look fro-zen'?

Apply the skills

8 Reread the two extracts. Write four or more further paragraphs exploring how Mansfield uses language to convey an impression of Miss Meadows. Explore patterns and focus on the implied meanings of particular phrases and techniques. Comment on: Miss Meadows; her surroundings; her interactions.

Check your progress:

▲ I can understand the ways a writer uses language, making relevant references to the text.

▲ I can very clearly understand the different ways a writer uses language, in close detail and across a whole text. I can respond in developed detail, integrating a wide range of well-selected textual references.

Lesson 3.10 Exploring language   **87**

Chapter 3 . Lesson 11

Extension: Exploring symbolism

How do writers use symbols and associations?

Start thinking

Some writers use language in a symbolic way. **Symbols** work through associated ideas – links we make between objects and abstract ideas.

> **Key term**
>
> **Symbols:** something used to represent something else, for example, a heart could *symbolise* love

1 What concepts might the following things **symbolise**?

a)   b)    c)

2 What associations helped you make these links?

3 Thinking of symbols:

a) What is meant by the word 'civilisation'?

b) What objects could symbolise civilisation? Write your associations around a spider diagram.

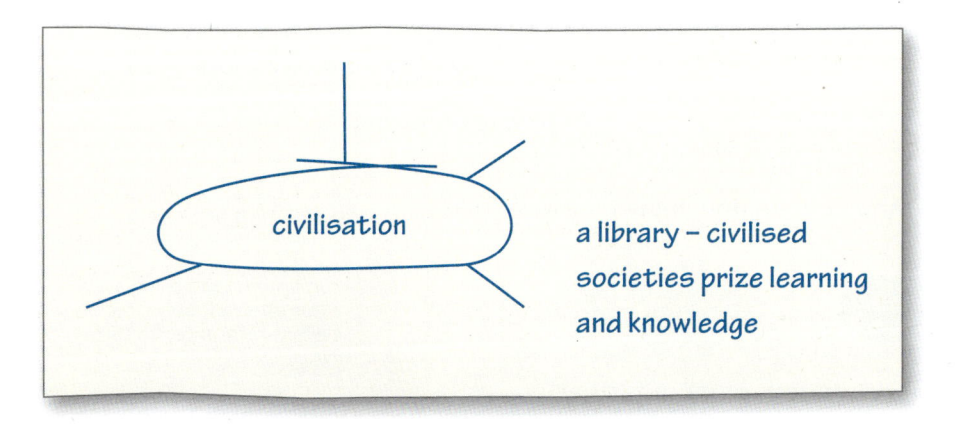

civilisation

a library – civilised societies prize learning and knowledge

88   Chapter 3 Studying prose

Chapter 3. Lesson 11

Explore the skills

Read this extract from a novel describing an upper-class community under siege, from the perspective of their leader, the Collector.

> Of all the ladies who had survived [...] none now displayed greater fortitude than Louise [...]. From this pale and anaemic-looking girl who had once thought only of turning the heads of young officers, and whom the Collector had considered insipid, he now saw a young woman of inflexible willpower emerging. He watched her as he passed the section of the hall reserved for the sick, the wounded, and the dying. Her cotton dress was rent almost from the armpit to the hem and as she leaned forward to bring a saucer of water to the lips of a wounded man, the Collector glimpsed three polished ribs and the shrunken globe of her breast; modesty was one of the many considerations which no longer troubled her. She stood up, mopping her brow with the back of a skeleton wrist. The Collector moved on, [...] and stood on the steps between the Greek pillars [...]. These pillars, he could not help noticing, were dreadfully pocked and tattered by shot. He thought contemptuously: 'So they weren't marble after all.' He lingered for a moment sneering at the guilty red core that was revealed beneath the stucco of lime and sand. He hated pretence.
>
> J. G. Farrell, from *The Siege of Krishnapur*

4 Start by exploring characters and setting:

a) What is Louise's physical condition?

b) How does she act?

c) Does she meet your expectations of an upper-class woman?

d) What does the Collector notice about Louise's appearance?

e) What is the Collector's opinion of Louise's personal qualities?

f) How is this different from what he thought about her before the siege?

g) What does the Collector notice about the appearance of the pillars?

h) How is this different from what he thought about them before the siege?

i) What is the Collector's opinion of the pillars now?

5 Explore symbols:

a) What ideas might you associate with 'Greek pillars'?

b) What does it suggest about the state of these concepts if the pillars are fake and crumbling?

6 Explore associations:

a) How is Louise's appearance comparable to a 'tattered' pillar?

b) How are her inner qualities affected by the siege, compared to those of the pillars?

Develop the skills

7 Civilisation is a key theme in the novel. Consider the Collector's views of Louise and the pillars.

a) What qualities does the Collector prize?

b) Is the *appearance* of civilisation important to him now?

c) How might the Collector define 'civilisation', in light of his experience?

Apply the skills

Now put all your findings together to complete the following task.

8 How has the writer conveyed ideas about what being civilised really means? Explore the following points, writing a paragraph on each one:

- the symbolism of the pillars
- links between Louise and the pillars; impact of the siege on both
- the Collector's views.

Chapter 3 . Lesson 11

Use these sentence starters to help you:

> The pillars could symbolise… because…
>
> The Collector notices…
>
> suggesting civilisation itself…
>
> Both Louise and the pillars… However, the siege has made the pillars… Whereas Louise…
>
> The Collector's attitude to Louise has changed…
>
> Now, his view of the pillars… The Collector now values…
>
> suggesting his view of civilisation…

Check your progress:

- I can understand a writer's use of symbolic language, making relevant references to the text.
- I can very clearly understand different ways a writer uses symbolic association. I can integrate a range of well-selected textual references, developing my response in considered detail.

Lesson 3.11 Extension: Exploring symbolism

Chapter 3 . Lesson 12

Viewing through context

How do I use my knowledge of context?

Start thinking

The context of a text is the situation surrounding it.

Context can be **social** or **historical**:	Context can be **literary**:
• The **life and times** of the writer which affects the way they write the text. For example, if a writer lived in the 1800s in England, they might write about scientific inventions and changes in industry that were happening at the time. • Events happening **at the time the text is read** which affect the way the reader views the text.	• Texts the writer has **read** which influenced them. For example, if a writer has read a poem or novel, they might refer to it in their own writing, or pick up on its themes. They might be influenced by other texts in the same form or genre. • Something **written** in response to or influenced by the text.

Writing about context should *not* be a history lesson. Your writing about context *must* be:

- directly linked to the text itself
- something which reveals further *meanings* in the text.

1 Consider how contexts contribute to meanings. Think about your favourite song.

   a) What is the song about?

   b) Is there anything about your life which makes this song very meaningful to you? Why?

   c) Do you know why the song was written, or information about people or places mentioned in it? How does this add to its meaning?

Explore the skills

Read the following extract from a novel. The main character, Newland Archer, arrives at a performance of the opera *Faust*.

> When Newland Archer opened the door at the back of the club box the curtain had just gone up on the garden scene. There was no reason why the young man should not have come earlier, for he had dined at seven, alone with his mother and sister, and had lingered afterward over a cigar in the Gothic library with glazed black-walnut bookcases and finial-topped chairs which was the only room in the house where Mrs. Archer allowed smoking. But, in the first place, New York was a metropolis, and perfectly aware that in metropolises it was "not the thing" to arrive early at the opera; and what was or was not "the thing" played a part as important in Newland Archer's New York as the [...] terrors that had ruled the destinies of his forefathers thousands of years ago.
>
> Edith Wharton, from *The Age of Innocence*

Chapter 3 Studying prose

Chapter 3. Lesson 12

2 Start by finding key information about characters and setting:

    a) What is Newland's approximate age?

    b) What do you find out about his family?

    c) What do you find out about his house?

    d) Where is the extract set?

    e) Why doesn't Newland arrive earlier?

    f) How does Newland feel about social and cultural rules?

Now consider social and historical contextual information relevant to the text:

- Newland has a 'club box' at the opera. A 'box' is a private balcony from which you can watch an opera, rather than sitting with the main crowd. A 'club box' is an opera balcony belonging to a club, so members of the club can use it.
- Being a member of a club was a social activity for upper-class men in the 1870s, when the story is set.
- Being a club member cost a lot of money.
- Going to the opera is often expensive. Occupying a 'box' at an opera is even more expensive.

3 What does the above contextual information suggest about the character of Newland?

Read the response paragraph below, examining the character of Newland. Notice how the contextual information is linked to the analysis of language.

> Newland Archer is a young man, living with his 'mother and sister', in a house with a 'Gothic library' implying the house is large and old-fashioned. The 'black-walnut bookcases' and 'finial-topped chairs' also sound expensive, suggesting the family is wealthy. He also has a 'club box' at the opera. In the 1870s, male members' clubs were for the upper-classes, so we can infer that Newland has high social status. As opera boxes are very costly, it further adds to our impression that he is rich, particularly as, despite the cost, he does not rush to get to the opera but arrives late, having 'lingered' over his cigar.

- selects relevant quotations
- infers from the text
- selects relevant contextual information
- links contextual information to relevant inference

Lesson 3.12 Viewing through context

4 How does the writer of the response link contextual information to inferences? Identify key phrases which help them join their ideas together.

5 Now consider the following literary context.
- The opera Newland goes to see is *Faust*.
- *Faust* is the story of a man who sells his soul to the devil for material things and worldly power. His fame and riches on earth come at a high price – he is eternally damned.

Why might the writer pick this opera for Newland to watch? What connections can you make between the plot of *Faust* and the rich, upper-class Newland, who conforms to worldly expectations?

6 How does this literary context influence your ideas about Newland? Complete the paragraph.

> Newland seems concerned with status and worldly rules as he is 'perfectly aware' it is '"not the thing" to arrive early at the opera', suggesting the rich upper-classes of 1870s New York follow certain social expectations. The fact that the author chooses to make the opera Faust could be significant as…

Develop the skills

Read the following extract from Maya Angelou's autobiography, *Mom & Me & Mom*. The author describes a conversation with her mother:

> I looked down at the pretty little woman, with her perfect makeup and diamond earrings, and a silver fox scarf. She was admired by most people in San Francisco's black community and even some whites liked and respected her. She continued. "You are very kind and very intelligent and those elements are not always found together. Mrs. Eleanor Roosevelt, Dr. Mary McLeod Bethune, and my mother—yes, you belong in that category. Here, give me a kiss." She kissed me on the lips and turned and **jaywalked** across the street to her beige and brown **Pontiac**.
>
> Maya Angelou, from *Mom & Me & Mom*

Glossary

jaywalked: crossed the road without using a designated crossing

Pontiac: American car brand

94 Chapter 3 Studying prose

Chapter 3 . Lesson 12

7 Explore ideas about Angelou's mother.

  a) How does Angelou describe her mother's appearance and clothing?

  b) Consider the adjectives 'perfect', 'diamond' and 'silver'. What associations do you think of?

  c) What opinions do people have of Angelou's mother?

  d) What opinion does Angelou's mother have of Angelou? What can you infer about Angelou's mother, that she tells her daughter this?

  e) What does the verb 'jaywalked' suggest about Angelou's mother's personality?

Now consider the following contextual information:

- The extract is set in San Francisco in America in 1950.
- In 1950s America, black people were kept separate from white people in most areas of public life (segregation). Black people were subject to systematic racist treatment and prejudice.
- San Francisco was highly segregated; most black people were on a very low income.
- Wearing animal furs as scarves was fashionable in 1950s America. Furs were usually expensive.
- Eleanor Roosevelt was an American politician. Her husband was President F. D. Roosevelt.
- Dr Mary McLeod Bethune was a stateswoman, educator and civil rights activist. She was in Roosevelt's Black Cabinet, advising him on the concerns of black people.

8 How does this information affect your reading of the text?

Apply the skills

9 Write three or more paragraphs, exploring how the writer has portrayed her mother. Comment on the meanings created in light of your contextual knowledge. Include ideas about:

- her appearance
- opinions others have of her
- the opinion she has of her daughter.

Check your progress:

▲ I can understand the meanings of literary texts and their contexts.

▲ I can confidently explore texts beyond surface meanings and selectively integrate contextual readings to show deeper awareness of ideas and attitudes.

Lesson 3.12 Viewing through context   95

Chapter 3 . Lesson 13

Making interpretations

How do I make interpretations?

Start thinking

Making interpretations is about giving an opinion on the meanings in the text. Some texts are **ambiguous**, leaving room for more than one **reading**.

Read the following ending of a novel. The narrator has been in love with an unavailable woman. The story closes with him meeting her in the house, now ruined, where they played as children:

Key terms

ambiguous: suggesting more than one interpretation

reading: a way of interpreting a text

> I took her hand in mine, and we went out of the ruined place; [...] the evening mists were rising now, and in all the broad expanse of tranquil light they showed to me, I saw no shadow of another parting from her.
>
> Charles Dickens, from *Great Expectations*

1 This ending has been interpreted in different ways. Sort the ideas below into either positive or negative atmospheres:

| a ruined house | mist | calm light |
| rising mist disappearing | shadow | leaving a ruined past behind |

Explore the skills

Look at this student's notes on the quotation 'I took her hand in mine'.

- Could be happy ending – they're holding hands – symbol of loving relationship.
- Is it unrequited? Narrator 'took' her hand 'in mine' – sounds possessive – is she even holding his hand?

Chapter 3 . Lesson 13

2 Explore the remaining highlighted phrases from the Dickens extract above. For each one, consider its use as evidence for these two interpretations:

a) They will stay together.   b) He will never see her again.

Develop the skills

Read the following extract from *Things Fall Apart* by Chinua Achebe.

> Unoka was, of course, a debtor, and he owed every neighbour some money [...]
>
> He wore a haggard and mournful look [...] He was very good on his flute, and his happiest moments were the two or three moons after the harvest when the village musicians brought down their instruments, hung above the fireplace. Unoka would play with them, his face beaming with blessedness and peace [...] Unoka loved the good fare and the good fellowship, and he loved this season of the year, when the rains had stopped and the sun rose every morning with dazzling beauty. [...] Unoka loved it all, and he loved the first kites that returned with the dry season [...] As soon as he found one he would sing with his whole being [...]
>
> Unoka, the grown-up, was a failure. He was poor and his wife and children had barely enough to eat. People laughed at him because he was a loafer, and they swore never to lend him any more money because he never paid back.
>
> Chinua Achebe, *Things Fall Apart*

Annotations:
- What is Unoka's relationship with his community?
- How does his appearance make you feel?
- How do you feel about his enjoyment of his musical talent?
- What impression does his appearance give here?
- Does this description of sunrise affect your view of Unoka?
- How does the repetition of 'loved' affect your view of Unoka?
- How does this affect your view of Unoka?
- Do you agree with this?
- How do you feel for his family?
- How do you feel about people's laughter?
- Does Unoka bring anything to his community?

3 Consider the annotated questions to explore how Unoka's character could be interpreted.

Apply the skills

4 Consider these interpretations:

A. Unoka is a sympathetic character.

B. Unoka fails his community and family.

C. Unoka's love of life and beauty makes him loveable.

D. Unoka is self-indulgent and feckless.

Which do you find most convincing? Write four or more paragraphs, explaining your interpretation of Unoka's character.

Check your progress:

▲ I can present a considered opinion about a text, making relevant textual references.

▲ I can confidently express a personal judgement about a text, supported by very clear understanding and integrated, well-selected textual references.

Lesson 3.13 Making interpretations   97

Chapter 3 . Lesson 14

Planning and writing a critical essay

How do I plan a response to a critical question on a prose text?

Understand the task

During your course, you may have to write a **critical essay** on your prose text.

The question may be worded in a number of ways, but will always ask you to explore **the writer's methods**.

Sample questions:

- How does [author] make [character name] such a memorable character?
- What does [author's] writing make you feel towards [character name] at the end of the novel?
- Explore the ways in which [author] creates such a striking contrast between [character 1] and [character 2].

1 Read this example question on the short story 'Miss Brill' by Katherine Mansfield. (You can read the full short story on Worksheet 3.14.)

> How far does Mansfield's writing make you sympathise with Miss Brill in 'Miss Brill'?

The first thing to do is identify the key things the question is asking you to focus on. Look at the highlighting. For this question, the key focuses are:

   a) your feelings of **sympathy** towards Miss Brill

   b) **how** the writer makes you feel sympathy through their **writing**

   c) how **far** you sympathise with Miss Brill.

98   Chapter 3 Studying prose

Chapter 3. Lesson 14

Gather your ideas and evidence

The next step is to plan what to include in your response.

Remember:

- You are *not* being asked to retell the story. Focus on several key parts of the story in detail, making links that bring in your wider knowledge of the story and its context.
- You must closely explore *how* the language and structure of key parts of the story make you feel sympathy for Miss Brill.

Here are some parts you could choose to explore that might affect the extent to which you feel sympathy for Miss Brill.

A. Miss Brill's arrival at the park. She sits alone and finds it 'disappointing' that no one talks to each other. She 'always looked forward to the conversation'.

B. Her reflections on how the park is like a theatre – it's her entertainment; she fantasises about being important to the other people.

C. The mocking comments of the young couple on the bench.

D. The ending of the story.

2 Consider what other parts of the story you can use to respond to the task. Which parts are the most interesting to explore?

Plan your response

Once you have chosen key parts to explore in detail, you can organise your ideas into an argument. There are several ways of doing this:

> Focus on *parts of the story* that made you feel sympathy.
>
> - Consider how **one part** has made you feel sympathy for Miss Brill. Build one or more analysis paragraphs around this point, making links to broader ideas.
>
> - Then move on to the **next part** of the story that made you feel sympathy. Build a further analysis paragraph around this point, making links to broader ideas.
>
> - Continue until you have covered several parts in detail, making sure you explore aspects of **language, structure and form** that made you feel sympathy.
>
> - Don't forget to explore any parts that **limit** the extent to which you feel sympathy for Miss Brill as well.

Lesson 3.14 Planning and writing a critical essay

Focus on *ways* that made you feel sympathy.

- Recall writers' methods (for example, narrative perspective, dialogue and reported speech, imagery, descriptive techniques, structural devices and sentences).

- Choose **one method or pattern of language** you feel is significant in the way it contributes to the extent to which you feel sympathy across your chosen parts of the story. Write an analysis paragraph on how this method or pattern of language affects your view, including references from **several parts of the story** to make your point.

- Next, consider how **a second method or pattern of language** contributes to the extent to which you feel sympathy across the parts you chose. Write one or more analysis paragraphs, including **several parts of the story** to make your point.

- Continue until you have covered a number of relevant writers' methods.

You can also write your essay in another way of your own.

3 Decide your approach now, and gather your ideas into your chosen form of plan.

The final step is to plan your paragraphs.

Checklist for success

Paragraphs should do the following:

✔ Focus on the question (here, how far you were made to feel sympathy for Miss Brill).

✔ Engage with the text and present your own viewpoint.

✔ Support ideas with understanding of the text and a range of relevant quotations.

✔ Explain how language/form/structure choices create an impression.

✔ Explore beyond surface meanings, making links to deeper ideas about character, theme or context where relevant.

4 Read the annotated paragraph on the following page. What do you notice about the paragraph structure? What is successful about the analysis paragraph?

100 Chapter 3 Studying prose

Chapter 3 . Lesson 14

The writer makes me feel a great deal of sympathy for Miss Brill through the conversation she overhears the couple having on the bench. The boy calls her a 'stupid old thing' with a 'silly old mug'. The insults 'stupid' and 'silly' are offensive and dismissive. The noun 'thing' suggests they don't even recognise her as a person, while the repetition emphasises that she is 'old' and therefore, as the young boy and girl see it, not needed in society anymore. The boy's rhetorical question 'who wants her?' might echo Miss Brill's own feelings, hearing this. We know she has already felt isolated as she finds it 'disappointing' earlier when no one talks. My sympathy is therefore increased by the fact that she was looking forward to listening in with a 'trembling smile', so the young couple's rudeness makes Miss Brill feel further excluded and disappointed– it is saddening to see an old woman cast aside by the younger generation.

- knowledge of and quotations from the text
- close analysis of language that creates sympathy
- clearly reasoned argument and opinions
- links to deeper understanding of character, themes and context

Write your response

5 Now plan and write your response to the following task in 45 minutes:

> How far does Mansfield's writing make you sympathise with Miss Brill in 'Miss Brill'?

Lesson 3.14 Planning and writing a critical essay · 101

Chapter 3 . Lesson 15

Evaluating your critical essay

How should I evaluate my response?

Before you evaluate how well you have done, check the table on page 124. It will help you decide if your work falls broadly into the first or second category – or outside them.

1 Go through your own response and write annotations around it, like the example paragraph in the previous chapter.

2 Read the following, thinking about what the writer of the response has done well and what advice they might need to make more progress.

> I am going to write about Miss Brill and how far the writer makes me feel sympathy for her. I feel really sorry for her because she is lonely. She sits on the park bench but nobody speaks. It says, 'They did not speak. This was disappointing, for Miss Brill always looked forward to the conversation.' The word 'disappointing' suggests she is sad about it and makes me feel sorry for her. The words 'always looked forward' make me think she often comes to sit in the park to listen to others and this why she comes to the park. This makes me sympathetic because she must be lonely with no one to talk to. The context links to this because she is called 'Miss' so she's not married. For a woman in her time to be unmarried means she doesn't feel she fits in, as she is expected to marry.
>
> The fur at the start is different compared to the end. Miss Brill loves her fur. She says 'Little rogue!' which suggests she feels friendly to it like it's her naughty pet. So do the words 'laid it on her lap and stroked it'. It's like it's her only companion – she doesn't even have a pet, just a fur. So it is really sad for her when the couple insult it. They say "It's her fu-fur which is so funny," giggled the girl.'

— clear response to the task, developing a personal view

— some comment on the writer's use of language

— developing response

— some exploration beyond surface meaning

— clear knowledge of whole text – could be more clearly expressed

— some exploration beyond surface meaning

— inference used clearly to build argument

102 Chapter 3 Studying prose

> The girl is laughing at her through the verb 'giggled' which is mean. The broken word 'fu-fur' shows she is laughing so much she can't speak. ————— clear focus on the task
>
> Laughing at Miss Brill's fur hurts her feelings. This ————— clear knowledge of whole text; lacking focus. Clunky expression
> makes me feel a lot of sympathy. Miss Brill notices strange old people in the park. The quote says they come from 'dark little rooms or even – even cupboards.' At the end Miss Brill is the same, her room is 'like a ————— starting to explore deeper meanings – needs clearer explanation and focus on the task
> cupboard'. It means she's like one of those sad people in the park and didn't know it. This is irony.

Comment:

The response shows understanding of the text and task, and includes several relevant quotations. The writer starts to explore language and their response is reasonably developed, although clearer focus and explanation is needed in parts. They show some understanding of the deeper meanings of the text.

3 How could this sample response be improved? Using the table on page 124 and the annotations on the sample response, think about what advice you might give the writer of the response to improve their work. Write your advice in three or more bullet points.

4 Now read a second response to the same question. Think about what is an improvement on the first response.

> Mansfield creates a great deal of sympathy for Miss ————— presents argument; deliberate focus on task
> Brill through her use of narrative form. The story is narrated in the third person limited voice, allowing us to hear Miss Brill's thoughts, but also to understand ————— close analysis of form and language
> her character across time. For example, we find out that 'she usually bought a slice of honey cake... if there was an almond it was like carrying home a tiny present'. This habit, and the excitement suggested by the simile 'tiny present' reveals she often relies on small, nice moments to look forward to and get her through her lonely days. This increases our sympathy as it suggests she is very sensitive, making her sense of rejection at the end even more painful. ————— confident response to character and task

Lesson 3.15 Evaluating your critical essay   103

The image of the fur is the most significant feature that makes us feel sympathy for Miss Brill. At the start, she is excited to wear the fur: she exclaims 'Dear little thing!' The word 'dear' and the exclamation suggest its value to her. She almost seems to view it as a pet: 'she could have... laid it on her lap and stroked it'. She clearly takes care of it, keeping it in a box and giving 'it a good brush'. Furs were fashionable at the time, an expensive symbol of status. Miss Brill seems to only have this one: 'her fur', so it's probably her most fashionable, valuable item. This adds to the cruelty of the girl's mockery of it, calling it a 'fried whiting'. By comparing it to a dead fish, the girl's simile devalues the fur in the eyes of Miss Brill. At the end, she 'unclasped the necklet quickly; quickly'. The repetition of the adverb suggests she cannot bear to look at the fur anymore, making us pity her since something she once loved is spoiled for her.

One of Miss Brill's less sympathetic qualities is her eavesdropping on others, and her judgemental comments on other silent old people in the park as 'funny' and 'odd'. This is one of the sources of irony in the story as Mansfield later creates pity for Miss Brill through her silently eavesdropping on the dialogue of the couple on the bench. The boy calls her a 'stupid old thing' with a 'silly old mug'. The insults 'stupid' and 'silly' are offensive and dismissive. The noun 'thing' suggests they don't even recognise her as a person, while the repetition emphasises that she is 'old' and, as the young couple see it, not needed in society anymore. The boy's rhetorical question 'who wants her?' might echo Miss Brill's own feelings. We know she has already felt isolated as she finds it 'disappointing' earlier when no one talks. She was looking forward to listening with a 'trembling smile' so the young couple's rudeness make Miss Brill feel further excluded and disappointed, increasing my sympathy. Perhaps Mansfield makes us pity her to highlight the isolation of unmarried, elderly women in society.

Annotations:
- sustained focus on task
- integrated range of references; confident analysis
- sensitive understanding of deeper meanings
- sustained response; sensitive analysis of character and language
- evaluative response to task and text
- integrated range of references; confident analysis
- character overview
- sensitive link to context and authorial intent

The portrayal of her room at the end of the story emphasises her isolation, increasing our sympathy. Mansfield describes it as 'the little dark room – her room like a cupboard'. The adjectives 'little' and 'dark' make it sound cramped and dingy. The simile 'like a cupboard' implies she is being packed away and dismissed, just like her fur. This makes the final line more ambiguous: is the 'something crying' the fur, or Miss Brill? Like the fur, she is shut away in a box-like space, no longer fashionable, and unwanted.

— sustained response; sensitive analysis of character and language

— explores ambiguity

Comment:

The response shows sustained personal engagement with the task and text and a confident critical understanding, incorporating well-selected references. The writer of the response demonstrates detailed analysis, an insightful overview of the text, and appreciation of deeper implications.

5 What advice might the writer of this response need to make even more progress? Use the table on page 124 to guide your ideas.

Lesson 3.15 Evaluating your critical essay

Chapter 3 . Lesson 16

Planning and writing a passage-based essay

How do I plan a response to an extract-based question on a prose text?

Understand the task

During your course, you may have to write an **extract-based essay**.

The question may be worded in a number of ways, but it will always ask you to explore **the writer's methods:** *how* the writer achieves something.

For example:

- How does the author make this such a dramatic moment in the novel?
- How does the author's writing make [character name] such an entertaining character at this moment in the novel?
- How does the author vividly convey [character name]'s feelings at this moment in the novel?
- How does the author make this conversation between [character 1] and [character 2] so intriguing?

1 Read the extract from the short story 'Miss Brill' by Katherine Mansfield:

> Behind the rotunda the slender trees with yellow leaves down drooping, and through them just a line of sea, and beyond the blue sky with gold-veined clouds.
>
> Tum-tum-tum tiddle-um! tiddle um! tum tiddley-um tum ta! blew the band. Two young girls in red came by and two young soldiers in blue met them, and they laughed and paired and went off arm-in-arm.
>
> Two peasant women with funny straw hats passed, gravely, leading beautiful smoke-coloured donkeys.

A cold, pale nun hurried by. A beautiful woman came along and dropped her bunch of violets, and a little boy ran after to hand them to her, and she took them and threw them away as if they'd been poisoned. Dear me! Miss Brill didn't know whether to admire that or not! And now an **ermine toque** and a gentleman in grey met just in front of her. He was tall, stiff, dignified, and she was wearing the ermine toque she'd bought when her hair was yellow. Now everything, her hair, her face, even her eyes, was the same colour as the shabby ermine, and her hand, in its cleaned glove, lifted to dab her lips, was a tiny yellowish paw. Oh, she was so pleased to see him – delighted! She rather thought they were going to meet that afternoon. She described where she'd been – everywhere, here, there, along by the sea. The day was so charming – didn't he agree? And wouldn't he, perhaps?... But he shook his head, lighted a cigarette, slowly breathed a great deep puff into her face, and even while she was still talking and laughing, flicked the match away and walked on. The ermine toque was alone; she smiled more brightly than ever. But even the band seemed to know what she was feeling and played more softly, played tenderly, and the drum beat, 'The Brute! The Brute!' over and over. What would she do? What was going to happen now? But as Miss Brill wondered, the ermine toque turned, raised her hand as though she'd seen someone else, much nicer, just over there, and pattered away. And the band changed again and played more quickly, more gaily than ever, and the old couple on Miss Brill's seat got up and marched away, and such a funny old man with long whiskers hobbled along in time to the music and was nearly knocked over by four girls walking abreast.

Oh how fascinating it was! How she enjoyed it! How she loved sitting here, watching it all! It was like a play. It was exactly like a play. Who could believe the sky at the back wasn't painted? But it wasn't till a little brown dog trotted on solemn and then slowly trotted off, like a little 'theatre' dog, a little dog that had been drugged, that Miss Brill discovered what it was that made it so exciting. They were all on the stage. They weren't only the audience, not only looking on; they were acting. Even she had a part and came every Sunday. No doubt somebody would have noticed if she hadn't been there; she was part of the performance after all.

Katherine Mansfield, from 'Miss Brill'

Glossary

ermine toque: ermine is a pale fur; a toque is a type of hat

2 Now read this example question on the extract:

> How does Mansfield convey such a vivid impression of the scene in the park here?

The first thing to do is identify key things the question is asking you to focus on.

Look at the highlighting. For this question, the key focuses are:

a) the vividness of the scene in the park

b) **how** the writer makes it vivid through their use of language, structure and narrative form.

Gather your ideas and evidence

The next step is to plan what to include in your response.

Remember:

- You are *not* being asked to retell the story. Focus on several key parts of the extract in detail, not forgetting the beginning and end.
- You must closely explore *how* the language and structure of key parts of the extract gave a vivid impression of the scene in the park.

Here are some parts you could choose to explore and the methods used:

A. the colours and sounds at the start of the extract

B. the lists of people and their movements

C. the meeting and dialogue of the 'ermine toque and a gentleman'

D. the ending of the extract and Miss Brill's feelings towards the park.

3 How do the methods used in these parts of the extract give us a vivid impression of the park? Note down your ideas for each of the suggested areas to explore given above.

4 Recall writers' methods, for example, narrative perspective, dialogue and reported speech, imagery, descriptive techniques, structural devices and sentences. Annotate any other relevant sections of the extract for further methods used by Mansfield to create a vivid impression of the park.

Chapter 3 . Lesson 16

Plan your response

Once you have chosen key parts to explore in detail, you can organise your ideas into an argument. There are several ways to do this:

> a) Focus on *parts of the extract* that convey a vivid impression of the scene in the park.
>
> - Consider how **the start of the extract** conveys a vivid impression of the scene in the park. Build one or more analysis paragraphs around this point, making links to broader ideas.
>
>   ↓
>
> - Then move on to the **next part** of the extract that conveys a vivid impression of the scene in the park. Build a further analysis paragraph around this point, making links to broader ideas.
>
>   ↓
>
> - Continue until you have covered several parts in detail, **including the end**, making sure you explore aspects of **language, structure and form** that convey a vivid impression of the scene in the park.

> b) Focus on *methods* that convey a vivid impression of the scene in the park.
>
> - Consider how the **structure of the extract** conveys a vivid impression of the scene in the park across your chosen parts. Write an analysis paragraph including **several parts of the extract** to make your points.
>
>   ↓
>
> - Next, consider how **imagery and figurative language** convey a vivid impression of the scene in the park across your chosen parts. Write an analysis paragraph including **several parts of the extract** to make your points.
>
>   ↓
>
> - Next, consider how **other language choices or character dialogue** convey a vivid impression of the scene in the park across your chosen parts. Write an analysis paragraph including **several parts of the extract** to make your points.

You can also write your essay in another way of your own.

5 Decide your approach now and gather your ideas into your chosen form of plan.

6 The final step is to plan your paragraphs.

Checklist for success

Analysis paragraphs should do the following:

✔ focus on the question (here, how the scene in the park is made to seem so vivid)

✔ engage with the text and present your own viewpoint

✔ support ideas with understanding of the text and a range of relevant quotations

✔ explain how language/form/structure choices create an impression

✔ explore beyond surface meanings, making links to deeper ideas about character, theme or context where relevant.

Chapter 3 . Lesson 16

7 Read this annotated paragraph. What do you notice about the paragraph structure? What is successful about the analysis paragraph?

> The writer conveys a vivid impression of the park through their use of sound imagery. We hear the band play at the start of the extract through the onomatopoeia 'tum-tum-tum tiddle-um! tiddle-um!' The exclamations and 'tum' sounds suggest the music is loud and cheery which creates a pleasant atmosphere in the park. Later in the extract, the music is personified: it 'seemed to know what she was feeling' and the sounds seem to talk: 'the drum beat 'The Brute!' The Brute!' over and over'. Giving the music feelings and dialogue makes it seem to come alive. Perhaps Miss Brill's character likes to imagine the music as a person as she is so lonely, and this may be why the park seems so vivid and exciting for her.

- clearly reasoned argument; strong focus on the question
- close analysis of language that created a vivid impression of the scene in the park
- knowledge of and quotations from the text
- link to deeper understanding of character

Write your response

8 Now plan and write your response to the following task in 45 minutes:

> How does Mansfield convey such a vivid impression of the scene in the park here?

Lesson 3.16 Planning and writing a passage-based essay

Chapter 3 . Lesson 17

Evaluating your passage-based essay

How should I evaluate my response?

Before you evaluate how well you have done, check the table on page 124. It will help you decide if your work falls broadly into the first or second category – or outside them.

1. Go through your own response and write annotations around it, like the example paragraph in the previous chapter.

2. Read the following response, thinking about what the writer has done well and what advice they might need to make more progress.

> At the start, the park is described as colourful. The quote says 'yellow leaves down drooping' and 'beyond the blue sky with gold-veined clouds' this shows it is colourful because of the yellow, blue and gold. The writer does this to give you a picture in your mind. — *reasonable focus on task, though expression is a bit vague and repetitive; relevant references*
>
> The next thing that gives me an impression of the park is the noise the band's making 'tu-tum-tum' this is onomatopoeia. It makes it sound loud. 'Blew the band' is alliteration. The noise of the band makes it vivid. Because you can hear the sounds in the park and see the colours it makes the park come to life. — *understands text and methods but analysis lacks full focus on the task* / *response is more focused here*
>
> The park is busy and vivid because it is full of people. There is a list of people in the third paragraph of the extract. For example, 'girls', 'soldiers', 'women', 'nun' and a woman who is called by her hat 'ermine toque' and a 'gentleman'. The writer fills the park with people to show what a busy place it is. All the characters make it seem full and very social. In those days a park was a place you went to be seen and show off. The scene in the park is vivid because it's busy with people showing off. — *range of references; analysis is focused* / *some consideration of deeper meanings*

112 Chapter 3 Studying prose

Chapter 3 . Lesson 17

> The next thing that shows the park is vivid is the rhetorical question. Miss Brill asks 'what would she do? what was going to happen now?' This shows she is thinking about the events and the people in the park. She is worried. The park is interesting to her. This gives us a vivid impression. The ermine toque woman is sad because the man left her and it's like the band gets sad too it says 'even the band seemed to know what she was feeling and played more softly' this makes it seem like when one person in the park is sad everyone is sad. This makes the impression of the park more interesting because there are feelings in the park.

— reasonable focus on task, clear analysis, appropriate quotation

— personal response developed; reasonable focus

Comment:
This response shows reasonable understanding of the text and task, and includes several relevant quotations. It improves as it progresses and the focus and analysis becomes clearer and more developed. Understanding of some deeper meanings is shown. It would have been good to have covered more of the extract and considered deeper implications further.

3 How could this sample response be improved? Using the table on page 124 and the annotations on the sample response, think about what advice you might give the writer of the response to improve their work. Write your advice in three or more bullet points.

4 Now read a second response to the same question. Think about what is an improvement on the first response.

> The vividness of the scene is shown through the metaphor of the park being like a play at the theatre. The structure of the extract takes us from the 'backdrop' of luxurious 'gold-veined clouds', through a crowd, followed by a conversation between two characters, the 'ermine toque' and the grey gentleman. Finally we see the characters exit to music and a dog trots across the scene. This structure echoes Miss Brill's belief that 'It was exactly like a play. Who could believe the sky at the back wasn't painted?' The zoom out from the backdrop through to Miss Brill watching implies that the park is a show and she is the audience, which makes it seem a vivid scene.

— confident grasp of key method; strong focus on task

— perceptive overview of extract

— confident analysis of structure

Lesson 3.17 Evaluating your passage-based essay

Miss Brill also believes she is 'part of the performance' – but the extract ends with her sitting and thinking by herself. The scene is as vivid as a play, but is Miss Brill really involved? — *deeper implications explored; explores ambiguity*

Mansfield's use of colours and clothing allows us to imagine a brightly-coloured, vivid scene in the park. Bright — *sustained focus on question*
colours such as 'girls in red', 'soldiers in blue', 'violets', 'yellow' contrast with paler, washed-out colours: 'smoke-coloured donkeys', 'pale nun', 'gentleman in grey', 'the same colour as the shabby ermine'. The contrast emphasises all the different types of people in the scene, suggesting its vividness. Miss Brill takes particular notice of others' — *range of relevant references; careful sustained analysis*
clothing, unsurprisingly since at the time the park was a place to be seen in your most fashionable clothes. It seems more youthful characters have brighter clothing, while the — *deeper implications explored*
paler colours seem for the characters who are less social, older, or somehow excluded from the liveliness of the scene. This reflects the later exclusion of Miss Brill who becomes identified with her pale, shabby fur, and experiences rejection — *deeper implications explored; explores ambiguity*
from the young couple.

The writer conveys a vivid impression of the park through — *sustained focus on question*
her use of sound imagery. We hear the band play at the start of the extract through the onomatopoeia 'tum-tum-tum tiddle-um! tiddle-um!' The exclamations and 'tum' sounds suggest the music is loud and cheery creating a pleasant mood in the park. Later in the extract, the music is personified: it 'seemed to know what she was feeling', the sounds seem to talk: 'the drum beat 'The Brute!' The Brute!' over and over. Giving the music feelings and dialogue makes — *range of relevant references; careful sustained analysis*
it seem to come alive. Perhaps Miss Brill likes to imagine the music in the park as a person because she is lonely, which may be why the park seems so exciting for her. — *deeper implications explored; sustained personal response*

Mansfield's use of lists makes the park seem action-packed: lists of verbs at the start and end of the extract suggest the park is full of movement, for example, 'got up and marched away... hobbled along... knocked over'. Lists of people emphasise how popular the park is, for example, 'two young girls', 'two young soldiers', and so on. All the people are described with adjectives: 'young', 'beautiful', 'cold', helping — *range of relevant references; sustained analysis; focused*

114 Chapter 3 Studying prose

us to picture them. Miss Brill seems particularly interested in pairs and couples. The vivid portrayal of the park as a busy social scene contrasts with her passive stillness and isolation, foreshadowing her later rejection by the young couple.

— sense of overview; deeper implications explored

Comment:

The response shows sustained personal engagement with the task and extract. The writer of the response gives an insightful overview of the extract and how it fits into the text, incorporating well-selected references from across the extract. They demonstrate detailed analysis and a perceptive grasp of deeper implications.

5 What advice might the writer of the response need to make even more progress? Use the table on page 124 to guide your ideas.

Chapter 3 . Lesson 18

Planning and writing a critical commentary on unseen prose

How do I plan a response to an unseen prose question?

Understand the task

During your course, you may have to write a response to an unseen prose passage.

You are advised to spend around **20 minutes reading the question and text and planning your answer** before starting to write.

The text will be **literary prose,** such as an extract from a **short story, novel, autobiography or travelogue.**

The question is constructed in three parts, as annotated on the sample question below:

> Read carefully the following extract from a novel. A Victorian scientist is telling his dinner guests about a journey he took in his invention, a Time Machine, travelling millions of years into the Earth's future.

The first part tells you to carefully read the given extract and gives you some **information** about what is happening. **Read this information carefully.**

> How does the writer make this moment so memorable?

The second part is **the question itself**. It will ask **how does the writer** convey a certain **impression** in the extract, for example, of **tension, vividness, intrigue**. Therefore, you need to explore **the writer's methods.**

> To help you answer this question, you might consider:
> - how the writer portrays the Earth in this future world
> - how he conveys the feelings and experiences of the narrator
> - how he portrays the crab-like creatures.

The third part of the question gives you **three bullet points of possible areas of the extract to explore.** Use these bullet points to build your response.

Read carefully the following extract from *The Time Machine* by H. G. Wells. A Victorian scientist is telling his dinner guests about a journey he took in his invention, a Time Machine, travelling millions of years into the Earth's future.

Chapter 3 . Lesson 18

'I stopped very gently and sat upon the Time Machine, looking round. The sky was no longer blue. North-eastward it was inky black, and out of the blackness shone brightly and steadily the pale white stars. Overhead it was a deep Indian red and starless, and south-eastward it grew brighter to a glowing scarlet where, cut by the horizon, lay the huge hull of the sun, red and motionless. The rocks about me were of a harsh reddish colour, and all the trace of life that I could see at first was the intensely green vegetation that covered every projecting point on their south-eastern face. It was the same rich green that one sees on forest moss or on the lichen in caves: plants which like these grow in a perpetual twilight.

'The machine was standing on a sloping beach. The sea stretched away to the south-west, to rise into a sharp bright horizon against the wan sky. There were no breakers and no waves, for not a breath of wind was stirring. Only a slight oily swell rose and fell like a gentle breathing, and showed that the eternal sea was still moving and living. And along the margin where the water sometimes broke was a thick incrustation of salt—pink under the lurid sky. There was a sense of oppression in my head, and I noticed that I was breathing very fast. The sensation reminded me of my only experience of mountaineering, and from that I judged the air to be more rarefied than it is now.

'Far away up the desolate slope I heard a harsh scream, and saw a thing like a huge white butterfly go slanting and fluttering up into the sky and, circling, disappear over some low hillocks beyond. The sound of its voice was so dismal that I shivered and seated myself more firmly upon the machine. Looking round me again, I saw that, quite near, what I had taken to be a reddish mass of rock was moving slowly towards me. Then I saw the thing was really a monstrous crab-like creature. Can you imagine a crab as large as **yonder** table, with its many legs moving slowly and uncertainly, its big claws swaying, its long antennae, like carters' whips, waving and feeling, and its stalked eyes gleaming at you on either side of its metallic front? Its back was corrugated and ornamented with ungainly **bosses**, and a greenish incrustation blotched it here and there. I could see the many **palps** of its complicated mouth flickering and feeling as it moved.

'As I stared at this sinister apparition crawling towards me, I felt a tickling on my cheek as though a fly had lighted there. I tried to brush it away with my hand, but in a moment it returned, and almost immediately came another by my ear. I struck at this, and caught something threadlike. It was drawn swiftly out of my hand. With a frightful qualm, I turned, and I saw that I had grasped the antenna of another monster crab that stood just behind me. Its evil eyes were wriggling on their stalks, its mouth was all alive with appetite, and its vast ungainly claws, smeared with an **algal** slime, were descending upon me.'

H. G. Wells, from *The Time Machine*

Now read this example question on the extract:

> How does the writer make this moment so memorable?

Glossary

yonder: that over there
bosses: lumps
palps: mouth-parts
algal: like algae, a slimy sea-plant

To help you answer this question, you might consider:

- how the writer portrays the Earth in this future world
- how he conveys the feelings and experiences of the narrator
- how he portrays the crab-like creatures.

The first thing to do is identify the key thing the question is asking you to focus on.

Lesson 3.18 Planning and writing a critical commentary on unseen prose

Look at the highlighting in the question above. For this question, the key focuses are:

　　a) the **memorable** nature of this moment

　　b) **how** the writer uses methods to make it so memorable.

Gather your ideas and evidence

The next step is to reread the extract carefully, annotating anything that creates a very striking or memorable impression.

Remember, you are not being asked to retell the story; focus on the three suggested key ideas in the extract carefully:

- the portrayal of the Earth
- the feelings and experiences of the narrator
- the portrayal of the crab-like creatures.

Think about how these parts of the text make it very *memorable*. You must closely explore *how* the language and structure in these parts create a memorable impression.

1 Annotate the text. Consider what other parts of the extract make it memorable. Pay particular attention to the **beginning** and **end** of any extract. Have any **changes** taken place across the extract which create a memorable impression?

Plan your response

Once you have annotated the three areas of the extract for how they create a memorable impression, you can organise your ideas into an argument.

The simplest way to do this is to write one or more analysis paragraphs for each of the three bullet points suggested in the question.

If you have time, write a final paragraph on anything else that adds to the memorable impression. You could think about the passage as a whole and any changes that have taken place.

2 Decide the order in which you want to write about these memorable moments now.

3 Next, plan each section of your response.

Checklist for success

Each analytical section should:

✔ focus on the question (here, how this moment has been made so memorable)
✔ engage with the text and present your own viewpoint
✔ support ideas with understanding of the text and a range of relevant quotations
✔ explain how language/form/structure choices create an impression
✔ explore deeper ideas, going beyond surface meanings.

Read the example plan for the first bullet point given in the question:

What you need to cover	How the portrayal of the Earth makes this moment so memorable
• Focus on the question – how the moment is so memorable. • Engage with the text and present your own viewpoint.	• The Earth is memorable as it seems strange, almost lifeless, an alien world.
• Support ideas with understanding of the text and range of relevant quotations.	• The colours show a strange world: sky: 'deep Indian red'; sun: 'red and motionless'; rocks: 'harsh reddish colour'. • The only life is the 'rich green' of leaves. The sea is dead, covered with 'a thick incrustation of salt'. It's very still: 'motionless', 'not a breath of wind'.
• Explain how language/form/structure choices make it so memorable.	• Red feels oppressive, reminding us of blood, or a dying sun. • Stillness and dead sea suggest Earth is almost lifeless. Adjectives: 'rich', 'thick' suggest a great deal of time has passed for plants and salt to build up.
• Explore deeper ideas, going beyond surface meanings.	• Lifeless appearance of the Earth increases shock later in the passage when crab-creature appears – 'reddish… rock' is a monster! Sun described as 'red and motionless' – also somehow monstrous? • Writer maybe makes this memorable so we think about this future – what happened? Has humanity caused this?

Write your response

4 Now plan and write your response to the following task in 1 hour 15 minutes:

> How does the writer make this moment so memorable?

To help you answer this question, you might consider:
- how the writer portrays the Earth in this future world
- how he conveys the feelings and experiences of the narrator
- how he portrays the crab-like creatures.

Chapter 3 . Lesson 19

Evaluating your critical commentary on unseen prose

How should I evaluate my response?

Before you evaluate how well you have done, check the table on page 124. It will help you decide if your work falls broadly into the first or second category – or outside them.

1 Go through your own response and write annotations around it.

2 Read the following response, thinking about what the writer has done well and what advice they might need to make more progress.

> The first thing that's so memorable is the Earth in the future is really different which is really shocking. There aren't any people and the sky looks strange, it is 'deep Indian red and starless'. Everything is red except the plants. It doesn't look like anything is alive. It says 'all the trace of life I could see at first was the intensely green vegetation'. This means that the plants are the main thing alive. The sea is completely still which is strange because normally the sea has waves but here it says 'there were no breakers and no waves'. There is repetition of the word 'no' to show there's no waves. I think the writer is making us wonder where all the life has gone to.
>
> There is a lot of tension which makes it feel scary. There is a 'huge white butterfly' which scares him with a 'harsh scream'. The word 'harsh' is an adjective and makes it sound nasty and loud. Also butterflies don't scream so it's really strange. Then it gets more scary and the narrator is really frightened by a big crab. The simile 'as large as yonder table' shows the crab is enormous which is frightening. The simile 'like carters' whips' makes the antenna sound like they can whip you and hurt you. We get scared the narrator might die.

- understanding of extract; some focus on task
- several relevant quotations – could be more focused
- some language analysis
- attempts to explore deeper meanings
- some developed analysis
- relevant quotations; some language analysis
- beginning and end of this paragraph could be more focused on task; implicit understanding of task, however

Chapter 3 . Lesson 19

> He feels scared, it says the crab is a 'monster'. This makes it sound dangerous. He grabs it by mistake and it gets angry. 'Its evil eyes were wriggling on their stalks, its mouth was all alive with appetite'. The eyes sound gross and they are wriggling on stalks like a snail. It's covered in slime, it's disgusting which means it is memorable. It wants to eat him, it says the claws 'were descending upon me.' It ends on a cliff-hanger which makes it suspenseful. But actually we know he made it because he is telling this story at dinner.

— some consideration of effects of structure and narrative form

— some developed analysis and personal response; reasonable focus on task

Comment:

This response shows understanding of the extract and task, and includes some relevant quotations. The writer starts to explore language and their response is reasonably developed, although further exploration is needed and they could maintain clearer focus on the task with more precise expression, particularly in the middle. They show some understanding of the deeper implications.

3 How could this sample response be improved? Using the table on page 124 and the annotations on the sample response, think about what advice you might give the student to improve their work. Write your advice in three or more bullet points.

4 Now read a second response to the same question. Think about what is an improvement on the first response.

> The portrayal of the Earth makes this moment very memorable as it seems frighteningly strange, like an alien world. The colours of the sky and land show how much the Earth has altered in the future: the sky is 'deep Indian red'; the sun is 'red and motionless'; the rocks are 'harsh reddish colour'; the sea is 'pink'. This pattern of red colours seems unnatural – more like the planet Mars than the Earth. The adjectives 'deep' and 'harsh' make the red feel oppressive and threatening, reminding us of blood, or a dying sun. The only visible life is the 'rich green' of the leaves; the sea is dead, covered with 'a thick incrustation of salt'. The stillness of the place is emphasised through negations: 'no breakers or waves', 'motionless', 'not a breath of wind'. The negativity and lack of movement feel creepy: the stillness and salt sea suggest the Earth is almost lifeless, devoid of animals and people. The adjectives 'rich' green and 'thick' layer of salt suggest a great deal of time has passed, for the plants and salt to build up so much. The Earth's still and lifeless appearance increases the shock we feel later in the passage when a crab appears right next to the narrator – the 'reddish mass of rock' is really a monster! We might revisit the description of the sun as a 'red and motionless' – is it also somehow monstrous? Perhaps the writer makes this moment memorable so we consider this bleak future of the Earth carefully – what has happened to civilisation? Has humanity caused this barren world?
>
> The first person narrative makes the narrator's uneasy sensations more immediate and therefore more memorable for the reader. He feels a 'sense of oppression' and is 'breathing very fast' which might make us fear for him. His experiences are memorably creepy. He sees a 'thing like a huge' butterfly and hears its 'harsh scream' and 'dismal' voice. The noun 'thing' suggests life on this future Earth is indescribably strange, and the adjectives 'harsh' and 'dismal' make the cry sound terrible. It seems appalling that a butterfly can 'scream'. The scientist's sense of unease is emphasised by his shift from scientific verbs 'I noticed', 'I judged' to admitting 'I shivered', underlining his fear.
>
> This gradually increasing sense of unease contrasts with the sudden and terrifying appearance of 'vast' crab-like creatures, creating a memorable impact. The narrator draws attention to their frightening size through a rhetorical question 'can you imagine a crab as large as yonder table', reminding us this story is being told on an earlier Earth, at dinner, creating a memorable juxtaposition with this strange world.

Annotations:
- confident focus on task and understanding of text
- range of well-selected references
- close language analysis
- confident and sustained, detailed language analysis
- perceptive sense of overview; sensitive and exploratory comment
- confident engagement and exploration beyond surface meanings
- confident understanding of narrative form; sustained focus on task
- detailed close language analysis; range of well-selected and integrated references
- sustained focus on task; sense of structural overview
- confident grasp of text and narrative structure

122 Chapter 3 Studying prose

Chapter 3 . Lesson 19

> The narrator is shocked by their closeness, feeling 'frightful' when an antenna is 'tickling' him, which is shocking for the reader too as seconds ago it seemed he was alone. The alliteration of 'flickering and feeling' emphasises his fixation on the crabs' mouths, which he assumes are 'alive with appetite', creating a memorable close-up visual for the reader. He calls them 'sinister' and 'evil', making a moral judgement of them, yet ironically it is he who is an alien invader in their world — he is the real 'apparition', appearing suddenly from the past on their beach. This confrontation between past and future emphasises the distance between the two worlds, creating a very memorable impression.

— close analysis; sustained focus on task

— original response; confident reading and analysis with perceptive exploration of meanings

Comment:

The response shows perceptive, sustained personal engagement with the task and extract. The analysis is detailed, incorporating well-selected references and expresses ideas with clarity and precision. The writer of the response has an overview of the extract and considers several deeper implications.

5 What advice might the writer of this response need to make even more progress? Use the table on page 124 to guide your ideas.

Lesson 3.19 Evaluating your critical commentary on unseen prose

Check your progress:

What are the features of a *reasonably developed, relevant* personal response?

Knowledge	• You show how you know the text **well** by making reference to it and/or by quoting from it.
	• You make points that are **relevant** (close textual reference and/or quotation) to the task set.
Understanding	• You show a **sound** understanding of the text, reading beyond the surface to explore implicit meanings.
	• You **develop your ideas** on themes, characterisation or ideas.
Language and effects	• You write about **some** of the ways in which the writer uses **language, structure and form**.
	• You make **some exploration** of the **effects of the writer's choices** and how these effects are created.
Personal response	• You make your own honest and **considered** response to the text, appropriate to the task.
	• You show **some development of your own ideas** about the text and task.

What are the features of a response showing *sustained personal and evaluative engagement* with task and text?

Knowledge	• You show a **detailed** grasp of the text as a whole and a **deep** understanding of the task.
	• You support your **original** ideas with **carefully selected, well-integrated reference** to the text.
Understanding	• You show a **sophisticated understanding** of the implicit meaning of the ideas, characterisation and themes in the text.
	• You show your ability to **analyse, evaluate and interpret** the text in an **original** and **perceptive** way.
Language and effects	• You examine **in depth** the way the writer uses **language, structure and form** and you explore different **interpretations**.
	• You show the ability to make a **close analysis** of extracts from the text and (where appropriate to the question) respond to the writer's effects in the text as a whole.
Personal response	• You make a **convincing** response, showing deep interest, understanding and an involvement with both text and task.
	• You have your own individual **ideas and judgements** about the text and express them with **confidence and enthusiasm**.

Studying poetry 4

This chapter explores in depth the key concepts of Literature in English in relation to poetry. You will learn how to develop and express your ideas about poetry texts. You will also be guided through planning, writing and evaluating example responses to exam-type questions.

4.1 What to expect when you read a poem

4.2 Exploring themes and ideas

4.3 Exploring language

4.4 Exploring form, sound, rhyme and rhythm

4.5 Exploring structure in poetry

4.6 Exploring setting in poetry

4.7 Viewpoint and perspective

4.8 Exploring speaker, voice and character in poetry

4.9 Understanding context in poetry

4.10 Making different interpretations

4.11 Planning and writing a critical essay

4.12 Evaluating your critical essay

4.13 Extension: Developing an overview

4.14 Evaluating your work

4.15 Planning and writing a critical commentary on an unseen poem

4.16 Evaluating your critical commentary on an unseen poem

Chapter 4 . Lesson 1

What to expect when you read a poem

What should I expect when I read a poem?

Start thinking

1 Use the mind-map below to write down what you think about when you consider poetry.

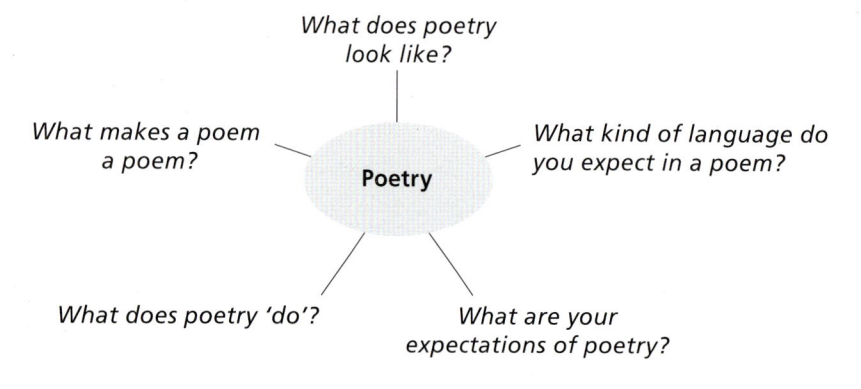

- What does poetry look like?
- What makes a poem a poem?
- What kind of language do you expect in a poem?
- Poetry
- What does poetry 'do'?
- What are your expectations of poetry?

Explore the skills

While you may have different ideas, many people's conception of poetry may be something like this famous piece from the 1590s:

> Shall I compare thee to a summer's day?
> Thou art more lovely and more temperate.
> Rough winds do shake the darling buds of May,
> And summer's lease hath all too short a date.
>
> William Shakespeare, from 'Sonnet 18'

Key terms

pathetic fallacy: when human emotion is attributed to a natural scene, often the weather

archaic language: words no longer in everyday use, and which give the impression of coming from a historical time period

2 Look at the table below, showing classic features of poetry.

a) Circle or highlight any of the features you can identify from the four lines of the Shakespeare sonnet above.

rhyme	onomatopoeia	**archaic language**	themes of death
themes of love	metaphor	repetition	rhyme scheme
alliteration	simile	**pathetic fallacy**	rhythm

126   Chapter 4 Studying poetry

Chapter 4 . Lesson 1

   b) Compare these with the ideas you wrote down in your mind-map.

   c) Generally, what is your impression of this poem? Does it conform to or go against your impressions of what poetry is?

Develop the skills

Read the poem to the right, written in 1934.

3 a) Take a look at those classic features of poetry listed in the table on the previous page. Do any of those apply to this text?

   b) Do you think this is a poem? Why or why not?

   c) What makes Williams's text different from Shakespeare's?

   d) Write two to three sentences summarising this text. What is it 'about'?

   e) What makes 'This Is Just To Say' different in terms of form and organisation from just a note left on the kitchen counter?

Apply the skills

It may seem surprising but 'This Is Just To Say' is one of the most famous American poems of the 20th century. Williams was known for challenging ideas of classic poetry and sought to write poems about everyday life.

4 Reread 'This Is Just To Say'.

   a) Circle or highlight the key adjectives in the last stanza. What **ideas** or **images** do they bring to mind?

   b) Consider the phrase 'Forgive me' in the last stanza. Who is the speaker addressing here? Does the speaker *really* sound sorry? If the speaker was *really* sorry, what might they have said instead?

   c) Why do you think the poet repeats the word 'so'? What effect does it have on the reader and on understanding the poem? Does it strike an apologetic **tone** or a triumphant **tone**?

5 Write a paragraph summarising your conclusions about 'This Is Just To Say'. How do the themes and ideas behind it make it a poem? Consider:
   - how the language used makes it a poem
   - how the structure and form make it a poem.

This Is Just To Say

I have eaten
the plums
that were in
the icebox

and which
you were probably
saving
for breakfast

Forgive me
they were delicious
so sweet
and so cold

William Carlos Williams

Check your progress:

▲ I can understand and identify features of poetry.

▲ I can clearly explain and analyse how a writer uses features of poetry to create meaning.

Lesson 4.1 What to expect when you read a poem   127

Chapter 4 . Lesson 2

Exploring themes and ideas

What is poetry 'about'?

Start thinking

When reading a poem, one of the first things you should do is think: 'What is this poem about? What **themes, ideas or feelings** are being expressed here?' Poems can tackle any number of subjects: from love and hate, to life and death… even, to fruit in a fridge!

Looking at how themes, ideas or feelings are developed through a poem will give you a valuable sense of overview that can earn you high marks.

Often, the title of a poem is the first step towards understanding a poem's themes and ideas.

1. You are going to read a poem called 'When I Heard the Learn'd Astronomer'.

    Before you read the poem, think about what the title might tell you and what it might lead you to expect.

    > **'When I Heard the Learn'd Astronomer'**

    a) Who might be the speaker in the poem? What might their attitude be to the 'Astronomer'?

    b) What does the term 'Learn'd' tell you? Is it in everyday usage?

    c) What sort of occasion do you imagine might be described?

    d) What sort of themes or ideas might this poem be about?

Explore the skills

Now read the poem, focusing your first reading on simply understanding what the poem is about and what ideas are introduced.

Chapter 4 . Lesson 2

When I Heard the Learn'd Astronomer

When I heard the learn'd astronomer
When the proofs, the figures, were ranged in columns before me,
When I was shown the charts and diagrams, to add, divide, and measure them,
When I sitting heard the astronomer where he lectured with much applause in the lecture-room,
How soon unaccountable I became tired and sick,
Till rising and gliding out I wander'd off by myself,
In the mystical moist night-air, and from time to time,
Look'd up in perfect silence at the stars.

Walt Whitman

2 How does the poem meet your expectations suggested by the title? What differences did you find with what you expected?

In this poem, the poet develops the themes of space and science. However, you need to say more than this when you outline a theme.

For example, you could say:

> The poem explores the relationship of humanity to the stars, and whether you understand space better by measuring and making charts, or simply by observing and feeling part of a mystical universe.

3 What other themes can you identify in the poem?

As you look more closely at the poet's language and technique, you will see how the theme develops. Writers will often build a **semantic field** of associated words to develop a theme throughout a text.

4 Complete the table below to catalogue words in the poem that fit each semantic field.

Maths, science and learning	Individual experiences, feelings, perceptions
'Learn'd'	'unaccountable'
'astronomer'	'tired and sick'

Key term

semantic field: a set of words or phrases that can be grouped by their meaning, linked to a particular subject, for example, 'battle', 'helmet', 'gun', 'enemy' are from the semantic field of war

Lesson 4.2 Exploring themes and ideas

Read this example of how the associated words from the semantic field of maths, science and learning build your understanding of the theme of humanity's relationship to the stars.

> The poem opens with the speaker sitting in a lecture theatre listening to the learn'd astronomer as he lectures. The poet creates the speaker's experience of the precise, measured, orderly world of the expert through a listing of terms from the semantic field of maths, science and learning. He is shown 'proofs', 'figures… ranged in columns' and 'charts and diagrams to add, divide and measure them'. This suggests that the learn'd astronomer is very certain of his way of understanding the stars.

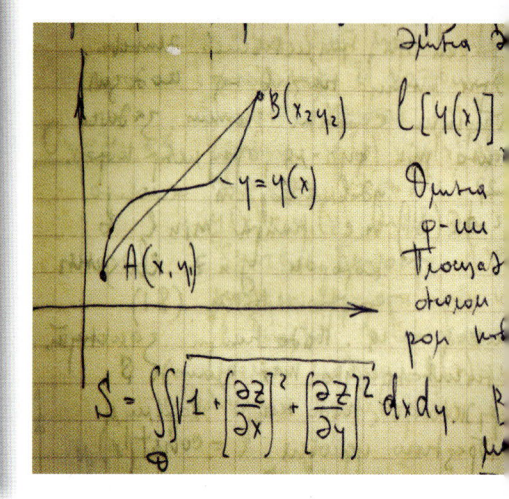

5 Now write a few sentences about the effect of the poet's use of the semantic field of individual experiences, feelings and perceptions.

Develop the skills

A theme will also be developed and explored through a range of poetic techniques.

6 Read the poem again, this time aloud, highlighting the following poetic techniques and making notes about how they affect the reader (what they make you think, feel or imagine).

- repetition of sentence starts (**anaphora**) in the first four lines
- the effect of using a single sentence and how it develops, is punctuated and runs on (enjambment) later in the poem
- the use of the passive voice and its effect in the first lines of the poem ('When I was shown…') compared with the active voice 'I wandered off' later in the poem
- imagery, sounds and sensations.

For example:

> The use of the passive voice in the lines, 'the figures, were ranged before me,/When I was shown the charts', makes the reader experience the speaker's lack of engagement and sense of bombardment.

Key term

anaphora: the deliberate repetition of the first part of a sentence for effect

Chapter 4 . Lesson 2

7 How does the language you identified relate to the poem's themes?

8 Consider the poem's final lines. What do you think they mean? How is the idea of learning different from the experience of learning presented earlier in the poem?

Extend your notes to include how you think the techniques develop your understanding of key **themes**.

Apply the skills

Read these two opening sentences, addressing the question 'How does Whitman present the theme of learning?'

Response A

> He finds learning boring because he is told things in a boring, stuffy way. He's not interested.

Response B

> The poet presents the theme of learning by introducing and developing the contrasting themes of active learning versus passive learning, suggesting in the poem his clear preference for the former.

Response A lacks specificity, direct links to the question and a comprehensive view of the poem. How does Response B improve on the first?

9 Using Response B above as a model, write a paragraph explaining how Whitman develops the key theme of science and/or passive learning in the first half of the poem.

10 Write another paragraph explaining how Whitman develops his theme in the second half of the poem towards the idea of mysticism and experiential learning.

Check your progress:

▲ I can understand some of the ways thoughts, feelings and ideas are portrayed and start to explore meaning.

▲ I can confidently analyse how thoughts, feelings and ideas are portrayed and explore deeper implicit meanings with sensitivity.

Chapter 4 . Lesson 3

Exploring language

Why do poets use the language they do?

Start thinking

The word 'home' is a loaded word; that is, it is full of meaning and **connotations** that go beyond its dictionary definition. Just think about this: what's the difference between a house and a home?

When this teacher thought of home once – a lovely little city in the southern US called Charleston – these words sprung to mind.

> Key term
>
> **connotations:** suggested meanings or associated ideas

> Where I come from
> The sunset hangs like a
> Pomegranate, ruby-red,
> In the starry-leaved sky.
> It soon ripens to an alabaster peach
> Pavilioned above the city's spires,
> Sharp and shadowed, swallowed up
> By the adjacent blackened harbour,
> The water slick and smooth to your caresses
> On a sultry summer's night.

1   **a)** When you think of home, what do you think of? Make a list of features, feelings and images.

      b) Now write your own poem about your hometown. Write at least 12 lines and use as many different poetic techniques as you can. It need not be flattering to your hometown.

Explore the skills

Poets choose their language with great care and, as attentive and perceptive readers, we need to be extremely sensitive to the meanings each word may carry or suggest.

132   Chapter 4 Studying poetry

Chapter 4 . Lesson 3

Word choice – denotation and connotation

When considering word choice in a poem, start with the word's **denotation** (that is, its literal meaning or dictionary definition), then think about its associative **connotations**.

Consider the word 'fist'. A 'fist' **denotes** a hand tightened into a ball. However, it **connotes** ideas of violence, aggression and animosity. Are there any additional **connotations** you can think of linked with a 'fist'?

Language techniques

Authors choose their words carefully, but they develop their meaning by using a range of language techniques.

2 Match each language technique in the left-hand column with an appropriate example on the right.

Technique	Example
1. imagery	a. The sky *brooded* in dark-grey clouds, and *sighed* a heavy wind.
2. metaphor	b. *Alone together*, I kept myself away from myself.
3. simile	c. *pink*-laced *petals*
4. personification	d. *plumed, wispy orbs*
5. alliteration	e. The peony blooms *like feathery ash*.
6. consonance / assonance	f. If we never fail, we can never *succeed*.
7. opposition & contrast	g. *the starry-leaved sky*
8. oxymoron	h. the *brittle rattle* of *sleepless dreams*

3 Read through the examples below, which use a 'fist' as a subject.

- **imagery and alliteration:** The hard, flinty fist shook in anger.
- **metaphor:** The fist – a hard, flinty rock – shook in anger.
- **simile:** The hard, flinty, rock-like fist shook in anger.

a) What impression do the adjectives 'hard' and 'flinty' add to the image of the 'fist'?

b) How does the /f/ alliteration of 'flinty' and 'fist' add to the harsh image of the 'fist'?

Lesson 4.3 Exploring language

c) Which image of the fist do you prefer: the metaphor or the simile? Why? How are they similar? How are they different?

d) How do these techniques develop further the connotations of a fist? Do they emphasise or change them in any way?

Develop the skills

Read the poem below.

> **The Fist**
>
> The **fist** clenched round my heart
> **loosens a little**, and I gasp
> **brightness**; but it tightens
> again. When have I ever **not loved**
> the **pain of love**? But this has moved
>
> past love to mania. This has the strong
> clench of the madman, this is
> gripping the ledge of unreason, before
> plunging howling into the abyss.
>
> Hold hard then, heart. This way at least you live.
>
> Derek Walcott

Annotations:
- 'fist' used here as a metaphor; suggests violence and tension
- alliteration of /l/; mimics the release of tension around the heart; the 'fist' is relaxing – perhaps falling out of love?
- 'pain of love' = contrast / opposition. Usually love thought to be pleasant and joyful, not painful; narrator loves not love, but the pain it brings – why?

4 Reread the poem, this time aloud. What other words does the poet use to develop the denotations and connotations of 'fist' throughout the poem?

5 Read the annotations of the first stanza, then continue to read and annotate the word choices and language techniques you notice in the second stanza.

6 Now work closely on the poem to answer these questions:

a) How does the short, enjambed sentence, 'but it tightens / again' add tension to the first stanza?

b) The poet also develops a **semantic field** of insanity in the move from the first to the second stanza. What language demonstrates this theme?

c) Look up the word 'abyss'. What does it mean? How does it develop the ideas of violence or insanity set up earlier in the poem?

134   Chapter 4 Studying poetry

7 **a)** The entire poem is a **metaphor** – one object has been substituted for another. What is the 'fist' a metaphor for?

b) What do you think the **images** of a fist and insanity have to do with love?

8 Read the poem again. What do you think the final line means? How does it relate to the connotations of a 'fist'?

Apply the skills

Read the response below, which analyses how key techniques develop meaning and themes.

> In the poem 'The Fist', the poet uses the metaphor of a fist to describe his feelings of being in love. The noun 'fist' has connotations of tension and aggression, which the poet introduces when he writes 'The fist clenched around my heart'. Here, the poet compares the feelings of being in love to the violent act of a fist holding and squeezing his heart – the organ most associated with love. Initially this strikes the reader as a negative, sad, even depressing image; in fact, we feel a sense of relief when the grip 'loosens a little', the alliterative /l/ sound mimicking the 'loosening' of tension here. However, we soon learn that the narrator 'loved / the pain of love.' The contradictory feelings of 'pain' and 'love' create an interesting irony here – the poet actually enjoys the aggressive ups and downs of falling and being in love. In the first stanza at least, the metaphor of a fist is used to represent the intense, forceful, even painful emotions that being in love makes him feel.

9 **a)** What key theme does this response focus on?

b) What language techniques does this response identify?

c) What does the response say about how each technique affects the reader?

10 Using the model above, write a second paragraph, which explains how the poet uses language techniques, such as semantic fields, imagery and metaphors, to develop the theme of love in the second and third stanzas.

Check your progress:

▲ I can identify the effect of language techniques and understand how they connect to the poet's ideas.

▲ I can convincingly analyse the effects of language techniques and show a sophisticated understanding of how they create meaning.

Chapter 4 . Lesson 4

Exploring form, sound, rhyme and rhythm

How do form and sound affect meaning?

Start thinking

The American Modernist poet Wallace Stevens wrote that:

'poetry is words; and that words, above everything else, are, in poetry, sounds.'

For Stevens, the *sound* of words in poetry was vital to understanding the *meaning* of the poem.

1 The following techniques focus mainly on the sound words create. Match each term with its appropriate definition.

Technique	Definition
alliteration	a. words that imitate or reflect sounds
consonance / assonance	b. repetition of the /s/ sound
sibilance	c. when words near each other begin with the same letter
onomatopoeia	d. the repetition of consonant / vowel sounds to create internal rhyme within phrases or sentences

2 Now, match the technique with an appropriate example.

Technique	Example
alliteration	a. The soft, sullen seas slowly churn.
consonance / assonance	b. The chirps and twits of goldfinches ring through the air.
sibilance	c. The dark night drew nigh.
onomatopoeia	d. The rustling curtain swirled, then came still.

Explore the skills

Sound – particularly techniques such as alliteration, assonance, sibilance and onomatopoeia – is vital to creating a rhythm or soundscape that helps the reader identify the themes, **tone** or **atmosphere** of the poem.

Key terms

tone: the voice, attitude or feeling created by the writer's language choices

atmosphere: the mood of a text

form: the type of poem, which may follow rules about a set number of lines, a set rhyme scheme, and a set metre or rhythm for each line

Chapter 4 . Lesson 4

However, the sound of words isn't the *only* way rhythm is created. Often, the **form** in which a poet decides to set the poem greatly affects word choice and rhyme – and thus, meaning.

> **Key term**
>
> **non-metrical:** without a regular rhythm

3 Below are some key poetic forms. Match the form with an explanation of its specific features.

Poetic form	Definition
sonnet	a. a poem in which an imagined speaker addresses a silent listener
free verse	b. a six-line stanza, or the final six lines of a 14-line sonnet
dramatic monologue	c. a rhyming four-line stanza
quatrain	d. a 14-line poem, with a variable rhyme scheme, and which 'turns' in terms of tone, usually after the first eight lines
sestet	e. an eight-line stanza, or the first eight lines of a 14-line sonnet
ballad	f. **non-metrical** (1), non-rhyming lines that closely follow the natural rhythms of speech
octave	g. a popular narrative song passed down orally. It usually follows a form of rhymed (abcb) quatrains alternating four-stress and three-stress lines

4 Read through the three excerpts from poems below. Which is:

a) a dramatic monologue: a poem that seems to be talking to someone else

b) a ballad: a poem that seems to begin telling a story

c) free verse: a poem that sounds like everyday speech?

This is a lifeskill, and I will learn
to go back to sleep without crying.
It is normal to find myself alone
at night. It is normal to call out
and for no one to come. I will adjust.

Sian Hughes, from 'Sleep Training'

But do not let us quarrel any more,
No, my Lucrezia; bear with me for once:
Sit down and all shall happen as you wish.
You turn your face, but does it bring your heart?

Robert Browning, from 'Andrea Del Sarto'

"But they are dead; those two are dead!
Their spirits are in heaven!"
'Twas throwing words away; for still
The little Maid would have her will,
And said, "Nay, we are seven!"

William Wordsworth, from 'We are Seven'

Lesson 4.4 Exploring form, sound, rhyme and rhythm 137

Develop the skills

Students responding to poetry often identify key features of poetic form or a rhyme scheme, without explaining the relevance of those elements to the meaning of the poem. Whenever you're discussing poetic form or rhyme, you must demonstrate *why* it is relevant and *how* it is relevant.

5 Which of the responses below better develops *how* and *why* the poetic form is relevant?

A

> The poem 'We are Seven' by Wordsworth is a ballad. It describes a conversation between the narrator and a little girl, 'the little maid', about death. She insists that she has seven siblings even though two of these are dead: 'And said, "Nay, we are seven!"'. This story makes the reader feel sad for the tragic loss, but happy that the girl gets on with her life. Moreover, the fact that the poet writes this as a ballad shows that he's creating a specific rhyme scheme – ABBA. This makes the poem flow better and helps the situation make sense.

B

> In the opening lines to 'Andrea Del Sarto', the poet introduces the idea of a lover's 'quarrel' between the narrator and his wife, 'Lucrezia'. The poet writes the poem as a dramatic monologue, whereby the narrator speaks directly to us. His use of direct address and the second-personal pronoun 'you' places the reader directly into the poem; in essence, we become Lucrezia, sitting down to listen to the narrator wax on about his career. This immediately draws our sympathies to the narrator, who, as is common in Browning's poems, may not necessarily deserve them. For example, his use of imperatives – 'bear with me for once' and 'Sit down' –suggests a tone of control in his voice which is belied by the calm and colloquial nature of his language.

6 Reread the excerpt from 'Sleep Training'. This poem is in **free verse**. Using the following notes, write a paragraph like the better response above, explaining how the form informs meaning.

- **What's it about?** The 'sleep training' of the title is a technique used with babies who cry a lot in the night. The idea is that, by ignoring their screams, parents train their child to get themselves back to sleep without help. This poem seems to be spoken by a person who is suffering and cannot sleep, but who is determined to train herself to sleep again. Is the speaker an adult or a child?
- **Form:** free verse, following the patterns of natural speech. This makes the expression of the poem feel more personal.
- **Techniques:**
  - Lines of verse **run on** – look and see where this happens and which words are emphasised. How does this affect meaning?
  - **Repetition**: find examples of words or phrases that are repeated. What tone of voice or feeling is created through the repetition?

Chapter 4 . Lesson 4

Apply the skills

Now practise those skills with another poem, one with a conventional form. Read the poem below.

> **What lips my lips have kissed, and where, and why**
>
> What lips my lips have kissed, and where, and why,
> I have forgotten, and what arms have lain
> Under my head till morning; but the rain
> Is full of ghosts tonight, that tap and sigh
> Upon the glass and listen for reply,
> And in my heart there stirs a quiet pain
> For unremembered lads that not again
> Will turn to me at midnight with a cry.
>
> Thus in winter stands the lonely tree,
> Nor knows what birds have vanished one by one,
> Yet knows its boughs more silent than before:
> I cannot say what loves have come and gone,
> I only know that summer sang in me
> A little while, that in me sings no more.
>
> Edna St. Vincent Millay

7
a) What do you think the poem is about? What does it describe?

b) What **form** does this poem take? How do you know?

c) Identify and annotate the rhyme scheme. Where do you see a big change in the scheme? How might that change be relevant to **meaning as it** develops in the poem?

d) What is the poem's **tone** and **theme(s)**?

e) Identify and annotate key techniques including **metaphors**, **similes**, **imagery**, **alliteration** and **sibilance**. How do these techniques help inform the meaning?

8 Write a paragraph addressing this question:

How does the poet portray the loss and loneliness of the narrator?

Make reference to the poetic **form** as a means of understanding the theme of loneliness.

Check your progress:

▲ I can identify aspects of form, sound, rhyme and rhythm and explain their effects.

▲ I can sensitively analyse aspects of form, sound, rhyme and rhythm and confidently link them to key meaning.

Lesson 4.4 Exploring form, sound, rhyme and rhythm

Chapter 4 . Lesson 5

Exploring structure in poetry

How does structure inform meaning?

Start thinking

Read the poem on the right aloud.

Even if you can't read it aloud, can you still *read* it? What does it say?

```
l(a
le
af
fa
ll
s)
one
l
iness
```
e. e. cummings

1 Write the poem out so that you can read it normally. How does this change its impact?

Explore the skills

The poem by e. e. cummings is an extreme example of how structure affects meaning. The way cummings has organised the poem quite literally makes it unreadable. However, that presentation – and even that inability to read to it – creates meaning.

2 The key theme is isolation and loneliness. But how does the poet express this idea?

   a) What key **image** does cummings employ?

   b) How does the poet use **enjambment** to emphasise these themes?

   c) What number does the structure of the poem resemble? Why might that be important to the poem?

   d) How does the inability to read the poem aloud reflect the key ideas within the poem?

> **Key term**
>
> **enjambment:** the continuation of a sentence without a pause beyond the end of a letter, word, line, couplet or stanza

Develop the skills

3 Look at these two responses on cummings's poem. Which do you think employs the term enjambment to the greatest effect? How and why do they do this?

A

> In 'l(a', the poet uses enjambment after the close parenthesis – 's) / one' – in order to develop the theme of isolation. In doing so, the poet places prominence on the word 'one' within the larger word 'loneliness'. Here, 'one' emphasises the dramatic and intense sense of loneliness the narrator feels.

B

> In 'l(a', the poet uses enjambment when he goes from one line to another while still in the same sentence. He does this throughout the entire poem, breaking up one word into different parts. This creates a sense of separation, which suggests he is apart from things. This affects the reader because we feel sad for him.

Chapter 4 Studying poetry

Chapter 4 . Lesson 5

Read the poem below.

> **Quickdraw**
> I wear the two, the mobile and the landline phones,
> like guns, slung from the pockets on my hips. I'm all
> alone. You ring, quickdraw, your voice a pellet
> in my ear, and hear me groan.
>
> You've wounded me.
> Next time, you speak after the tone. I twirl the phone,
> then squeeze the trigger of my tongue, wide of the mark.
> You choose your spot, then blast me
>
> through the heart.
> And this is love, high noon, calamity, hard liquor
> in the old Last Chance saloon. I show the mobile
> to the sheriff; in my boot, another one's
>
> concealed. You text them both at once. I reel.
> Down on my knees, I fumble for the phone,
> read the silver bullets of your kiss. Take this …
> and this … and this … and this … and this …
>
> Carol Ann Duffy

caesura

enjambment

4 What are the key themes developed in this text?

5 Notice where Duffy uses enjambment. How does the poet use each instance to create tension? How does this contribute to the meaning of the poem?

6 Notice where the author uses caesuras. What effect does this have on how you read the poem?

7 What is happening in the closing lines?

Key term

caesura: a pause at or near the middle of a poetic line

Check your progress:

▲ I can identify key features of structure and I understand how they can create meaning.

▲ I can confidently analyse how structural features create meaning.

Apply the skills

8 Now write a paragraph on the use of caesura in 'Quickdraw', using one or two examples.

Lesson 4.5 Exploring structure in poetry   141

Chapter 4 . Lesson 6
Exploring setting in poetry

What is the importance of setting within a poem?

Start thinking

Places often inspire poets, either because they believe the place tells a unique story or because the beauty or significance of the place captures their imagination.

1 Which of these famous places that form the setting and subject of a poem do you recognise?

2 **a)** Can you think of a place that particularly inspired or moved you? Where was it and why did it inspire you?

b) Write a short description (about 50 words) of that place – the sights you saw, the sounds you heard, the emotions you felt. What language – or even literary techniques – have you used to convey the emotional impact of that place?

Explore the skills

Setting can be concerned with time, place and **mood**. In poetry, the setting is often important to the way a poet introduces and develops key themes and ideas.

In many cases, the setting of a poem is the subject of the poem – that is, it is what the poem is about. However, poets often use setting metaphorically to introduce more complex ideas. In this sense, as a reader, you want to be aware of the ways in which poets may use setting to move from the concrete or **literal**, to the **metaphorical** or perhaps even symbolic.

Read the following poem written in 1803, and set on Westminster Bridge in London, near the Houses of Parliament.

> **Key terms**
>
> **mood:** the feeling or atmosphere of a piece of writing
>
> **literal:** the usual, basic meaning of a word or image
>
> **metaphorical:** symbolic or figurative meaning of a word or image

142   Chapter 4 Studying poetry

Chapter 4 . Lesson 6

Composed Upon Westminster Bridge, September 3, 1802

Earth has not anything to show more fair:
Dull would he be of soul who could pass by
A sight so touching in its majesty:
This City now doth, like a garment, wear
The beauty of the morning; silent, bare,
Ships, towers, domes, theatres, and temples lie
Open unto the fields, and to the sky;
All bright and glittering in the smokeless air.
Never did sun more beautifully steep
In his first splendour, valley, rock, or hill;
Ne'er saw I, never felt, a calm so deep!
The river glideth at his own sweet will:
Dear God! the very houses seem asleep;
And all that mighty heart is lying still!

William Wordsworth

3 What is the initial mood of the setting? Is it calm, peaceful, chaotic or hectic? Pick out words, phrases or images that give you this impression.

4 a) Wordsworth was a poet who loved nature and the rural countryside. However, in this poem he is in the middle of a major city. What emotions and thoughts are produced by this particular setting?

b) What language does he use to celebrate the city environment?

c) What about the rural environment?

d) Why do you think this city environment was so moving?

5 What techniques does the poet use to show his appreciation of the setting? What effect do these techniques have on the reader and your understanding of what the poem is about? Complete the table below.

Language / Image	Technique	Effect on the reader
'All bright and glittering in the smokeless air.'	imagery, adjectives	suggests a clean, pristine environment (ironic as it's a large city?)
'A sight so touching in its majesty'		suggests a sense of grandeur & magnificence
'The river glideth at his own sweet will'	personification	
'This City now doth, like a garment, wear / The beauty of the morning'		

Lesson 4.6 Exploring setting in poetry

Develop the skills

Read the following poem written in 1899 at a time of great change and industrialisation in Britain.

The Darkling Thrush

I leant upon a coppice gate
   When Frost was spectre-grey,
And Winter's dregs made desolate
   The weakening eye of day.
The tangled bine-stems scored the sky
   Like strings of broken lyres,
And all mankind that haunted nigh
   Had sought their household fires.

The land's sharp features seemed to be
   The Century's corpse outleant,
His crypt the cloudy canopy,
   The wind his death-lament.
The ancient pulse of germ and birth
   Was shrunken hard and dry,
And every spirit upon earth
   Seemed **fervourless** as I.

At once a voice arose among
   The bleak twigs overhead
In a full-hearted evensong
   Of joy **illimited**;
An aged thrush, frail, gaunt, and small,
   In blast-beruffled plume,
Had chosen thus to fling his soul
   Upon the growing gloom.

So little cause for carolings
   Of such ecstatic sound
Was written on terrestrial things
   Afar or nigh around,
That I could think there trembled through
   His happy good-night air
Some blessed Hope, whereof he knew
   And I was unaware.

Thomas Hardy

a) The poet uses personification here. What effect might this have on how the reader sees the landscape?

b) What do you notice about the imagery highlighted in grey?

c) The landscape here symbolises the century that has passed. What might the symbolism express?

d) What does the metaphor of the 'germ' or seed represent for the future?

Glossary

fervourless: passionless, without strong feeling

illimited: infinite, without limit

Chapter 4 . Lesson 6

6. What is the setting? Think about the time of day, the season, the weather and what can be seen.

7. What mood is created in the first two stanzas? Answer questions a)–d) annotated on the first two stanzas of the poem.

8. a) How does the mood change in the third and fourth stanzas?
   b) How is the thrush and its song described?
   c) What might be the significance of the beautiful song coming from the ageing bird in the gloomy landscape?

9. What might the ending of the poem suggest about hope?

Apply the skills

10. Which response below do you think more adequately addresses the effects of the setting on the poem 'Composed Upon Westminster Bridge'? Explain why.

A

Wordsworth vividly conveys the setting in 'Composed Upon Westminster Bridge' by comparing an urban landscape with a rural one. For example, the 'Ships, towers, domes, theatres, and temples lie / Open unto the fields, and to the sky.' Here, Wordsworth creates an image where the cityscape setting transitions seamlessly into the surrounding landscape, suggesting their equivalence in terms of beauty and inspiration; the fact that the city opens 'to the sky' moreover suggests to the reader that the city is a place of transcendence, or divine perfection.

B

Wordsworth shows that the city and nature are the same. Wordsworth loved nature and thought it more important, but here, he is in the city and says the city is just as good as nature. We see that the nature around the city is important, but so is the city itself. This proves then that Wordsworth thought the city setting as important as the natural setting.

13. Using the better example as a model, write a paragraph about the setting in 'The Darkling Thrush', and how it is used to represent the poet's thoughts and feelings.

Checklist for success

Make sure you include:
- ✓ key techniques you can identify
- ✓ effects on the reader.

Check your progress:

▲ I can understand the way a writer uses language to convey setting and show some understanding of implicit information, making reference to the text.

▲ I can very clearly understand the different ways a writer uses language to convey setting, including implicit information. I can include a range of well-selected references to the text and thoughtfully develop my response in detail.

Lesson 4.6 Exploring setting in poetry

Chapter 4 . Lesson 7

Viewpoint and perspective

In what ways does viewpoint influence meaning?

Start thinking

Just as poets agonise over language choices, they also very carefully choose the **perspective** or **viewpoint** from which a poem is narrated.

1 In the table below, match each viewpoint with an appropriate example:

Viewpoint	Example
1. first person perspective: told from the point of view of 'I', 'me', 'we' and 'us'	a. 'You must change your life'
2. second person perspective: told from the point of view of 'you' and 'your'	b. 'It is an ancient mariner, / And he stoppeth one of three'
3. third person perspective: told from the point of view of 'he/she', 'they' and 'them'	c. 'I wondered lonely as a cloud'

Explore the skills

The speaker and narrative perspective the poet chooses will be crucial to understanding key **themes** introduced and developed throughout the poem.

Read the opening stanzas from Samuel Taylor Coleridge's poem 'The Rime of the Ancient Mariner'. In this opening, the **third person speaker** tells the reader about an old sailor who stops a happy wedding guest ('one of three'), bewitches him with a crazed stare, and begins telling him a fantastical story. In this story he kills an albatross, whereupon his ship then gets lost at sea; his crewmates die, turn into ghosts and disappear; his ship sinks and he's rescued; and he becomes cursed to tell his tale throughout the lands forever as penance for his unprovoked crime against nature.

146 Chapter 4 Studying poetry

Chapter 4 . Lesson 7

It is an ancient Mariner,
And he stoppeth one of three.
'By thy long grey beard and glittering eye,
Now wherefore stopp'st thou me?

The Bridegroom's doors are opened wide,
And I am next of kin;
The guests are met, the feast is set:
May'st hear the merry din.' — *Here, you hear the wedding guest speaking to the Ancient Mariner, having been grabbed by him. What does the wedding guest say to the old man?*

He holds him with his skinny hand,
'There was a ship,' quoth he. — *What is the Ancient Mariner saying here? Does he take any notice of what the wedding guest says to him? Why or why not?*
'Hold off! unhand me, grey-beard loon!' — *The wedding guest is speaking again. What impression of the Ancient Mariner does he have here?*
Eftsoons his hand dropt he.

He holds him with his glittering eye—
The Wedding-Guest stood still,
And listens like a three years' child:
The Mariner hath his will. — *How has the wedding guest's attitude towards the Ancient Mariner changed by this point?*

The Wedding-Guest sat on a stone:
He cannot choose but hear; — *What does this line suggest about the wedding guest? Is he able to resist listening to the Ancient Mariner's story? Why or why not?*
And thus spake on that ancient man,
The bright-eyed Mariner.

Samuel Taylor Coleridge, from 'The Rime of the Ancient Mariner'

2 This poem is told by a third-person, **omniscient** – or all-knowing and seeing – speaker. Rewrite this episode in a prose paragraph or a rhymed/unrhymed poem from the first person perspective of the wedding guest. Consider:

- What is your speaker doing just before meeting the Ancient Mariner?
- What does the Ancient Mariner look like to your speaker?
- How does your speaker react to the Mariner?

Make sure you use details from the original poem in your reconstructed perspective.

3 How has the altered perspective changed your understanding of the story?

Glossary

Eftsoons: soon afterwards

Lesson 4.7 Viewpoint and perspective   147

Develop the skills

Read the excerpts from the poems below.

The Chimney Sweeper (*Songs of Innocence*)

When my mother died I was very young,
And my father sold me while yet my tongue
Could scarcely cry "'weep! 'weep! 'weep! 'weep!"
So your chimneys I sweep & in soot I sleep.

There's little Tom Dacre, who cried when his head
That curled like a lamb's back, was shaved, so I said,
"Hush, Tom! never mind it, for when your head's bare,
You know that the soot cannot spoil your white hair."

And so he was quiet, & that very night,
As Tom was a-sleeping he had such a sight!
That thousands of sweepers, Dick, Joe, Ned, & Jack,
Were all of them locked up in coffins of black;

And by came an Angel who had a bright key,
And he opened the coffins & set them all free;
Then down a green plain, leaping, laughing they run,
And wash in a river and shine in the Sun.

Then naked & white, all their bags left behind,
They rise upon clouds, and sport in the wind.
And the Angel told Tom, if he'd be a good boy,
He'd have God for his father & never want joy.

And so Tom awoke; and we rose in the dark
And got with our bags & our brushes to work.
Though the morning was cold, Tom was happy & warm;
So if all do their duty, they need not fear harm.

William Blake

The Chimney Sweeper (*Songs of Experience*)

A little black thing among the snow,
Crying "weep! weep!" in notes of woe!
"Where are thy father and mother? Say!"
"They are both gone up to the church to pray.

Because I was happy upon the heath,
And smil'd among the winter's snow,
They clothed me in the clothes of death,
And taught me to sing the notes of woe.

And because I am happy and dance and sing,
They think they have done me no injury,
And are gone to praise God and his Priest and King,
Who make up a heaven of our misery."

William Blake

In these two poems, the first written in 1789 and the second in 1794, Blake uses the same poetic subject, but uses a slightly different perspective.

4 Which poem starts in a first person perspective and then 'switches' to third person, and which one starts in third person, but then 'switches' to first person?

5 Reread the 'The Chimney Sweeper' (*Innocence*). What do you learn about the speaker in the first stanza?

6 Reread the 'The Chimney Sweeper' (*Experience*). What do you learn about the speaker in this poem?

7 How are the two speakers different? How are they similar?

In Blake's day, children were often used for dirty and dangerous jobs such as chimney sweeping; this appalled Blake. As a result, he often used his poetry to give a voice to vulnerable people who were exploited by those in power.

8 What effect does the first person perspective in these poems have on you, as a reader? Why do you think Blake uses a third person perspective in *Experience*? Who do you think is talking to the young boy and listening to his story?

Apply the skills

9 In the following response, the writer notes that Blake's use of perspective in the two 'Chimney Sweeper' poems:

> allows the reader to see the dire situation of child chimney sweepers from both the child's point of view as well as the concerned adult on the street.

Do you agree with this assessment? Write a paragraph, with reference to key quotations, explaining why or why not.

Check your progress:

- I can identify viewpoint in poetry and make inferences about its impact in a poem.
- I can confidently explore the effect of viewpoint and perspective in a poem.

Chapter 4 . Lesson 8

Exploring speaker, voice and character in poetry

Who's speaking in a poem and why does it matter?

Start thinking

Read the poem below.

> **I'm nobody! Who are you?**
>
> I'm nobody! Who are you?
> Are you – Nobody – too?
> Then there's a pair of us?
> Don't tell! they'd advertise – you know!
>
> How dreary – to be – Somebody!
> How public – like a Frog –
> To tell one's name – the livelong June –
> To an admiring Bog!
>
> Emily Dickinson

1
a) To whom is the **speaker** speaking in the poem?
b) Who do you think 'they' are?
c) Why do you think the speaker wants to be a 'Nobody'? What are the advantages? What are the disadvantages?

Key terms

speaker: the person in a poem who 'speaks' or describes the events

tone: the style and the opinions or ideas expressed in a piece of writing

diction: the speaker's style of expression and the wording or phrasing they use

Explore the skills

Closely linked to perspective are the concepts of poetic voice, speaker and character.

Voice encompasses the speaker's **tone**, **diction** and rhythm. This should give you an impression of the speaker's character.

2 Which of the following adjectives would you use to describe the **character** of the speaker?

> self-centred   internal   self-promoting   isolated
> superficial   private   introverted   extroverted

150   Chapter 4 Studying poetry

Chapter 4 . Lesson 8

3 Reread the poem aloud. Is the speaker being playful or serious? Which words or phrases suggest a playful tone? Which suggest a serious tone?

4 Consider the line: 'Don't tell! they'd advertise – you know!'

   a) Do the exclamations and hyphen emphasise the playfulness or the seriousness of the tone?

   b) How does the hyphen change the rhythm of the phrase? If you take it away, does it change how you say the phrase – or how you interpret it?

5 How do you think the speaker voices the phrases 'Don't tell!' and 'you know!' Angrily? Flirtatiously? Quietly? Frantically?

6 Do you agree with this student who wrote that the speaker, 'rejects the idea of fame and notoriety, and enjoys her status as a "nobody", an invisible person'?

7 Write a paragraph explaining your impression of the speaker, of her voice and character and of what you think the speaker's intentions are in this poem.

Develop the skills

Below is another poem where **voice** is a key feature of the poem: Carol Ann Duffy's 'Mrs Faust'. First, read the summary of the story of Doctor Faust (sometimes Doctor Faustus).

> Originally a German legend, the story of Dr Faust concerns a scholar who is successful, but largely dissatisfied with life. Using his interest in science and alchemy, Faust summons the Devil, and decides to sell his soul for unlimited knowledge and worldly pleasures during his life. However, in the end, the Devil comes to collect his due and carries Faust down to Hell for all eternity.

In her poem, Duffy retells the well-known story of Dr Faust, but changes the perspective and the voice to tell the Faust story from Faust's wife's **point of view**.

8 Read the excerpt from the poem below, then answer the questions in the annotations.

> **Mrs Faust**
>
> First things first –
> I married Faust.
> We met as students,
> shacked up, split up,
> made up, hitched up,
> got a mortgage on a house,

Lesson 4.8 Exploring speaker, voice and character in poetry   151

flourished academically,
BA. MA. Ph.D. No kids.
Two toweled bathrobes. Hers. His.
We worked. We saved.
We moved again.
Fast cars. A boat with sails.
A second home in Wales.
The latest toys –
computers,
mobile phones. Prospered.
Moved again. Faust's face
was clever, greedy, slightly mad.
I was as bad.

I grew to love the lifestyle,
not the life.
He grew to love the kudos, not
the wife.
[…]
I felt, not jealousy,
but the chronic irritation.
I went to yoga, t'ai chi,
Feng Shui, therapy, colonic
irrigation.
[…]
He wanted more.
I came home late one winter's
evening,
hadn't eaten.
Faust was upstairs in his study,
in a meeting.
I smelled cigar smoke,
hellish, oddly sexy, not allowed.
I heard Faust and the other
laugh aloud.
[…]
As for me,
I went my own sweet way,
saw Rome in a day,
spun gold from hay,
had a facelift,

[…]
went to China, Thailand, Africa,
returned enlightened.
Turned 40, celibate,
teetotal, vegan,
Buddhist, 41.
Went blonde,
redhead, brunette,
went native, ape,
berserk, bananas;
went on the run, alone;
went home.

[…]
At this, I heard
a serpent's hiss
tasted evil, knew its smell,
as scaly devil's hands
poked up
right through the terracotta
Tuscan tiles
at Faust's bare feet
and dragged him, oddly
smirking, there and then
straight down to Hell.

Oh, well.
Faust's will
left everything –
the yacht,
the several houses,
the Lear jet, the helipad,
the loot, et cet, et cet,
the lot –
to me.

C'est la vie.
[…]
I keep Faust's secret still –
[…]
[Faust] didn't have a soul to sell.

Carol Ann Duffy

a) What impression of the speaker's character and of her relationship with Faust do you get at this point in the poem?

b) What impression of Faust does the speaker create by this point in the poem?

c) By this point in the poem, does the speaker seem different from or similar to the character introduced in the opening of the poem?

d) By the end of the poem, what do you think Mrs Faust's opinion of Mr Faust is? Is she concerned with his fate? Why or why not?

152 Chapter 4 Studying poetry

Chapter 4 . Lesson 8

9 What adjectives would you use to describe the speaker of the poem?

> a. superficial b. considerate c. cynical
> d. loving e. doting f. manipulative
> g. indecisive h. vain i. selfless
> j. sincere k. materialistic l. unambitious

10 Following the example provided, use the table below to organise quotations around these key adjectival descriptions, as well as their effects.

Key adjectival description	Evidence	Effects
superficial	'Fast cars. A boat with sails. / A second home in Wales.'	Suggests to the reader that the speaker only likes luxurious, premier items.
cynical		
indecisive		She's had so many hairstyles and lifestyles – she's following fashionable 'trends' – that she's lost any true sense of self.
vain		

Apply the skills

11 Write a paragraph explaining why you think Duffy retells the Faust story from his wife's perspective.
- How is the story similar? How is it different?
- What do you learn of Mrs Faust as a wife? As a person? As a narrator?

Check your progress:

▲ I can identify key features of voice and character and link them to meaning.

▲ I can confidently analyse how aspects of voice and character create tone and meaning.

Chapter 4 . Lesson 9

Understanding context in poetry

What is context and how do I write about it?

Start thinking

1 Look at the picture below.

a) What do you think is happening here?
b) Why do you think Friedrich, the artist, painted it?
c) What do you think it signifies, suggests or 'means'?

To many people looking at this painting, it probably 'means' nothing. It is just someone standing on a mountain looking at some clouds.

Often, to understand a piece of literature, just like a piece of art, we need **context** – that is, some background information that helps us understand how and why it was created.

Friedrich's 'Wanderer over a sea of fog' is considered a masterpiece of **Romanticism** – a style of art (in literature and painting alike) that values the role of the individual over society, the power of nature over technology, and the mystical influence of the imagination over the rational rules of science.

Chapter 4 . Lesson 9

2 With that **context** in mind, consider these questions:

   a) Why does the painting's subject have his back turned to us? Why is he in such a beautiful, but remote environment? What might his standing over the fog represent?

   b) How does this contextual information help you appreciate this painting better?

> **Key term**
>
> **context:** background to a text that aids in understanding the text

Explore the skills

Cultural information can help you make sense of a poem. Read the poem below.

We Real Cool

THE POOL PLAYERS.
SEVEN AT THE GOLDEN SHOVEL.

We real cool. We
Left school. We

Lurk late. We
Strike straight. We

Sing sin. We
Thin gin. We

Jazz June. We
Die soon.

Gwendolyn Brooks

Brooks opens the poem here with an **epigraph** – information that prefaces the poem that is relevant to the poem's content. It provides some key context that helps the reader to understand the poem better.

'POOL PLAYERS' references the main subjects in the poem, a group of young men playing pool. 'SEVEN AT THE GOLDEN SHOVEL' lets the reader know that there are seven young men in this group, and that the name of the bar where they play pool is The Golden Shovel.

> **Key term**
>
> **epigraph:** a short phrase at the beginning of a text that summarises the content or themes

3 a) Why is this contextualising information helpful to your understanding of the poem?

   b) How does it help you understand the pool players' way of speaking, or dialect, in the poem?

Lesson 4.9 Understanding context in poetry   155

4 a) Where do you see the number 'seven' play some importance in the poem?

b) Where do you see language linked to pool playing?

c) What impression of the young men do you get from this poem?

d) Are they hard-working, studious types? Or are they irresponsible, cavalier rebellious types? What language suggests this?

5 The last lines of the poem – 'We / Die Soon.' may also read as an **epitaph** – that is, a memorial inscription often found on a grave or tombstone. How does Brooks' presentation of the language perhaps suggest this idea?

> **Key term**
>
> **epitaph:** a phrase written in memory of a person who has died

Develop the skills

6 Highlight and annotate instances of rhyme, alliteration and repetition. A student noted that these techniques give the poem a feeling of alternating dialogue, like people having a conversation. Do you agree?

Another piece of contextual information that might affect your understanding and response to the poem concerns the voice of the speaker(s). Phrases like 'We real cool' could be judged to be grammatically incorrect, with this reflecting negatively on the players. However, the missing verb from 'We real cool' (rather than 'We *are* real cool') is a feature of a language dialect spoken by some African-American communities.

7 a) How does this contextual information affect your response to the poem and its meaning?

b) Do you think the poem might be suggesting that some African-Americans had limited opportunities due to a racist society?

Finally, this additional biographical and historical context might influence your understanding of the poem: Brooks, an African American, wrote this poem in 1960 when jazz was a popular form of music and the fight for civil rights for Black Americans was growing.

8 Can you hear the ways in which Brooks gives this poem a musical quality?

9 Given the ending of the poem, do you think Brooks is celebrating the young men's rebellion or is she mourning it? Why do you think this?

Chapter 4 . Lesson 9

Apply the skills

While knowing about a writer's biographical information can be helpful, it can also hinder, limit or close down possible interpretations. Just like anything you write, you need to make sure that you put that information to useful purposes.

Read these two responses:

A

> In 'We Real Cool', Brooks talks about some people playing pool and drinking 'Thin gin'. This is important because Brooks was an African-American poet writing during Civil Rights.

B

> In 'We Real Cool', Brooks suggests that the 'Seven At The Golden Shovel' are poor teenagers who are wasting their lives. As an African-American poet writing during the struggle for Civil Rights, Brooks suggests we can see these seven as symbolic of the injustice towards poor black people at that time.

10 a) Which of these responses uses context to add to the understanding of the poem?

b) Which response helps develop a key theme?

Check your progress:

▲ I can understand the meanings of literary texts and their contexts.

▲ I can explore texts confidently beyond surface meanings and selectively integrate contextual understanding.

Lesson 4.9 Understanding context in poetry   157

Chapter 4 . Lesson 10

Making different interpretations

How can poems be interpreted in different ways?

Start thinking

1 Consider the phrase 'Stopping by woods on a snowy evening'. Which of the following interpretations of this phrase could you agree with?

  a) The person is stopping to warm up from the cold.
  b) The person is stopping because they are tired.
  c) The person is stopping to appreciate the natural environment.
  d) The person is stopping to see if anyone is following them.
  e) The person stopping is lonely.
  f) The person stopping wants to enjoy the peace and quiet.
  g) The person stops because they are contemplating their own mortality.
  h) The person stops because they are very busy but want a brief rest.
  i) The person is stopping because they have a flat tyre.
  j) None of the above.
  k) All of the above.

2 Why do some of these interpretations seem plausible – that is, more likely to be a valid interpretation – while others seem implausible?

3 Is it possible that two or more of these interpretations can be plausible at the same time? Why is that so?

Explore the skills

Read the poem below.

Stopping by Woods on a Snowy Evening

Whose woods these are I think I know.   A
His house is in the village though;   A
He will not see me stopping here   B
To watch his woods fill up with snow.   A

My little horse must think it queer   B
To stop without a farmhouse near   B
Between the woods and frozen lake   C
The darkest evening of the year.   B

He gives his harness bells a shake   C
To ask if there is some mistake.   C
The only other sound's the sweep   D
Of easy wind and downy flake.   C

Chapter 4 . Lesson 10

> The woods <mark>are lovely, dark and deep,</mark> **D**
> But I have promises to keep, **D**
> And miles to go before I sleep, **D**
> And miles to go before I sleep. **D**
>
> Robert Frost

One popular interpretation of this poem is that it is simply about a weary traveller who decides to take a much-needed respite to enjoy the natural scenery.

4 How might the highlighted language choices support this interpretation? Using the example below, create mind-maps for these highlighted phrases to tease out connotations suggesting an appreciation for the surrounding natural scene.

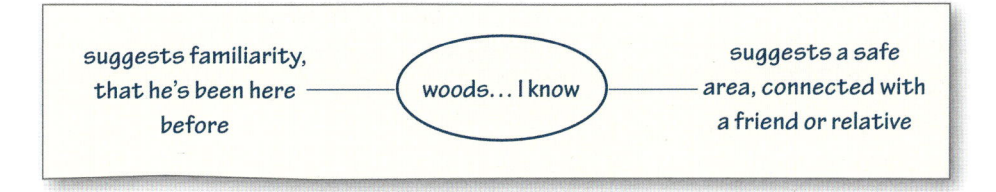

suggests familiarity, that he's been here before — **woods… I know** — *suggests a safe area, connected with a friend or relative*

5 Which of the following adjectives do you think captures the **mood** of the poem, following this interpretation. Explain why.

  a. gloomy   b. reflective   c. tranquil
     d. sinister   e. relaxing

6 The rhyme scheme of the poem has been annotated for you. Note how the rhyme scheme changes, and how the rhythm of the poem swings and sways. How does the rhyme and rhythm help create a peaceful and calming **mood** to the poem?

7 What **images** or other techniques does the poet use that would help you argue that this poem is about the loveliness of a natural scene?

Another popular interpretation of this poem is that it is not about appreciating nature but about death.

Lesson 4.10 Making different interpretations   **159**

8 How might the highlighted language support this alternative interpretation? Using the example provided below, create mind-maps for these phrases to tease out connotations suggesting death.

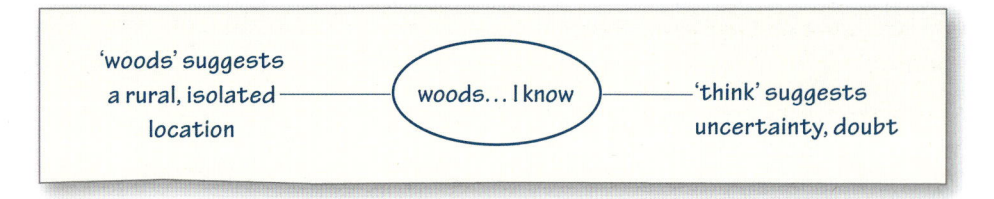

> 'woods' suggests a rural, isolated location — woods… I know — 'think' suggests uncertainty, doubt

9 Which of the following adjectives do you think captures the **mood** of the poem, following this interpretation? Explain why.

> a. lonely   b. reflective   c. depressed
> d. ominous   e. relaxing

10 Note how the rhyme scheme changes, suggesting something's 'off', and how the rhythm swings and sways, perhaps like the speaker's thoughts. How might the **rhyme scheme** and **rhythm** of the poem support the idea that this poem is about death?

11 What **images** or other techniques does the poet use that would help you argue that this poem is about the death?

12 If this poem is about death, what do you make of the repetition of the final lines? What do they mean in this case?

Develop the skills

13 Read the following two responses, each of which begin analysing the poem a different way. For each, write the second paragraph, trying to follow a similar line of argument. Prompts have been provided for the first response to help guide you.

> The poet introduces the key theme of natural appreciation in the first stanza. For example, the narrator says how he's 'stopping here / To watch his woods fill up with snow.' Here, the poet creates a peaceful and calm image of a person observing snow fall. The alliteration of the /w/ sound in 'watch' and 'woods' emphasises this by creating an equally peaceful and calm tone – the /w/ sound perhaps onomatopoeically mimicking the soft 'whoosh' of the snow falling. Moreover, the use of the verb 'stopping' suggests rest and repose, further highlighting the peaceful scene.
> The poet further develops this idea of natural appreciation when he writes '_____.'

160 Chapter 4 Studying poetry

a) Choose another quotation that may link to this point about the appreciation of nature, for example, 'The woods are lovely, dark, and deep'.

b) What key language or technique does Frost use in this quotation?

c) What does this key language or technique mean, suggest and/or connote?

d) What effect does this key language or technique have on the reader?

> The poet introduces the key theme of death in the first stanza. For example, the narrator says how no one will 'see me stopping here' to 'watch [the] woods fill up with snow'. Here, the poet creates an image of isolation and loneliness: the narrator is alone in the forest without anyone nearby to witness his activities. Here, the verb 'stopping' suggests a cessation of activity, which introduces connotations of death; the narrator will be 'stopping' here for the rest of his life. The passivity of 'watching… woods fill up with snow' could be symbolic of time passing away. The snow collecting on the ground is like an hour glass counting down the final moments of his life.
>
> The poet further develops this idea of death when he writes…

Apply the skills

Believe it or not, there is one further interpretation of this poem. While it's rather silly, it only serves to prove the point that if you have the evidence to support your argument, any sensible and reasonable interpretation can be valid.

14 Find evidence and write up to two paragraphs making the case that 'Stopping by Woods on a Snowy Evening' is actually about Father Christmas or Santa Claus.

Check your progress:

▲ I can understand that poems can be interpreted in different ways and I can find the necessary evidence to support my interpretation.

▲ I can confidently express a personal interpretation of a text, supported by very clear understanding and integrated, well-selected textual references.

Lesson 4.10 Making different interpretations 161

Chapter 4 . Lesson 11

Planning and writing a critical essay

How should I respond to a question on a poem I know well?

Understand the task

When you answer a question on a poem you have studied already, the first thing you should do is read the question carefully.

To start off, highlight or underline key words in the question, so you know specifically what you need to look for in the poem.

For example, look at one student's annotations of the following question:

Focus on authorial method; what techniques used?

Focus on characteristics; my opinion; how is the character portrayed? How is she portrayed in different ways?

> How does Duffy convey vivid impressions of Mrs Faust in these lines?

'vivid' means clear, vibrant; focus on imagery, adjectives, similes & metaphors

Titular character; main character; focus must be on her as:
*protagonist – wife of Dr Faust;
*speaker – first person, female perspective
*voice/tone

1 Practise this 'engaged reading' with the following question.

> How does Dharker powerfully portray the excitement of the people in these lines?

a) Highlight or underline all the key words in the question.

b) Annotate the question with ideas that help you understand what you need to do.

c) List all the techniques you can think of which might be relevant as you read through the poem.

Gather your ideas and evidence

After you have read the question in Question 1, highlighted or underlined key words in the question, made any appropriate notes, *then* you should reread the poem with the question in mind.

162   Chapter 4 Studying poetry

Chapter 4 . Lesson 11

Make annotations in the margins to record your thoughts and ideas on the poet's techniques, their effects and the meanings created that clearly link to the question.

2 Practise these skills on the poem below.

Blessing

The skin cracks like a pod.
There never is enough water.

Imagine the drip of it,
the small splash, echo
in a tin mug,
the voice of a kindly god.

Sometimes, the sudden rush
of fortune. The municipal pipe bursts,
silver crashes to the ground
and the flow has found
a roar of tongues. From the huts,
a congregation: every man woman
child for streets around
butts in, with pots,
brass, copper, aluminium,
plastic buckets,
frantic hands,

and naked children
screaming in the liquid sun,
their highlights polished to perfection,
flashing light,
as the blessing sings
over their small bones.

Imtiaz Dharker

intros idea of a lack of basic necessity; simile: lack of water creates problems – dry, painful skin pops – intros idea of drought, famine; image of people like dried-up, drying plants. Here, there is no excitement or joy – only despair and desperation – clearly contrasting with the excitement and joy that comes in the third and fourth stanzas

Lesson 4.11 Planning and writing a critical essay   163

> **Plan your response**

Drafting a quick plan helps you organise your ideas and provides a road map to develop your argument and analysis.

Generally, your response should consist of the following:

> An **introduction** that:
> a) addresses the key terms expressed in the question
> b) links clearly to the poem's content
> c) potentially provides a brief summary of the poem's main points to demonstrate your understanding.
>
> Three or so **main body** paragraphs that:
> a) develop key observations linked to the question
> b) make reference to a range of quotations and techniques used within the poem
> c) examine, explain and analyse *how* meaning is created through language and techniques.
>
> A **conclusion** that:
> a) summarises your key observations and explains effects on the reader.

Try this with the following exam-style question:

> How does Dharker powerfully portray the excitement of the people in these lines?

So, firstly, you need to track through the poem with the key terms of the question in mind:

- **the excitement** of the people – (what feature of the poem to focus on)
- **How…** powerfully portray – (poetic techniques and language that create the excitement).

Read the student's annotation of the opening lines. As the poem opens, you may notice at first the lack of excitement – indeed, the desperation and need that is clearly apparent – which contrasts with the joy which is so evident later on.

3 a) Now continue to annotate the poem, picking out details that relate to the idea of excitement and how the people feel.

b) Notice when and where there are changes in the levels or types of excitement.

164   Chapter 4 Studying poetry

Chapter 4 . Lesson 11

You could track your observations using a table like this:

Key theme	Introduced: *first stanza*	Develops: *second stanza*	Develops further/ changes: *third stanza*
lack of joy, excitement / only dire need	'There is never enough water' = intros idea of a lack of a basic necessity; 'Skin cracks like a pod' = simile; lack of water creates problems – dry, painful skin pops – intros idea of drought, famine; a clear lack of joy and excitement	'Imagine drip of it' – people so desperate for water, they're constantly thinking about it; 'Imagine' also suggests illusion – the water's not real, such a lack they can only think about it	'sudden rush of fortune' – metaphor: water = fortune, wealth, money, gold; an unexpected flood of water – abrupt change from lack to abundance, from desperation to joy and excitement

4 For each observation, think about *how* the feeling is created through poetic techniques such as language, structure, form, sound, voice or perspective. Add comments to your annotations, or to your table.

The main body of your response should follow the focus of the question in relation to how it develops as you move through the poem, from beginning to end.

Write your response

5 Using that framework, write a response to the poem using any of the practice questions above.

Checklist for success

- ✔ Have you identified the key terms of the question?
- ✔ Have you tracked through or annotated the poem with the key terms in mind?
- ✔ Have you identified key language and techniques in the poem?
- ✔ Have you identified a range of key quotations that link to the question?
- ✔ Have you created mind-maps for that key language or those key techniques to help tease out meaning?
- ✔ Have you linked your observations to the focus of the question?

Chapter 4 . Lesson 12

Evaluating your critical essay

How can I assess and improve my own work?

Your task

> Read 'Blessing' by Imtiaz Dharker.
> How does Dharker powerfully portray the excitement of the people in these lines?

Evaluating your work

Before you make an evaluation of how well you have done, check the table on page 186. It will help you decide if your work falls broadly into the first or second category – or outside them.

1. Go through your own response and, if possible, write your own brief annotations around it.

2. Now read the following response, thinking about what the writer of the response has done well and what advice they might need in order to make more progress.

> The poet shows the excitement in many different ways. For example, the poet writes, 'the sudden rush of fortune.' Here, the poet uses language to suggest that the water coming is unexpected and this suggests excitement. 'Fortune' shows that they are lucky that this water has come. This makes me think that the people really needed water, that there was a drought, and that this water coming was almost like a life saver for them. The author also writes that when the pipe bursts, 'silver crashes to the ground / and the flow has found / a roar of tongues.' This shows how valuable the water was; it was like 'silver'. 'Roar of tongues' suggests that the water was flowing very quickly, gushing and making a lot of noise. This suggests excitement because the water itself is making a lot of noise. The people also show excitement with the water being available. They are 'frantic.' They all grab whatever they can to put the water in. This shows that they were so desperate,

Annotations:
- key quotations
- some response to language
- understanding of the text and some deeper implications
- key quotations
- some response and development of language relevant response to the question
- some use of key quotations

166   Chapter 4 Studying poetry

Chapter 4 . Lesson 13

Extension: Developing an overview

How do I develop an overview and build an analysis in a poetry response?

Understand the task

This section focuses in detail on how to develop an overview and build your analysis, while working closely with the text.

One way to create a response that links your ideas together and connects them to the question, is by using **signposting** – that is, using language specific to the question and to your argument at the beginning and ending of your paragraphs.

1 Read the example **introductory** paragraph below on 'Mrs Faust', which begins to address the question:

> How does the writer convincingly portray the character of Mrs Faust in the poem?

> The writer convincingly portrays the character of Mrs Faust as materialistic, greedy and soulless. The poem retells the famous story of Dr Faust, a scientist who sells his soul to the Devil in order to obtain godlike knowledge and worldly possessions. However, Duffy chooses Faust's hypothetical wife as her narrator, and we see Faust's rise and fall from her unique perspective. Duffy shows the ways in which Mrs Faust's moral character is corrupted because of her marriage to Faust.

a) Underline words in the introduction that reflect the language of the question.

b) Circle words which you think constitute the main ideas of an argument.

c) Double underline phrases which concisely summarise the plot of the poem.

2 Now read the ensuing first **body paragraph**. What language in this paragraph links back not only to the question, but also to the previous paragraph? Underline these words or phrases.

Lesson 4.13 Extension: Developing an overview   169

> The poet introduces the idea of Mrs Faust being a materialistic, greedy and soulless character in the first stanza. For example, Duffy has the narrator say, 'I married Faust'. Here, the reader sees Mrs Faust as in control – she marries him, rather than the other way around. This is emphasised when the narrator refers to 'Two towelled bathrobes. Hers. His.' in that 'Her' bathrobe comes before the usual 'His'. This suggests her tendency to put herself first and get whatever she wants. Here, the poet demonstrates Mrs Faust's greedy nature by suggesting that she treats Faust almost as a possession himself – a trophy husband to show off with his 'PhD.'

Your **body paragraphs** should continue to build and link to ideas you introduced at the very opening of your response. Before you apply this approach to any poem, make sure you read and plan carefully to ensure that this approach will work to effectively address the question.

3 If you were carrying on from the paragraph above to write the second body paragraph to 'Mrs Faust', which would be the best paragraph opener?

a)
> We also see Mrs Faust's character when she talks about going to 'yoga' and 't'ai chi' and see how she is only going to these activities because she 'loves the lifestyle' and doesn't have anything better to do with her life because she knows that her husband no longer loves her.

b)
> Another key idea of the poem is that of good and evil.

c)
> In the fourth stanza, the poet develops the idea of Mrs Faust's greedy and materialistic character when she writes, 'I went to yoga, t'ai chi, / Feng Shui, therapy, colonic irrigation.'

d)
> Duffy also uses short sentences, caesuras and enjambment to create effects on the reader.

Chapter 4 . Lesson 13

4 a) Why did you choose the sentence you did? How does that sentence connect with what came before?

b) Why did you reject the other ones?

Writing a conclusion can add a great dynamic and sense of purpose to your response. To have a purposeful conclusion, you need to draw an overview, together with your own personal opinions about the poem's effectiveness.

Read the example below.

> In conclusion, it's clear to me that Mrs Faust is an immoral, dishonest, and even wicked character. Duffy seems to use her to comment on the materialistic nature of modern society – of how people have come to value things and experiences over other people and even themselves. I think Duffy's portrayal of this idea is a powerful one because it shows how easily material possessions can take over your life. In this way, materialism is the Devil coming to take away your soul.

5 a) What broad or general idea has this response introduced to try to tie together the analysis? Highlight or circle key words which you think show this.

b) Where do you see the response offering a personal opinion? Underline these instances.

Gather your ideas and evidence

Read the question and the poem on the following page, in which the poet deals with ideas and feelings concerning love, isolation and anxiety over the passage of time.

6 Annotate:

a) where you think those ideas and feelings are conveyed

b) how those thoughts and feelings are introduced, develop or change (if indeed they do develop or change) throughout the poem

c) what key techniques you can identify.

Lesson 4.13 Extension: Developing an overview   171

How does the poet powerfully convey his thoughts and feelings in this poem?

Bright star! would I were steadfast as thou art

Bright star! would I were steadfast as thou art—
Not in lone splendour hung aloft the night,
And watching, with eternal lids apart,
Like Nature's patient sleepless **Eremite**,
The moving waters at their priestlike task
Of pure **ablution** round earth's human shores,
Or gazing on the new soft fallen mask
Of snow upon the mountains and the moors—
No—yet still steadfast, still unchangeable,
Pillow'd upon my fair love's ripening breast,
To feel for ever its soft fall and swell,
Awake for ever in a sweet unrest,
Still, still to hear her tender-taken breath,
And so live ever—or else swoon to death.

John Keats

Glossary

Eremite: a Christian hermit or recluse

ablution: a ceremonial act of washing oneself

Plan your response

7 Use the table below to organise your own thoughts about 'Bright star!'.

Thoughts and feelings	Introduced:	Develops?	Develops further/ changes?
anxiety over the passage of time			

172   Chapter 4 Studying poetry

Chapter 4 . Lesson 13

Write your response

8 Using the framework below, write a response to the poem, addressing the question above. Use the sentence starters provided to help build your analysis as outlined in this section, if you need to.

Introductory paragraph

> The poet powerfully conveys his ideas and feelings in this poem through the themes of love, isolation and the passage of time. The poem is about…

- Write the rest of the sentence summarising the poem in your own words.
- Close the introductory paragraph with a sentence which links back to the opening sentence, **highlighting** your key themes again and **signposting** the ideas you are to develop.

First body paragraph

> The poet introduces ideas of love, isolation and time in the opening lines. For example, the poet writes…

Second body paragraph

> The poet develops these ideas further near the middle of the poem, when he writes…

Third body paragraph

> However, the poet changes the tone of his feelings nearer the end when he writes…

Conclusion

> To conclude, I think that the poet is saying that love should be…

Lesson 4.13 Extension: Developing an overview   173

Chapter 4 . Lesson 14

Evaluating your work

How can I assess and improve my own work?

Evaluating your response

Before you make an evaluation of how well you have done, check the table on page 186. It will help you decide if your work falls broadly into the first or second category – or outside them.

1 Go through your own response to the question you considered in Lesson 4.13, and write your own brief annotations around it.

> How does the poet powerfully convey his thoughts and feelings in this poem?

2 Now read the following, thinking about what the writer of the response has done well and what advice they might need in order to make more progress.

> The poet conveys his thoughts and feelings in a number of ways. Firstly, he compares himself to a 'Bright star'. **'Bright' suggests being shiny, and full of light, which could suggest the way he wants his love to be. By comparing himself to a 'Bright star', the poet wants to be noticed. We know this because in the third line, the poet writes 'Not in lone splendour'.** This means that he doesn't want to be alone in his 'splendour' but wants to share it, just like he wants to share his emotions. The poet also says he doesn't want to be a 'Eremite', which is a Christian hermit. A hermit is someone who lives alone, and the poet uses this simile to show his fear of being alone. Therefore, here, the poet shows feelings of wanting his love to be noticed, but also fear of being alone.
>
> This poem is a sonnet, which means it has 14 lines and a specific rhyme scheme. **The rhyme scheme for this poem is ABAB CDCD in the octave, and EFEF GG in the sestet.** Sonnets are also usually about love, and a major theme of this poem is love.

— some thoroughness in the use of supporting evidence

— missed opportunity to comment on the effects of the rhyme scheme

174 Chapter 4 Studying poetry

Chapter 4 . Lesson 14

We see this when the poet writes, 'pillow'd upon my fair love's ripening breast.' Here, the poet says he wants to rest his head on his lover's chest for all time, thereby being with them forever. Here, he feels his lover's breast's 'soft fall and swell', a key image showing how connected they are and how connected he wants them to be. This shows his emotions to be profound in that the poet loves this person so much that he wants to spend the rest of his life with them. — *some response to the writer's use of language*

However, the poet also introduces the idea of death at the end – 'or else swoon to death'. Here, the poet says that if he can't be 'steadfast' like a star – that is, to be around forever – then he at least wants to be with his love until he dies. It could also suggest, however, that if he can't be with her forever, then he would rather just be dead, because he can't live without his love. This shows how powerful his emotions are, as 'swoon' suggests passing out from extreme emotion. His love is so powerful that it has the capacity to keep him alive, but it also — *some understanding of the text and its deeper implications*
has the ability to kill him. This is ironic as usually we think of love — *personal response*
as a positive thing that most people want to live their life.

Comment:
This is a reasonably developed and relevant personal response, although just. The writer demonstrates thoroughness in their use of supporting evidence with the use of the quotations throughout the response. They also make some response to how the poet uses language, although at times this can be quite general and sweeping rather than specific. However, there is some understanding of deeper implications.

3 How could this sample response be improved? Using the table on page 186, think about what advice you might give the writer of the response to improve their work.

4 Now read a second response to the same question. As you read, think about what has been done that is an improvement on the first response.

Lesson 4.14 Evaluating your work

The speaker powerfully conveys conflicted feelings concerning his love and his fears surrounding the passage of time. He does this through his use of a central image – the 'bright star' to which the poem is addressed – and the sonnet form. The star's radiance and beauty are emphasised immediately through the adjective 'bright' placed right at the start of the poem, suggesting the powerful strength of the star's light, making it an appropriate metaphor for his desire to be strong, pure and constant in his love. The iambic rhythm of a sonnet is also immediately broken by the stress placed on this first word, 'bright', suggesting again the powerful force of the star's light, and also creating the impression that the poem is bursting from the speaker's lips, as if he is suddenly compelled to address the star because of the strength of his feelings.

[annotation: confident focus on task and understanding of key writer's methods]

[annotation: language analysis revealing confident understanding of central ideas in the poem]

[annotation: detailed structural analysis]

However, the speaker's feelings are conflicted, as demonstrated by the fact that he almost immediately qualifies his choice of the star as an image for his commitment to his love. He thinks that a star is actually too distant and 'lone', isolated like a hermit or 'Eremite'. He uses images associated with purity, such as 'priestlike... ablution' and 'new... snow' to describe the star's 'eternal-lidded' watching. Yet these images suggest sterility as well as purity – priests bless and cleanse but they do not marry; snow is bright and white like the star itself, but cold and, as it is a 'mask', untouched and hiding the warm earth beneath. The speaker wants to have the star's constancy and 'steadfast' nature, but does not want to be cold and distant like a star, denied the touches of his lover. He feels a conflict between the purity of an eternal love and his desire to be 'pillow'd' on the 'soft' and 'ripening breast' of his lover, images suggesting embraces and fertility, as though lying with his lover in bed. The adjective 'ripening' sums up his fears – if his lover's breast is 'ripening' then at some point it must become 'ripe', but like all soft, ripe fruit, it must also then eventually start to decay. He fears to lose his lover.

[annotation: perceptive understanding of ideas, focused on the task]

[annotation: well-selected range of references explored perceptively and in detail]

[annotation: perceptive sense of overview, maintaining focus on task]

[annotation: detailed close language analysis; range of well-selected and integrated references; sustained focus on task]

His conflicted desires, caught between an eternal yet cold and sterile love, like a distant unchanging star might feel, and a strong desire to embrace the 'fall and swell' of his lover's chest, are emphasised by the repetition of 'still, still'. This repetition suggests his desperation to keep things as they are, listening to the 'fall and swell' of his lover's breath. The repeated 'll' sounds of 'fall and swell' and 'still' create a lulling sense of continuity, like a lullaby soothing him into a comforting 'sweet unrest'. However, the 'fall and swell' of the breath itself reminds us that life is proceeding, and must end in 'death', as the final rhyming couplet emphasises. The only way the speaker can ever really gain 'still' eternity is through dying, leading him to his final feelings of impossible conflict – either attempt to remain hugging his lover forever or die.

The sonnet form itself emphasises how trapped he feels by this oxymoronic choice – rather than a single volta between the octet and sestet, there is this further final twist, emphasised by the caesura in the last line, as well as the two earlier rejections of his image of the star. His desire to be steadfast whilst repeatedly turning from each choice creates an overall sense of irony, which powerfully conveys his conflicted thoughts and feelings.

Annotations:
- sustained focus on task; confident grasp of ideas; well-selected references
- confident engagement; perceptive analysis of patterns of language
- perceptive exploration of meanings; detailed focus on text and task
- confident understanding of form
- sustained focus on task; sense of overview

Comment:
The response shows perceptive, sustained personal engagement with the task and poem. The analysis is very detailed, incorporating well-selected references. The writer of the response demonstrates a critical understanding of the poem and the techniques the poet uses, as well as a clear sense of overview and the way in which meanings develop across the poem.

5 What advice might the writer of this response need to make even more progress? Use the table on page 186 to guide your ideas.

Chapter 4 . Lesson 15

Planning and writing a critical commentary on an unseen poem

How can I organise a response to an unseen poem?

Understand the task

One big difference between tackling a question on a poem you have studied and one on an unseen poem is the amount of time you need to read, plan and prepare your response. For an unseen question, you are advised to spend 20 minutes reading and planning your response.

Take a look at the example question below on a poem called 'Harmonium' by Simon Armitage.

> Read carefully the following poem. The narrator discusses how he and his elderly father moved an old harmonium (a church organ), which was due to be scrapped, from a church.
>
> **How does the poet's writing powerfully show the relationship between father and son?**
>
> To help you answer this question, you might consider:
> - how the poet describes the harmonium and its history
> - how the poet describes his father
> - how the poet conveys his feelings.

Most unseen questions provide some brief **context** – or additional information – which explains the basic premise of the poem. *Don't forget to read this!*

Unseen poetry questions provide bullet points after the question which help you focus your response. Treat these bullet points more as instructions rather than suggestions.

Again, the first thing you need to do is read the question carefully, highlighting or underlining key words, so you know specifically what to look for in the poem.

1 a) Highlight or underline all the key words in the question – *including* the context and the bullet points.

  b) Annotate the question with definitions or ideas that help you understand what you need to do. Perhaps even rewrite the question in your own words if you think that would be helpful.

Gather your ideas and evidence

Again, *after* you have:

1) read the question,

2) highlighted or underlined key words in the question, and

3) made any appropriate notes,

then you should read the poem.

178   Chapter 4 Studying poetry

And for the unseen poem, the mantra of reading it, rereading it and then reading it again, is vital to ensure you have a solid grasp of the poem's content.

Harmonium

The **Farrand Chapelette** was gathering dust
in the shadowy porch of Marsden Church.
And was due to be bundled off to the skip.
Or was mine, for a song, if I wanted it.

Sunlight, through stained glass, which day to day
could **beatify** saints and raise the dead,
had aged the harmonium's softwood case
and yellowed the fingernails of its keys.
And one of its notes had lost its tongue,
and holes were worn in both the treadles
where the organist's feet, in grey, woollen socks
and leather-soled shoes, had pedalled and pedalled.

But its hummed harmonics still struck a chord:
for a hundred years that organ had stood
by the choristers' stalls, where father and son,
each in their time, had opened their throats
and gilded finches – like high notes – had streamed out.

Through his own blue cloud of tobacco smog,
with smoker's fingers and dottled thumbs,
he comes to help me cart it away.
And we carry it flat, laid on its back.
And he, being him, can't help but say
that the next box I'll shoulder through this nave
will bear the freight of his own dead weight.
And I, being me, then mouth in reply
some shallow or sorry phrase or word
too starved of breath to make itself heard.

Simon Armitage

Glossary

Farrand Chapelette: the brand of the organ

beatify: in the Roman Catholic church, a step towards turning someone who is already deceased into a saint; or, to make someone extremely happy

2 Read the poem and make some notes. In the first reading, you want to get a good sense of the poem's basics:

- What's happening? What is the poem 'about'?
- Who's speaking? And from what perspective and with what 'voice'?
- Where is it set? When is it set? Is it in the past or present tense?
- How is the poem organised? How many stanzas are there? To what extent may this be relevant to what the poem is about?
- Does it have a rhyme scheme and a particular rhythm?
- Is the poem written in a particular form – a sonnet perhaps?
- How might any or all of these questions help you understand the question focus?

Read the poem again. Your second reading should look to get into more detail.

3 Work through the poem closely, annotating any observations you make about the focus of the question. In this case, you need to look at:

- the **relationship** between **father** and **son**
- **how** it is **portrayed** through:
    - how the poet describes the harmonium and its history
    - how the poet describes his father
    - how the poet conveys his feelings.

When you consider *how* the relationship is portrayed, you should show how the poet's techniques (language, imagery, form, viewpoint, rhyme, and so on) create this relationship.

Read the poem again. Your third reading should be a chance to 'step back' and understand the poem as a whole.

4 a) How do all these poet's techniques work together to create this poem and link to the question asked?

b) Is there anything new that has sharpened or come more into focus because you've 'stepped back' from it? What is it and how does it help you address the question?

Plan your response

In your response for an unseen poem, make sure that it focuses on the question, and uses the bullet points to guide your organisation of the response. In many ways, however, it can be similar to that of a seen poem.

Chapter 4 . Lesson 15

Generally, you can include:

- an **introductory** paragraph that provides an overview of the poem and the question focus
- three or so **main body** paragraphs where you develop your analysis, focused on the bullet points from the question. Each bullet point could be the focus of a paragraph
- a conclusion to draw together your ideas and your own opinions of the poem. Again, make the **conclusion** purposeful rather than perfunctory.

Once more, being able to trace the focus of the question through the text – noting how it is introduced in the beginning of the poem, how it develops in the middle and then how it develops further or changes by the end of the poem – is key to a strong, solid response.

You want to demonstrate that, in the short amount of time you have had with the poem, you have a healthy understanding of it and can aptly apply your analytical skills.

5 Use the table below to organise your own thoughts about 'Harmonium'.

Bullet point from the question	Observation	Poet's techniques	What this shows about the father / son relationship
how the poet describes the harmonium and its history			
how the poet describes his father			
how the poet conveys his feelings			

Write your response

You should now have a plan for your response.

6 Using this framework, write your response to 'Harmonium'.

> **Checklist for success**
>
> Make sure you include:
> - ✔ clear points linked to the question
> - ✔ a range of quotations from throughout the poem
> - ✔ reference to a range of poetic techniques
> - ✔ explanation of how the poetic techniques create meaning and link to the question.

Chapter 4 . Lesson 16

Evaluating your critical commentary on an unseen poem

How can I assess and improve my own work?

Your task

Before you make an evaluation of how well you have done, check the table on page 186. It will help you decide if your work falls broadly into the first or second category – or outside them.

1 Reread the question on 'Harmonium' by Simon Armitage. Go through your own response and, if possible, write your own brief annotations around it.

> **How does the poet's writing powerfully show the relationship between father and son?**
>
> To help you answer this question, you might consider:
> - how the poet describes the harmonium and its history
> - how the poet describes his father
> - how the poet conveys his feelings.

Evaluating your work

2 Now read the following, thinking about what the writer of the response has done well and what advice they might need in order to make more progress.

> The poet shows the relationship between the father and son to be centred around the harmonium, which is a church organ. The poet writes how 'for a hundred years that organ has stood / by the chorister's stalls, where father and son, / each in their time, had opened their throats'. This suggests the harmonium has been around for a long time and that it helped create a strong relationship between the father and his son. In this way, the organ represents something that kept them together. The son stops the harmonium being 'bundled off': the word 'bundled' suggests the harmonium is old and unimportant.

— focus on language and its effect

The poet also describes the relationship between father and son by describing the father. He has 'smoker's fingers and dottled thumbs'. This suggests that he is old and that he smokes. Because smoking is dangerous to your health, this could also suggest that he is close to death. The father seems to realise this when he jokes that 'the next box I'll shoulder through this nave / will bear the freight of his own dead weight'. This means that the father says to his son the next time he's in the church carrying something it will be the father's coffin with his dead body inside of it. This shows the reader that the father is waiting for his death, but the fact that he jokes about it suggests he's not that bothered by it. — *personal response*

However, this affects the son (who is also the narrator) because he doesn't say anything or know what to say, which suggests that he is sad about the idea that his father may die soon. In this way, the poet creates a link between the organ and the father – both of which are old and falling apart. The poet uses personification saying the keys are like 'yellowed… fingernails' and this personification links the harmonium to his father. — *focus on language and its effect*

However, whereas the organ has previously brought fathers and sons together, this organ being taken out of the church creates a strained relationship between the narrator and his father because the narrator doesn't want his father to die. — *understanding of ideas and some deeper implications*

Comment:

This is a reasonably developed and relevant personal response. The writer of the response demonstrates points using supporting evidence well throughout the response, although they could have used more precise, and less lengthy, quotations to augment their arguments. More could have been done to explore the language in detail. The reference to the metaphoric link between the organ and father is well-considered, if underdeveloped. The focus on the difference in relationships the organ creates, however, in the third paragraph clearly recognises some of the deeper implications of the poem.

3. How could this sample response be improved? Using the table on page 186, think about what advice you might give the writer of the response to improve their work.

4. Now read a second response to the same question. As you read, think about what the writer has done that is an improvement on the first response.

Lesson 4.16 Evaluating your critical commentary on an unseen poem

In 'Harmonium', the poet reveals his feelings about his ageing father through his attitude towards an old church organ which was going to be thrown away. Armitage introduces his feelings about age, and how we can consider things useless if they are too old, through his description of the harmonium. The phrases 'gathering dust' and 'bundled off' suggest the organ is neglected and unvalued by its owners. The porch is 'shadowy', suggesting no-one pays it any attention in the dusty gloom. The poet contrasts the organ in the present with its history in the following stanzas. Now abandoned in darkness, it used to be touched by 'sunlight'. Although this 'sunlight' was a 'day to day' occurrence, it has a miraculous quality: it seemed to 'beatify saints and raise the dead'. The fact that the organ used to be bathed in blessing and resurrecting light makes it sound holy. But despite this glory, the light has also 'aged' the harmonium. Armitage personifies its 'yellowed... fingernails' and 'lost... tongue' making us sympathise with the instrument as if it is a person, and value it more for its former glory and the suffering it has undergone, repeatedly 'pedalled' by the organist. The poet seems to want to save the harmonium and demonstrate someone cares for it after its hard life, just as later in the poem he wants to hold on to his relationship with his father.

Armitage portrays the harmonium's history as valuable to him, using musical imagery to convey the instrument's importance. The warm, alliterative sound of 'hummed harmonics' and the metaphor 'struck a chord' suggest his emotional attachment to it – and particularly to the memories it evokes of 'father and son' singing in church. The final image of this stanza suggests that, for the poet, the harmonium is a symbol of harmony, both musical and metaphorical, representing shared memories between his father and himself. Like the sunlight, it is given the power of performing miracles in the reversed simile 'gilded finches – like high notes', as if birds, not music, flew from their mouths when it was played. Father and son used to sing along to the organ with the beauty and freedom of golden birds, suggesting the harmonium has the power to transform their 'day to day' voices, and relationship, into something almost magical.

Armitage's description of his elderly father in the last stanza draws together his impressions of his father's physical ageing with his desire to salvage and value the harmonium. His father is described as being in 'his own blue cloud', echoing the dusty shadow the harmonium stands in, while his 'smoker's fingers,' which would be yellowed by nicotine, echo the personified harmonium's 'yellowed fingernails'. Even the adjective 'dottled', suggesting hands mottled with age, echoes the earlier sound of 'treadles' and 'pedalled'. These connections suggest the poet notices his father's ageing and compares it to the decaying organ, while the smoking hints at a possible future cause of his father's death. However, his father also draws this comparison, stating in a matter-of-fact way 'the next box' the poet will carry 'will bear the freight of his own dead weight'. The internal rhyme of 'freight' and 'weight' and the three stresses of 'own dead weight' create a sense of finality, which the father doesn't shrink from. — *insightful explanation of method, focused on task* / *integrated range of references; confident analysis; sensitive understanding of implications* / *close analysis of language and rhythm; carefully selected references*

However, Armitage clearly feels less able to confront his father's inevitable death, failing to 'mouth in reply' anything that could 'make itself heard.' Ironically, here, it is the poet who is most like the frail organ which has 'lost its tongue', scared to face up to the reality of losing his father. The poem as a whole can be seen as a metaphor for Armitage's desire to hang on to his ageing father, their relationship and valuable memories together, just as he wants to salvage the decaying organ for the sake of the value he places on its past. — *sustained response; evaluates patterns of language, demonstrating perceptive understanding* / *insightful overview*

Comment:

This response sustains a detailed personal and evaluative engagement with the task and the poem throughout.

The writer demonstrates a confident, critical understanding of the poem and the techniques the poet uses, sustaining an analytical understanding and incorporating well-selected references. The response demonstrates an appreciation of deeper implications as it develops and offers an insightful sense of overview.

5 What advice might the writer of the response need to make even more progress? Use the table on page 186 to guide your ideas.

Check your progress:

What are the features of a *reasonably developed, relevant personal* response?

Knowledge	• You show how you know the text **well** by making reference to it and/or by quoting from it.
	• You make points that are relevant (close textual reference and/or quotation) to the task set.
Understanding	• You show a **sound** understanding of the text, reading beyond the surface to explore implicit meanings.
	• You **develop your ideas** on themes, characterisation or ideas.
Language and effects	• You write about **some** of the ways in which the writer uses **language, structure and form**.
	• You make **some exploration** of the **effects of the writer's choices** and how these effects are created.
Personal response	• You make your own honest and **considered** response to the text, appropriate to the task.
	• You show **some development of your own ideas** about the text and task.

What are the features of a response showing *sustained personal and evaluative engagement* with task and text?

Knowledge	• You show a **detailed** grasp of the text as a whole and a **deep** understanding of the task.
	• You support your ideas with **relevant, well-selected, well-integrated reference to the text**, skilfully and with **flair**.
Understanding	• You support your **original** ideas with **carefully selected, well-integrated reference** to the text.
	• You show your ability to **analyse, evaluate and interpret** the text in an **original** and **perceptive** way.
Language and effects	• You examine in **depth** the way the writer uses **language, structure and form** and you explore different **interpretations**.
	• You show the ability to make a **close analysis** of extracts from the text and (where appropriate to the question) respond to the writer's effects in the text as a whole.
Personal response	• You make a **convincing** response, showing deep interest, understanding and an involvement with both text and task.
	• You have your own individual **ideas and judgements** about the text and express them with **confidence and enthusiasm**.

Studying drama 5

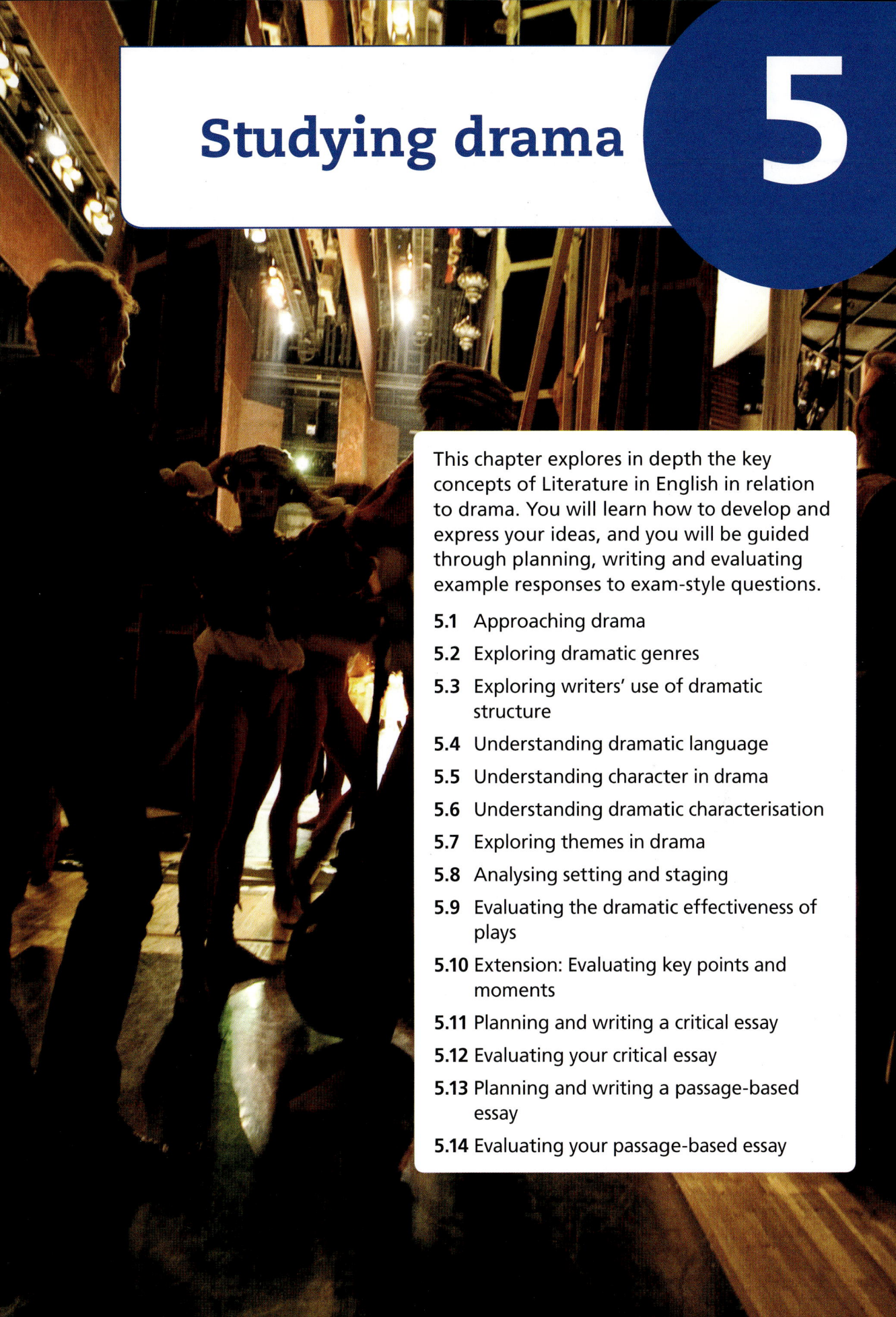

This chapter explores in depth the key concepts of Literature in English in relation to drama. You will learn how to develop and express your ideas, and you will be guided through planning, writing and evaluating example responses to exam-style questions.

- **5.1** Approaching drama
- **5.2** Exploring dramatic genres
- **5.3** Exploring writers' use of dramatic structure
- **5.4** Understanding dramatic language
- **5.5** Understanding character in drama
- **5.6** Understanding dramatic characterisation
- **5.7** Exploring themes in drama
- **5.8** Analysing setting and staging
- **5.9** Evaluating the dramatic effectiveness of plays
- **5.10** Extension: Evaluating key points and moments
- **5.11** Planning and writing a critical essay
- **5.12** Evaluating your critical essay
- **5.13** Planning and writing a passage-based essay
- **5.14** Evaluating your passage-based essay

Chapter 5 . Lesson 1
Approaching drama

What do I need to know about the drama element of my course?

Start thinking

1 a) What was the last play you saw? (Was it at school or at the theatre?)

b) What do you remember about it? Can you recall the plot – or the main characters? What was the **staging** like – if it had any?

Explore the skills

Play scripts – plays written down – are very different from the other types of text you will study. It is important that you do not forget that plays are meant for performance, so as you study them, you need to imagine how they might look and sound on stage.

You will need to focus on how characters and ideas are portrayed through:

- speech: what characters say, and how others react to them
- movements and gestures
- entrances and exits (how and when they arrive and leave the stage)
- the writer's **stage directions** (information about speech, movement, appearance and staging).

2 Which of the features above are deployed in this simple opening line from Shakespeare's play *Troilus and Cressida*? What does the information provided tell us?

> *Scene V1: The battlefield*
>
> ENTER Ajax.
> AJAX: Troilus, thou coward Troilus, show thy head!
>
> William Shakespeare, from *Troilus and Cressida*

> **Key terms**
>
> **staging:** the **set**, **props**, lighting and design that create the space in which the play takes place
>
> **set:** the objects – such as walls or furniture – which create the background for a play
>
> **props:** objects which are used by actors (for example, a cup or a letter)

Chapter 5 . Lesson 1

Develop the skills

You will need to deploy different sorts of skills during your course and assessment. For example, you may be asked to respond to two types of question.

Extract-based questions

You will need to learn how to focus on the way a specific moment or scene creates an impact on the audience in relation to key themes or characters.

For example, in relation to a question on a given passage from *Othello*:

> How does Shakespeare **make you feel sympathy for Othello** at **this moment** in the play?

Critical essay questions

Questions on the play as a whole or the writer's methods across the play may be more discursive – inviting you to consider the extent to which you agree or disagree with a statement. Or you may be asked to explore the writer's presentation of a character or an idea across the play as a whole.

> 'I am a man more sinned against than sinning.' How far do you agree with this description by Lear of himself?

OR

> **In what ways** does Shakespeare make Portia a strong and determined character?

3 Which of these questions is more likely to require you to:
   a) write about lots of different moments in the play?
   b) focus specifically on stage directions, movements, single words and phrases or how characters interact?

Apply the skills

4 Compare the opening 10–15 lines of any poem or novel you are studying with a play you have studied or are studying. What immediate differences in layout and presentation do you notice between them?

Check your progress:

▲ I can demonstrate knowledge of the basic requirements of the drama course.

▲▲ I can demonstrate clear critical understanding of how analysing a drama script differs from a poem or prose text.

Lesson 5.1 Approaching drama

Chapter 5 . Lesson 2

Exploring dramatic genres

What is 'genre' and why is it important when studying plays?

Start thinking

Imagine this beginning to a story...

> Two lovers agree to meet in secret in the woods. The girl sends the boy a note arranging the time and place. However, another boy intercepts the message...

1 Can you think of at least three different ways the story could develop?

Think of one sad way, one funny way, and one romantic way.

Explore the skills

How plays develop and end often gives us a clue to their **genre**. For example, in the story above, imagine if the first boy ended up seeing the girl and the second boy together. It is dark and he believes they are kissing. Jealous and angry, he confronts the girl and before she can explain, he does something terrible...

Tragedy

You could call such a story a **tragedy**. In fact, it has many of the **conventions** of dramatic tragedy.

Key terms

genre: category or type of story

conventions: standard features of a particular type of story or play

protagonist: the leading character in a drama

Main character	Often, but not always an important or noble person. He or she has a *key weakness* or *flaw* – in this case, it could be that he gets jealous too quickly, or that he is quick-tempered (or both).
Plot	The plot may contain *chance events* or *misunderstandings* that contribute to the tragedy – the first boy getting to the woods after it is dark, which means he can't see things properly. Sometimes a single, fatal error sets the **protagonist** on a path to their downfall.
Ending	In traditional tragedies, there is often a climax when the protagonist realises what they have done. Often this leads to the death of the protagonist and sometimes of others, too.

Chapter 5 . Lesson 2

2 Can you think of any stories or plays you know which have aspects of the tragic genre?

The idea of tragedy was developed in the time of the Ancient Greeks, and can be seen in many plays, both modern and old. Shakespeare adapted Greek ideas, for example. It is not difficult to spot the conventions of tragedy in plays such as *Romeo and Juliet*, *Othello* and *King Lear*.

Comedy

As you saw from the example at the start, funny and sad plays might both begin in the same way. But the way a comedy develops and ends is often quite different.

Main character	The main character may have a weakness or flaw, but this weakness endears the character to the audience. He or she is more likely to look ridiculous or silly than sad or dangerous.
Plot	The plot may also contain misunderstandings or things that go wrong, but these are designed to make the situation silly, and the audience laugh at the characters' errors. For example, in the dark the two boys bump into each other, thinking they have met the girl…
Endings	In comedies things are sorted out, secrets uncovered and order is (usually) restored. In many traditional comedies, lovers marry.

3 Here is part of the plot of Shakespeare's play *A Midsummer Night's Dream*. What elements of comedy *and* tragedy can both be seen?

A nobleman, Egeus, is furious that his daughter Hermia refuses to marry the man he has chosen, Demetrius. Hermia says she loves someone else, Lysander. Egeus asks the King of Athens to make her follow his orders, and says if she doesn't she should die.

The king makes a judgement: if she won't marry Demetrius, she must either die or become a nun. She chooses the latter.

However, later she arranges to meet with Lysander in a local forest and they will run away. Hermia's best friend, Helena, meanwhile loves Demetrius though he says he hates her. She finds out that Hermia and Lysander are about to run away together and tells Demetrius who follows them to the forest, with Helena not far behind.

The fairies of the forest, hoping to put things right, decide to sprinkle a love potion on Demetrius's eyes so that he will love Helena, not Hermia. Unfortunately, they get the wrong man…

Lesson 5.2 Exploring dramatic genres

4 How do you think the play might end? Is it more likely to be a tragic or a happy ending? Remember to explain reasons for your views.

Develop the skills

Genres are generally very wide – and as you have seen – the divisions between them can become blurred. Often the core aspects of comedy or tragedy can still be identified in plays from whatever era, but over time other types of drama have emerged.

In the Jacobean era (under the reign of King James I of England) **revenge dramas** were popular. Plays such as *The Duchess of Malfi* by John Webster and *Titus Andronicus* and *Hamlet* by Shakespeare featured characters who are so angered by something that has happened that they commit violent, terrible acts.

Historical plays might also feature some of the elements of tragedy and comedy, but because their focus is on particular 'real' characters and political events which are themselves of interest, they can be seen as a genre in their own right. Shakespeare's *Henry V* and Robert Bolt's *A Man for all Seasons* (about Sir Thomas More from Henry VIII's reign) or *The Madness of King George* by Alan Bennett, are good examples of this. These plays often explore what it is to be a monarch or politician and the opposition a ruler may face.

Much modern drama, especially just before and after the Second World War, began to present characters, events and ideas in a much less traditional way. Plots had no clear beginning, middle and end – and sometimes no real 'story' at all. Characters behaved in ridiculous or unpredictable ways, and weren't consistent. A movement called the **'Theatre of the Absurd'** tried to reflect the fact that life was difficult to understand and often appeared meaningless.

Plays also began to reflect the everyday lives of ordinary people. The term **'kitchen-sink drama'** gives an idea of where such plays were often set, and what their concerns were. The dialogue was much more like 'ordinary' conversation about money, relationships or work.

5 a) You are now going to read some short extracts from plays, then match them to their genres (or the ones they seem closest to). As you read each extract, consider its ingredients: does it share any conventions with the genres you have read about?

b) Write a brief sentence explaining *why* you think it most closely represents that category.

Chapter 5 . Lesson 2

Extract A

GIOV	He turn'd murderer!
	Away with them to prison, and to torture:
	All that have hands in this shall taste our justice,
	As I hope heaven.
LODO	I do glory yet,
	That I can call this act mine own. For my part,
	The rack, the gallows, and the torturing wheel,
	Shall be but sound sleeps to me…

Extract B

MRS E	(*lifting kitchen hatch*): Will you have boiled pork or boiled eggs?
PERCY	(*reading paper*) Nothing.
MRS E	You heard what I said – boiled pork or boiled eggs?
PERCY	And you heard what I said – nothing. Just a cup of tea

Extract C

DECIUS BRUTUS
Caesar, all hail! Good morrow, worthy Caesar:
I come to fetch you to the senate-house.
CAESAR
And you are come in very happy time,
To bear my greeting to the senators
And tell them that I will not come to-day:
Cannot, is false; and that I dare not, falser:
I will not come to-day: tell them so, Decius.

Apply the skills

6 What have you learned about 'genre' from this unit? Write a paragraph explaining what it means and how plays can be identified through their language or plot.

Check your progress:

- I can show understanding of the term 'genre' and use it correctly.
- I can demonstrate clear critical understanding of genre elements in plays and refer relevantly to how they are used.

Lesson 5.2 Exploring dramatic genres   193

Chapter 5 . Lesson 3

Exploring writers' use of dramatic structure

How does the way a play is structured contribute to its effect?

Start thinking

Think for a moment about poems and novels, and how they are organised. Novels often have chapters; poems have lines and verses. But what about plays? How are they divided up – and for what reasons?

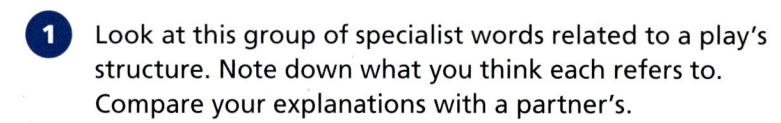

1 Look at this group of specialist words related to a play's structure. Note down what you think each refers to. Compare your explanations with a partner's.

act	entrance	exit	epilogue
	scene	line	prologue

Not all of these terms will be relevant to the play you study, but many will.

Explore the skills

Because plays were written to be performed in public spaces, people have always had strong views about what could be shown or how plays should look.

For example, the Greek writer and philosopher Aristotle established some core ideas about drama. Some later playwrights developed these into a set of rules, which they believed would make plays more truthful and realistic. They called these rules the **'unities'**.

unity of **action**	plays should have **one single story** or **plot**
unity of **time**	they should take place over the course of **one full day**/night (24 hours)
unity of **place**	they should take place in **one location** or setting

2 What do you think of these rules?

Consider:

- the advantages: would the rules make plays more or less realistic?
- the disadvantages: what wouldn't be possible within these rules? How interesting would the plays be?

Chapter 5 Studying drama

Chapter 5 . Lesson 3

Like novels and stories, traditional plays followed a well-established structure. Here is the main plot of *A Midsummer Night's Dream*.

Stage	Explanation	Example
exposition	Main characters are introduced – a problem or difficulty emerges.	Hermia wants to marry a different man (Lysander) from the one her father, Egeus, has chosen (Demetrius).
rising action	The plot develops as the characters seek to resolve the situation.	Hermia and Lysander run away to the forest. An attempt by the fairies to resolve the situation with a magic potion goes wrong as Lysander now falls in love with Helena (Hermia's best friend).
climax	This is the moment of highest drama or tension.	The couples fight – the men possibly with the intention of killing each other; the best friends (the women) seeming to hate each other. Lysander tells Hermia he never loved her.
falling action	Tension drops as matters begin to be resolved or clarified.	The fairies reverse the magic, and each lover is matched to the 'right' person.
conclusion	Everything is sorted out or explained, for better or worse.	The two couples watch a humorous play together as part of a celebration of their forthcoming marriages.

3 Look at these lines from the play. Match each one to the relevant stage in the table.

a) **PUCK:** … upon thy eyes I throw / All the power this charm doth owe…

b) **THESEUS:** Here come the lovers, full of joy and mirth. / Joy gentle friends! joy and fresh days of love / Accompany your hearts!

c) **HERMIA:** I would my father looked but with my eyes.

d) **PUCK:** On the ground / Sleep sound; / I'll apply / To your eye, / Gentle lover, remedy.

e) **LYSANDER:** (*struggling with Hermia*): Hang off, thou cat, thou burr! vile thing, let loose, / Or I will shake thee from me like a serpent!

Develop the skills

The success of most plays depends on **conflict**. Conflict can be presented in a number of ways, and how that conflict develops over the course of the performance is often what engages an audience.

For example:

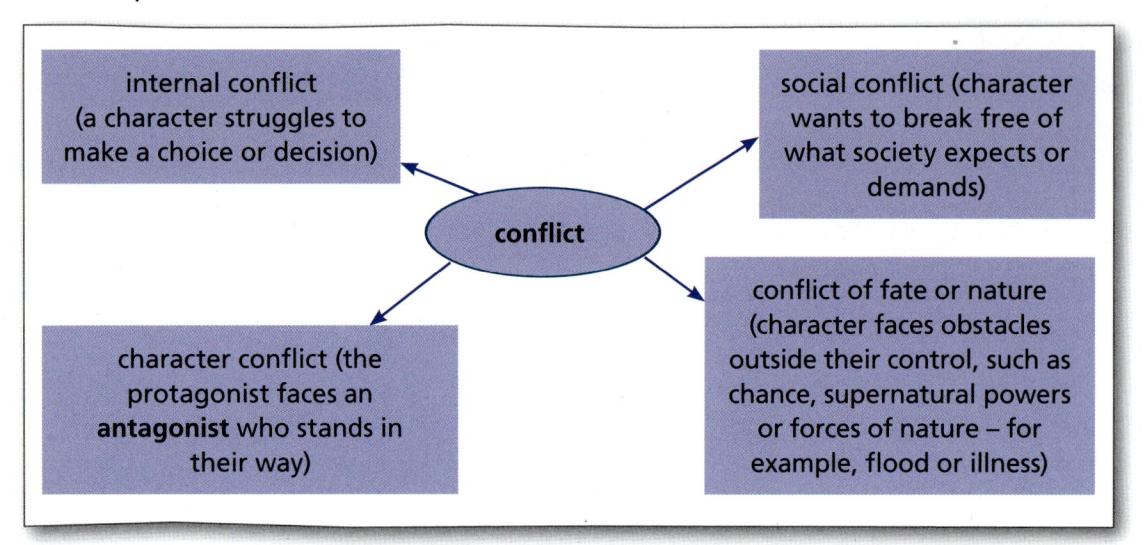

```
                    conflict
```

- **internal conflict** (a character struggles to make a choice or decision)
- **social conflict** (character wants to break free of what society expects or demands)
- **character conflict** (the protagonist faces an **antagonist** who stands in their way)
- **conflict of fate or nature** (character faces obstacles outside their control, such as chance, supernatural powers or forces of nature – for example, flood or illness)

These types of conflict are often linked and combined. So, for example, a main character finds someone who opposes him or stands in his way. This might lead to inner and social conflict: what should I do? What is right? What will society think?

In this dramatic version of the Cinderella story, the prince's mother (Princess Zehra) has invited people from around the kingdom to come to a party for Amir, the prince.

> **Key term**
>
> **antagonist:** a character who opposes the hero or heroine

Princess Zehra opens envelopes. A large pile is already thickening next to her.

ZEHRA   Everyone has accepted.

AMIR   Since the miserable day we settled here, not one person has come to welcome us.

ZEHRA   They're all coming now.

AMIR   No one has invited us. This country knows nothing of hospitality.

ZEHRA   There are two sides to hospitality, Amir: our hosts are not welcoming, so we must be generous guests. Every girl in the region is coming to dance and some will be beautiful.

AMIR   No one is beautiful here […], they all look like boiled potatoes.

ZEHRA   You must not speak like someone with a shrivelled heart.

Timberlake Wertenbaker, from The Ash Girl

4 a) What types of conflict can you identify from this conversation?

   b) How is the conflict conveyed through what the characters say and do? For example, how does Amir describe the day they 'settled' in the country?

5 Look again at the structure grid: where in the play would you expect this scene to come?

Chapter 5 . Lesson 3

Another structural technique to look for in plays is **contrast**. Good stories often benefit from:
- a change of tone or mood
- switching focus from one character to another
- moving to a new location or setting.

It would be very boring if *The Ash Girl* simply focused on Amir and his mother. How does the preceding scene from the play (below) contrast with the one you have just read? In this scene, Ruth and Judith, sisters of the ash girl, are planning to steal a key to their father's study.

Movement in the ashes. And now a figure emerges, grey, spectral, skeletally thin, a girl about seventeen.

JUDITH	Ashgirl. Eyeing us.
RUTH	Spying.
JUDITH	Look and tell.
ASHGIRL	I will tell Mother you're planning to steal the key.

They seize her arms.

RUTH	You won't!
JUDITH	She won't believe you.
ASHGIRL	I always tell the truth.

---

6 Make notes on:
- who appears in the scene, and what happens
- the style of speech – and how it is different from the scene with Amir and Zehra.

7 What effect does this contrast have? Think about:
- what it shows about how families treat each other (is one kinder than the other?)
- how the action is speeded up, or slowed down.

Apply the skills

8 Write about the conflict as shown in the scene above. Explain:
- what sort of conflict it is
- how it is shown.

Checklist for success
✔ Be specific about the extract you are talking about ('in this episode', 'in this dialogue between…').
✔ Consider where it might come in the action as a whole.
✔ Comment on the roles of the characters. (Is there a protagonist or antagonist? How can you tell?)

Check your progress:

▲ I can understand what structure is and can comment on aspects of its use.

▲ I can respond sensitively and in detail to how structural elements contribute to the impact of a play.

Chapter 5 . Lesson 4

Understanding dramatic language

How does a playwright's use of dramatic language create an impact?

Start thinking

1 Look at the image on the right from a play. What do you think is happening? What is each character thinking?

Explore the skills

In plays, the only way you can tell what a character is thinking is by interpreting their movements and, more importantly, analysing what they say.

The scene in this image comes from Shakespeare's *The Taming of the Shrew*, about two warring lovers. Here are their lines:

PETRUCHIO	Come, come, you wasp; i' faith, you are too angry.
KATHARINA	If I be waspish, best beware my sting.
PETRUCHIO	My remedy is then, to pluck it out.
KATHARINA	Ay, if the fool could find it where it lies.

2 a) What does the dialogue tell us about the lovers' relationship? Think about:
- what Petruchio compares Katharina to
- how she takes the insult and uses it to argue back.

b) How is the imagery continued in the lines that follow?

As you can see, you will be identifying and commenting on aspects of language that you would also encounter in novels or poetry.

For example:
- use of imagery, motifs and **symbols**
- simile and metaphor
- repetition and other patterns of language
- variety of lines or sentences.

Language can also be used in drama to heighten or release tension or to create suspense. One way in which playwrights do this is by using particular types of sentence in their dialogue, for example, in the way characters react to each other.

Key terms

symbols: when an image or description represents a wider or more general idea, such as spring flowers representing new life

suspense: anxious or fearful expectation

Chapter 5 . Lesson 4

In this extract from a play version of *Treasure Island*, pirates are searching for a map which reveals where treasure has been buried. Jim, a young boy, and his mother, who have the map, are hiding from them behind a curtain.

*The **Pirates** empty the chest onto the floor.*

BLACK DOG	I don't see it!
DEATH	It ain't' here no place!
HANDS	Look at the linin'. It's been ripped open. Somebody's took out the map already.
DEATH	Who?
MERRY	Who?!
BLACK DOG	Who?!
DEATH	Who was it?
BLIND PEW	… That little pup. It's him. I'll rip his head off. I'll pull his fingers from his hands! *I'll squeeze His neck until the pus runs out of his eyes!* Where is he?

*At which moment, out of fear, **Mother** makes a noise, shifting the curtains slightly.*

BLIND PEW	What was that?
BLACK DOG	What?
BLIND PEW	I heard somethin'.
MERRY	It was upstairs.
DEATH	Right above us.
BLACK DOG	Come on!

Ken Ludwig, adapted from *Treasure Island*

The extract starts with a very physical, visual action – the pirates emptying out the chest. But the suspense begins to build once they realise the map is missing.

3 Try acting this scene out as a group. Then, consider the following questions:
- What effect does the use of the repeated 'who' have at the start?
- How does Blind Pew's description of what he will do to Jim raise the tension even more?
- How does the noise affect the pirates' behaviour?
- How do the questions and short statements after they have heard the noise affect the mood?
- How easy was it to make the scene seem dramatic and full of suspense?

Lesson 5.4 Understanding dramatic language

4 Write a paragraph explaining how the writer uses language to make the scene tense and dramatic. (You could also mention the writer's use of stage directions, which are relevant here.)

> Start: The short, sharp repeated question 'Who?' creates suspense through dramatic irony as the audience know that…
>
> Continue: When Blind Pew realises it is Jim who stole the map, his violent language makes the audience…

Develop the skills

On occasions, writers use **soliloquies** or **monologues** to explore a character's thoughts and **motivations**.

Later in *The Taming of the Shrew*, Petruchio has married Katharina and has taken her back to his house to 'tame' her wildness. In this extract from a soliloquy, he explains his behaviour to the audience.

> My **falcon** now is sharp and passing empty;
> And till she stoop she must not be **full-gorged**,
> For then she never looks upon her **lure**.
> Another way I have to man my **haggard**,
> To make her come and know her keeper's call,
> That is, to watch her, as we watch these **kites**
> That bate and beat and will not be obedient.
> She eat no meat to-day, nor none shall eat;
> Last night she slept not, nor to-night she shall not;
> As with the meat, some undeserved fault
> I'll find about the making of the bed;
> And here I'll fling the pillow, there the bolster,
> This way the coverlet, another way the sheets:
> Ay, and amid this hurly I intend
> That all is done in reverend care of her;
> And in conclusion she shall watch all night:
> And if she chance to nod I'll rail and brawl
> And with the clamour keep her still awake.
> This is a way to kill a wife with kindness;

Key terms

soliloquies: longer speeches made by a character when they are on their own, which reveal their thoughts

monologues: any long speech made by a character

motivations: reasons for a character's behaviour

Glossary

full-gorged: fully fed

falcon, haggard, kites: all types of hawk or birds of prey

lure: a piece of clothing made to look like a smaller bird a hawk would prey upon

Chapter 5 . Lesson 4

Petruchio uses the **extended metaphor** of hawk training to explain how he will tame his wild wife.

Key term

extended metaphor: an image which is extended across a piece of writing

5 Begin by tracking the different ways he will train her, for example:

> a) He will keep her hungry ('empty') until she 'stoop' (accepts his rule).
>
> b) He will keep a constant eye on her…

Shakespeare uses the soliloquy to give the audience an insight into Petruchio's thoughts. For example, he states that last night Katharina 'slept not' and 'tonight shall not'. These short negatives suggest he is determined to follow through with his plan.

6 What overall impression do you get of him from this speech? Consider:

- what sort of personality he has (cruel? jokey? caring? dominant?)
- whether his behaviour is sexist: what do you think of him comparing Katharina to a wild animal?

Make notes explaining your ideas, including evidence from the speech in the form of key words or phrases.

Apply the skills

7 Write up your ideas in about 75–100 words on how Shakespeare uses language in Petruchio's speech to reveal his thoughts and character.

Check your progress:

▲ I can make some response to the way writers use language, supporting my ideas with relevant evidence.

▲ I can respond sensitively and in detail to the way a writer achieves their effects through language.

Checklist for success

✔ Explain what impression you get of Petruchio from the speech.
✔ Support what you say with well-chosen quotations from the speech.

Lesson 5.4 Understanding dramatic language   201

Chapter 5 . Lesson 5

Understanding character in drama

What do I need to know about different character types and roles?

Start thinking

Understanding the impact individual characters have on the action, themes and relationships within a play is key to your drama study. This understanding begins with exploring what 'character' means.

For example, look at the image in the margin from Shakespeare's play *Othello*.

1 What do you know about this character? You might think about:

- his story (if you know it at all)
- what ideas or feelings you associate with him
- any well-known things he says (if you know the play).

Explore the skills

Writers create characters to make an impression on audiences. Characterisation starts in a simple way: with their names or roles listed at the front of the play.

For example:

> *Othello, the Moor, in the service of Venice*

But as the play progresses, this outline is gradually filled in so that a picture emerges.
This is achieved through:

What the character says and does	... and the impact this has on others in the play, for example, do they help/love/kill/betray someone?
How often the character appears on stage	... and in what circumstances are they appearing, for example, how often are they the 'main person' on stage? Why do they first enter the stage? How does their story end?
How the character is seen in relation to others	Are they more or less powerful? Do they come into conflict with anyone? Are they part of a family group?

202   Chapter 5 Studying drama

2 Think about a character from a play you know or a play you are studying. Note down:
  a) **one thing** the character does which is linked to the plot
  b) **one event** which is going on when they first appear in the play
  c) **one person** or **group** they are linked with.

Develop the skills

Such simple facts about a character may begin to tell you something about their influence on the plot or about their feelings. Or they might reveal something about a theme (for example, love or revenge).

The extent of a character's influence depends on their role in the play. Do they lead or follow events? Do events have a direct or indirect impact on them? How much of a major or minor character are they? Look at these two lists.

A major character:	A minor character:
• will be involved in the **main events** of the plot, either as someone who **instigates** them or who is profoundly affected by them	• may be involved in **sub-plots**
• is likely to **explain** or **reveal** things about themselves, such as their **emotions**, **motives** or **worries**	• may be affected by the main plot, or contribute to it – but is unlikely to be the main person affected by it
• is likely to have more to **say** or **do** than other characters	• may act as a **confidante**, **friend** or 'sidekick' to one of the main characters (either as a good or bad influence)
• will be someone whose progress the audience follows closely across the play	• may reveal less of their feelings, or express them mainly in terms of how they affect the main character
• may be a character with **authority, money** or **high status** (for example, a princess or the head of a family).	• may be a **poorer** character, of **lower** or **working class** status (such as a servant or clown).

3 a) In many cases, the division between major and minor can be quite slight. Who would you regard as the main character or characters in the play you are studying or in a play you know? Why?

  b) Create a simple table for the play you chose.

Major characters	
Less important characters who have some influence on plot or themes	
Truly 'minor' characters	

> **Key terms**
>
> **instigates:** brings about or sets something in motion
>
> **sub-plots:** stories that run in parallel to the main plot

It is also worth considering typical character *types*. Sometimes these are referred to as **stock characters**. For example, in many traditional or older plays you might encounter:

The tragic hero or heroine	**The passionate lover**
A character, often but not always highly born (a king, princess or nobleman/woman), who has a key weakness that leads to their downfall or death (ambition, pride, vanity). They fight against their fate, but are unable to defeat it.	Usually a young man or woman who falls deeply in love with one of the other main characters. Obstacles are put in their way throughout the play (his or her own pride, others' jealousy) and the play is about whether they overcome or are destroyed by them.
The best friend or 'confidante'	**The strict or anxious parent**
An adviser or guide to a main character who takes part in their adventures or troubles, and may themselves be affected by it. Sometimes their stories mirror those of the main character, at other times they stand apart.	A father or mother (or someone who acts in the place of a parent) who struggles with the actions and desires of their children. In comedies, they can be figures of fun; in tragedies, they may create division or conflict.

4   a) Do any of the characters from the play you know fit these 'types'? In what ways are they similar or different?

   b) Are there other **stock** 'types' you can think of?

It can help to think of these categories, but most successful playwrights create **rounded characters** who do not always fit simply into one category. For example, in the play *Othello*, there are two main characters:

OTHELLO	*a noble soldier who loves his young wife deeply*
IAGO	*an ensign who serves Othello and tells him what is going on with other people*

Key term

stock characters: characters with very recognisable features or roles in stories (in fairy tales, these might be the evil stepmother or the handsome prince)

Glossary

ensign: flag bearer in the Army

5   Which categories do they seem to fit into above?

6   In the play, Othello murders his wife because he thinks she has been unfaithful. We learn that Iago has fed Othello lies about his wife because he hates him. How does this change your initial ideas about their character types?

Chapter 5 . Lesson 5

Another important aspect when considering a character is **status**. This can take several forms:

- social or political status: a king may have power and money through his position as ruler of a country: a father or mother may have power as the head of a family
- personal status: someone in a relationship may be weak or strong: for example, a man may love a woman who does not love him back.

> **Key term**
>
> **status:** level of power

Consider this short exchange in the play *Beauty and the Beast*, by Laurence Boswell. 'Beauty' is a humble village girl kept prisoner by the terrifying Beast.

BEAUTY	I spent the day exploring The Palace. It is like a dream.
	Beast, are you going to eat me?
BEAST	No! ... *(BEAST'S MAN serves BEAUTY with a glass of wine)* ... Forever?
BEAUTY	Beast, your Palace is the most magical place I've ever known, but I can't stay here forever. I want to see my Father again and I miss my brothers and sisters.
NARRATOR 3	Beast recoiled in pain...
NARRATOR 4	It hurt him to know that Beauty was unhappy.
NARRATOR 6	Beauty changed the subject.
BEAUTY	Why do you speak so... simply, Beast?

BEAST makes a groaning sound. He is clearly embarrassed.

Laurence Boswell, from *Beauty and the Beast*

7 a) In terms of position, wealth and social power, who should have higher 'status' in this scene?

b) Who actually seems to have the power? What phrases or lines indicate this?

Apply the skills

8 Write a paragraph about the Beast:
- Explain what sort of character he seems to be, based on this extract.
- Comment on the effect on the reader/audience of the way he is presented.

Check your progress:

▲ I can show understanding of how writers create different characters.

▲ I can demonstrate clear, critical understanding of how writers create a range of characters for different effects.

Lesson 5.5 Understanding character in drama

Chapter 5 . Lesson 6

Understanding dramatic characterisation

How do playwrights create characters?

Start thinking

Characterisation is a term we use to describe the different methods through which a writer creates a character. In drama, playwrights create character through the following elements.

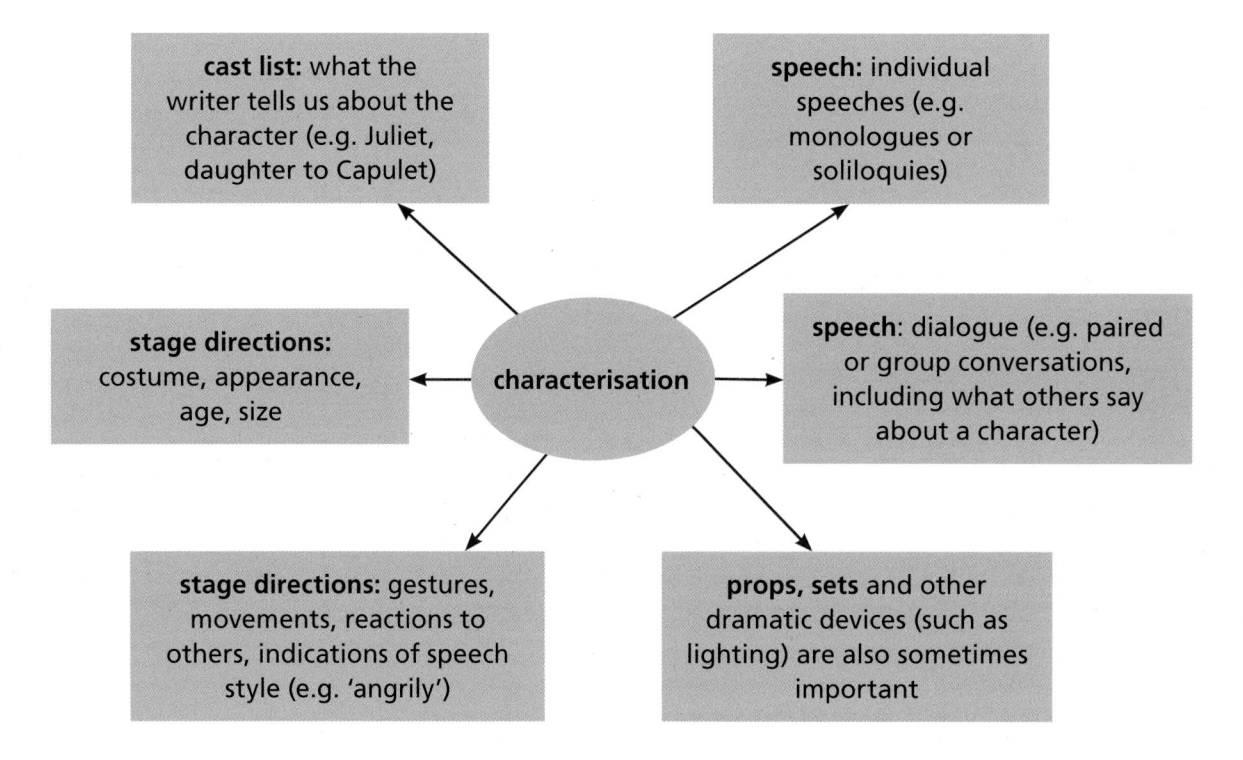

- **cast list:** what the writer tells us about the character (e.g. Juliet, daughter to Capulet)
- **speech:** individual speeches (e.g. monologues or soliloquies)
- **stage directions:** costume, appearance, age, size
- **characterisation**
- **speech:** dialogue (e.g. paired or group conversations, including what others say about a character)
- **stage directions:** gestures, movements, reactions to others, indications of speech style (e.g. 'angrily')
- **props, sets** and other dramatic devices (such as lighting) are also sometimes important

1 Select any character from a play you know or from a play you are studying. Look at their entry in the cast list, and at their first entrance or appearance in the play.

- What are you told about the character (if anything)?
- How easy would it be to play that part based solely on this first appearance?

206   Chapter 5 Studying drama

Chapter 5 . Lesson 6

2 Create a grid with these headings for the main characters in the play you are studying. As you go along, or as you look back at your reading, you could fill in the relevant details.

Character names	Costume / appearance	Notable gesture / movement	Important individual speeches	Important dialogues with other characters	Inferences that can be drawn

Explore the skills

Characterisation is made up of things we are told directly by the writer, and things we learn indirectly or have to **infer**.

For example, consider playwright Charlotte Jones's description of the character Mercy in her play *Humble Boy*.

Think about:

- what we are told about her appearance
- what we are told by the writer about her actions or behaviour.

> Mercy Lott enters the garden. She is ==wearing black clothes with brown shoes==. She is in ==her late fifties, a petite== and ==timid, mousy== woman. She ==watches Felix with concern. She approaches him, but doesn't get too close==. Felix glances at her then returns his attention to the hive.
>
> Charlotte Jones, from *Humble Boy*

Key term

infer: work out from clues

3 Decide which of the highlighted sections provide:
- *direct* information about Mercy's character (look for adjectives)
- *indirect* information (look for things that suggest or support what we have been told directly, or hint at other things about Mercy).

4 On the basis of this evidence, what is the overriding impression you get of Mercy? Write a sentence summing up your thoughts.

The stage directions in *Humble Boy* are vital evidence in your understanding of Mercy's character. So far, they have been about her appearance and behaviour. But characterisation is also about how *others* **interact** with the character.

Key term

interact: how people behave towards each other

5 Reread the extract. How does the character Felix respond to Mercy?

Lesson 5.6 Understanding dramatic characterisation   207

6 Which of the following would be sensible inferences to draw from his behaviour? You could consider the idea of her status in the household.

   a) Mercy is a cruel, unpleasant person who others avoid if they can.

   b) Mercy is a respected friend who people can easily turn to for advice.

   c) Mercy is well-meaning, but rather irrelevant and easily ignored.

Develop the skills

Speech and dialogue are central to characterisation. Dialogue is especially important when analysing relationships. In passage-based responses you will need to analyse such dialogue forensically, like a detective working through clues. Again, you should keep in mind what you are told directly and what has to be inferred.

7 Read this extract from the play *Ti-Jean and His Brothers* by Derek Walcott. You may wish to read it aloud or perform it. As you do so, consider your initial impressions of each character.

Ask yourself:

- How does each character behave? How does the other person respond?
- How do I feel about each character? Is this how the playwright wanted me to feel – and, if so, how did he achieve it?

Daybreak. The hut. The MOTHER and her sons asleep. GROS JEAN rises, packs a bundle. His MOTHER stirs and watches. He opens the door.

MOTHER   You will leave me just so,
               My eldest son?

GROS JEAN   Is best you didn't know.

MOTHER   Woman life is so. Watching and losing.

GROS JEAN   *Maman,* the time obliged to come I was to leave the house, go down the tall forest, come out on the high road, and find what is man work. Is big man I reach now, not no little boy again. Look this arm, but to split trees is nothing. I have an arm of iron, and have nothing I 'fraid.

208   Chapter 5 Studying drama

Chapter 5 . Lesson 6

> MOTHER The arm which digs a grave
> Is the strongest arm of all.
> Your grandfather, your father,
> Their muscles like brown rivers
> Rolling over rocks.
> Now they bury in small grass,
> Just the jaws of the ant
> Stronger than them now.
>
> Derek Walcott, from *Ti-Jean and His Brothers*

8 Now, copy and complete this table about Gros Jean.

Character: Gros Jean		What we can infer from this
Actions	Tries to leave without the rest of the family waking ('He opens the door')	He doesn't want a scene with his mother because…?
Speech	Explains why he didn't wake his mother ('Is best you didn't know')	Why is he saying it's for the best? For whom? Perhaps he feels guilty…
	Says 'Is big man I reach now'	He is saying that…
	'Look this arm, but to split trees is nothing…'	He seems to think that forest work is…

9 Based on the different elements – what he does and says – write a sentence or two about Gros Jean and how he is presented. Include at least one quotation from the extract and explain what it suggests.

10 Now complete a similar table for Gros Jean's mother. Think about what she is suggesting through lines such as:

- 'You will leave me just so, My eldest son?'
- 'Your grandfather, your father… now they bury in small grass… jaws of the ant stronger than them now.'

Apply the skills

11 Write 75–100 words explaining how Walcott reveals the relationship between mother and son.

Comment on:

- what we are told about the situation in the stage directions – and therefore the relationship
- what each character says and how the other person responds
- what you infer about the relationship from your evidence.

Check your progress:

▲ I can show understanding of some of the deeper implications in the ways writers use characterisation.

▲ I can demonstrate a clear, critical understanding of writers' use of characterisation, and respond sensitively to the effects created.

Lesson 5.6 Understanding dramatic characterisation

Chapter 5 . Lesson 7

Exploring themes in drama

How can I recognise and write about themes in drama?

Start thinking

1 Think about work you have done on themes. Can you name any themes in books you have studied? How did you identify them?

Explore the skills

Dramatists can develop themes in different ways from poets and novelists. For example:

- Drama is a medium of spoken language, so *what* people say, *how* they say it – and *how others respond* will take on extra significance.
- Drama is a physical medium: in performance, how people move, gesture, enter or leave a scene can have a big impact on meaning.
- Drama can also communicate through stage design or scene setting: these can reveal themes or ideas.

In the play *Private Peaceful*, two brothers go off to war. But the play starts when they are much younger. Look at these two very short extracts from different points in the play:

Scene 2	Scene 40
Tommo I don't want to go to school! *Tommo stamps his foot and stops – Charlie stops too.* **Charlie** Piggyback? *(Tommo hops up on Charlie's back trying hard not to weep or whimper)* First day's the worst, Tommo. It's not so bad. Honest.	*No Man's Land. The muffled sound of machine gun fire. Tommo lies in the mud.* **Charlie** Hang on, Tommo. Hang on. We'll get you out. *(Tommo is dragged into the open air by Charlie and Pete).* Thought we'd lost you. Michael Morpurgo, from *Private Peaceful*, adapted by Simon Reade

2 What can we learn about the theme(s) of the play from these extracts? For example:

- What does the spoken language tell us about the relationship between the two brothers in both scenes?
- How do the two brothers behave? (What does Charlie do in both scenes?)
- Where do the two scenes take place?

Chapter 5 Studying drama

Chapter 5 . Lesson 7

3 Which of the following general themes *might* be relevant to the play, based on these two snippets?

| Brotherly love | Weakness | Growing up |
| War | Friendship | |

Bear in mind that themes:

- are often revealed gradually
- intersect or overlap with each other
- can themselves be broken down into more specific ideas. (For example, a theme might be 'jealousy' but a more precise definition such as 'how jealousy destroys what you value most' would be more helpful.)

4 Think again about the general themes listed above. Here are some more specific thematic ideas. Are any relevant to both extracts?

- How brotherly love survives life's challenges.
- How friends are there when you need them.
- How war ruins lives.

Develop the skills

Now read this further extract from the play and the annotations around it. The action takes place in France during the First World War. Brothers, Tommo and Charlie Peaceful are stuck on the battlefield. Tommo is badly injured.

Tommo	(*whispering to Charlie*): Charlie, I don't think I can make it. I don't think I can stand up.
Charlie	It's all right. Don't you worry, we'll stay together, no matter what.
Sergeant Hanley	Right. This is it. We're going out. Make sure you've got a full **magazine** and one up the spout. Everyone ready? On your feet. Let's go. (*nobody moves*) What in Hell's name is the matter with you lot? On your feet, damn you! On your feet!
Pause.	
Charlie	I think they're thinking what I'm thinking, Sergeant. You take us out there now and the German machine guns'll just mow us down. They've seen us go in here, and they'll be waiting for us to come out. They're not stupid. Maybe we should stay here and go back after dark. No point in going out there and getting ourselves killed for nothing, is there, Sergeant?
Sergeant	Are you disobeying my order, Peaceful?
Charlie	No, I'm just letting you know what I think.

— sergeant's angry question shows he expects to be obeyed

— question emphasises disagreement between the two men

Lesson 5.7 Exploring themes in drama   211

> **Sergeant** And I'm telling you, Peaceful, that if you don't come with us when we go, it won't be field punishment again. ==It'll be a court martial for you. It'll be the firing squad. Do you hear me, Peaceful? Do you hear me?== — threat – and repeated shouting
>
> **Charlie** Yes, Sergeant. I hear you. But the thing is, Sergeant, even if I wanted to, ==I can't go with you== because I'd have to leave Tommo behind, and I can't do that. — Charlie's refusal
>
> Michael Morpurgo, from *Private Peaceful*, adapted by Simon Reade

5 Each of the annotations above suggest that 'conflict' is a key theme of the play. But what *sort* of conflict is being explored in these particular lines? Is it:

- conflict between the British and the Germans
- the stupidity of war
- conflict between particular characters
- inner conflict (someone who is struggling to make a choice about what to do)?

Glossary

magazine: a round of ammunition for a gun

6 Write a paragraph explaining what sort of conflict is shown, and use at least one of the highlighted annotations to support what you say.

7 Another key theme of the play, as you have seen, is 'brotherly love'. Can you find examples from the extract which indicate this? Complete the table below:

Evidence	What it tells us	What it might reveal about the theme
Tommo 'whispering to Charlie'	The fact he whispers shows Tommo only trusts his brother.	Brotherly love and trust is stronger than other ties of friendship.
Charlie: Don't you worry, we'll stay together, no matter what.	Charlie is prepared to…	
[add your own example]		
[add your own example]		

8 A student has begun to turn their findings in the table into a paragraph about the theme. Can you complete it by adding your own point and evidence from the grid?

> The theme of brotherly love is emphasised by Tommo's willingness to trust his brother rather than the other soldiers or the Sergeant. The stage direction tells the audience he is 'whispering', as if ashamed or frightened. Charlie's response is to tell him…

212 Chapter 5 Studying drama

Now read this speech from another play which explores a different sort of conflict. A character experiences inner conflict as he tries to decide what course of action to follow. In this scene, Hamlet has crept up on his uncle (the king) who is praying. Hamlet believes his uncle murdered his father (the old king). This is Hamlet's chance to get revenge.

> *The king kneels. Enter Hamlet*
>
> Now might I do it **pat**. Now he is a-praying.
> And now I'll do't. And so he goes to heaven.
> And so am I revenged.—That would be scanned.
> A villain kills my father, and, for that,
> I, his sole son, do this same villain send
> To heaven.
> Oh, this is hire and salary, not revenge.
> He took my father grossly, full of bread,
> With all his crimes broad blown, as flush as May.
> And how his audit stands who knows save heaven?
> But in our circumstance and course of thought
> 'Tis heavy with him. And am I then revenged
> To take him in the purging of his soul
> When he is fit and seasoned for his passage?
> No.
> **Up, sword**, and know thou **a more horrid hent**.
>
> William Shakespeare, from *Hamlet*

Glossary

pat: easily

Up, sword: Hamlet takes his sword away

a more horrid hent: a more violent grasp (wait for a more violent moment)

9 What evidence is there in this speech of Hamlet's inner conflict?

Think about:
- what happens – or what doesn't happen!
- why Hamlet cannot make up his mind to kill him
- what he says and how he says it (for example, what he says about taking revenge).

Check your progress:

▲ I can demonstrate knowledge of themes through the use of supporting textual detail.

▲ I can respond sensitively and in detail to the ways in which writers convey themes.

Apply the skills

10 Write up your ideas about Hamlet's inner conflict in two paragraphs.

Lesson 5.7 Exploring themes in drama

Chapter 5 . Lesson 8

Analysing setting and staging

How can a play's setting or staging help you understand its themes or impact?

Start thinking

1 Look at the following locations which appear in some of Shakespeare's plays.

a) Can you match them to the characters most likely to be seen in them? Some might fit more than one.

b) Do you recognise the play and/or the character(s)?

Settings	Characters
a busy Italian market-place	a powerful magician
an exotic island	a moneylender
castle walls	soldiers on patrol
a forest at night-time in the summer	a nobleman about to be murdered
a dungeon in a royal prison	lovers meeting in secret

Explore the skills

Some plays (especially Shakespeare's) have very little detail about the location or setting, and provide few details about the set or design. Others provide lengthy instructions to the director. It is important to interpret what these details reveal – however little information you are given.

In Brian Friel's play, *Making History*, we see the same character O'Neill, an Irish nobleman, at different stages of his life. The play is partly about the writing of O'Neill's biography.

Read these two openings to Act 1 Scene 1 and Act 2 Scene 1. The second scene happens some years after the first, just after O'Neill has lost an important battle with the English.

Chapter 5 Studying drama

Chapter 5 . Lesson 8

Act 1, Scene 1

A large living room in O'Neill's home in Dungannon, County Tyrone, Ireland. Late August in 1591. The room is spacious and scantily furnished: a large, refectory style table; some chairs and stools; a sideboard. No attempt at decoration.
O'NEILL moves around this comfortless room quickly and energetically, inexpertly cutting the stems off flowers, thrusting the flowers into various vases and adding water.

Act 2, Scene 1

*The edge of a **thicket** somewhere near the **Sperrin mountains**. O'NEILL is on his knees. He is using a wooden box as a table and he is writing – scoring out – writing rapidly, with total concentration, almost frantically. Various loose pages on the ground beside him. He looks tired and anxious and harassed.*

Brian Friel, from *Making History*

2 What obvious differences can you identify in the *settings* for both scenes?

Think about:
- which one is an interior setting; which an exterior
- which one 'belongs' to O'Neill
- what props or objects are mentioned.

3 What does the playwright tell the reader about O'Neill himself and how he looks? Think about:
- what he is doing in each case
- how he is described.

4 From these clues, you could say there has been a change in O'Neill. Write one or two sentences explaining how the setting and the stage descriptions show this change. You could use these prompts:

> In the first scene, the audience is presented with O'Neill in.........
>
> However, at the start of Act 2 Scene 1, O'Neill is.......

Glossary

thicket: a dense group of bushes or trees

Sperrin mountains: a range of mountains in Northern Ireland

Develop the skills

Often, the settings or situations characters find themselves in are conveyed through the character's descriptions of them. This is particularly important in plays when it isn't always possible to show locations realistically.

For example, in the next part of the second scene from *Making History*, O'Neill is joined by another defeated Irishman called O'Donnell. How does Friel give the audience more information about the setting here?

Lesson 5.8 Analysing setting and staging   215

O'Donnell	I had to make detours going and coming back – the countryside's crawling with troops. And then there were a lot of things to see to at home – disputes – documents – the usual. Look at my feet. These Sperrins aren't mountains – they're bloody **bogs**!
[…]	
O'Neill	Have you any food?
	(*O'Donnell opens his leather bag and produces a scone of bread. O'Neill goes to him, takes the bread and eats it hungrily.*)
O'Donnell	My mother made me half-a-dozen of them but I met a family begging on the roadside near **Raphoe**. Everywhere you go there are people scavenging in the fields, **hoking up** bits of roots, eating fistfuls of **watercress**. They look like skeletons.

5 What does O'Donnell have to say about:
- the countryside
- the local people?

How does this add to, or develop, what we learned earlier?

6 Which of the following words or phrases would best describe the environment the men find themselves in?

> inhospitable   welcoming   harsh   comforting
> isolated   nourishing   prosperous

Glossary

bogs: muddy marshland
Raphoe: another local town
hoking up: digging up
watercress: a salad vegetable which grows in rivers

7 Overall, what do these details suggest about the situation O'Donnell and O'Neill are in? Write a sentence explaining your ideas.

Waiting for Godot by Samuel Beckett is famous for being a play in which not very much happens. Two men are waiting for someone, and they remain in the same place throughout the play. The play is often said to be 'about' the meaning of life – what the point of it is, for example. The setting is very simple.

A country road. A tree.

Evening.

Estragon, sitting on a low mound, is trying to take off his boot. He pulls it with both hands, panting.

He gives up, exhausted, rests, tries again.
As before.
Enter Vladimir.

Estragon	(*giving up again*): Nothing to be done.
Vladimir	(*advancing with short, stiff strides, legs wide apart*) I'm beginning to come round to that opinion. All my life I've tried to put it from me, saying Vladimir, be reasonable, you haven't yet tried everything. And I resumed the struggle. (*He broods, musing on the struggle. Turning to Estragon.*) So there you are again.

Samuel Beckett, from *Waiting for Godot*

Chapter 5 . Lesson 8

8 Why do you think Beckett chose to describe the opening to the play in this way?

Think about:

- what a tree brings to mind
- what the road might symbolise
- why he chose 'evening' rather than 'morning'.

Although it is not strictly related to the staging, an important stage direction is Estragon is struggling with his boot as the scene opens.

9 How does Vladimir misunderstand Estragon's comment about the boots?

Apply the skills

10 Write a paragraph about the way Beckett sets his opening scene.

Comment on:

- the particular details he provides
- the atmosphere or mood these create
- how these specific details might stand for or symbolise larger ideas.

Check your progress:

▲ I can demonstrate knowledge of how writers use setting and staging through the use of supporting textual detail.

▲ I can respond sensitively and in detail to the ways in which writers achieve effects through staging and structure.

Lesson 5.8 Analysing setting and staging   217

Chapter 5 . Lesson 9

Evaluating the dramatic effectiveness of plays

How do I write about plays and show I have engaged with them thoughtfully?

Start thinking

1. Talk for two to three minutes with a friend or partner about their favourite band or singer, using these questions as prompts.
   - What do you think of his/her/their latest song?
   - How was it different from or similar to their previous song – or other songs they have written?
   - What makes the new song better – or not so good as the last one?

Explore the skills

In discussing the questions above, you expressed a personal opinion to begin with. This was probably straightforward – you liked or didn't like the music. However, in the second and third questions you were beginning to explore reasons – you were *evaluating* the songs. This skill is vital to your drama study.

When answering questions that require a personal response, make sure:

you **engage** with the text	This means you show interest in it, its themes, ideas and characters. The views should preferably be your own, rather than ones you repeat second-hand.
your response is an **informed** one	This means you demonstrate detailed knowledge of the play – you don't just assert things without evidence.
you consider **alternative interpretations**	This means you do not consider just one possibility but explore a range of ideas ('This might show... but it could also suggest...').
you understand that texts have **ambiguities**	You understand that not everything is crystal clear and that writers sometimes deliberately mislead or create characters whose motives are unclear or debatable.

218   Chapter 5 Studying drama

Chapter 5 . Lesson 9

2 Read the following extract from the play *A Slight Ache* by Harold Pinter. As you do so, think about your own response to it:
- how effectively the writer creates a sense of the characters
- the sort of mood or atmosphere created.

In the extract, a married couple have become aware of an old **match-seller** who stands at the end of their garden. Flora invites him into the house, and talks to him about the plants but he does not respond. He waits 'in the hall'.

Silence. She enters the study.

FLORA	He's here.
EDWARD	I know.
FLORA	He's in the **hall**.
EDWARD	I know he's here. I can smell him.
FLORA	Smell him?
EDWARD	I smelt him when he came under my window. Can't you smell the house now?
FLORA	What are you going to do with him, Edward? You won't be rough with him in any way? He's very old. I'm not sure if he can hear, or even see. And he's wearing the oldest –
EDWARD	I don't want to know what he's wearing.
FLORA	But you'll see for yourself in a minute, if you speak to him.
EDWARD	I shall.

[slight pause]

FLORA	He's an old man. You won't… be rough with him?
EDWARD	If he's so old, why doesn't he seek shelter… from the storm?
FLORA	But there's no storm. It's summer, the longest day…
EDWARD	There was a storm, last week. A summer storm. He stood without moving, while it raged about him.

Harold Pinter, from *A Slight Ache*

Now, read this exam-style task:

> To what extent does Pinter make you feel tension at this moment in the play?

Glossary

match-seller: (usually) a poor person who travelled around selling matches

hall: entrance space inside the front door which leads off into different rooms

Lesson 5.9 Evaluating the dramatic effectiveness of plays 219

- 'To what extent' means 'how much' – so you need to make a judgement.
- '…make you…' means 'what does Pinter do' – so you need to look at techniques.
- 'tension' = 'anxious suspense' – so focus on this aspect.

3 What possible elements in the scene create tension? Begin by making notes on how Flora and Edward speak to each other:

- Do they agree/disagree?
- Do they speak lovingly or in some other way?
- Is there anything notable about the length of lines/sentences?
- Does one character seem to have more status or control than the other?

Develop the skills

Read these two responses to the question.

A

Edward and Flora speak to each other in a stilted, cold way. However, Flora is warmer than Edward and is worried about what he might do to the old man. She says, 'You won't be rough with him?' which shows her caring side. Pinter presents Edward as blunt and unfriendly, for example when he says, 'I don't want to know what he's wearing.'

B

Pinter creates a real sense of tension from the first line through the short, blunt dialogue between Flora and Edward. To me, Flora is almost like a child, reporting back to Edward, 'He's here', but Edward seems to cut her off in an abrupt way – 'I know'. It is as if she is nervous in front of him, worried she'll anger him. However, Pinter could be suggesting he is anxious too – about a stranger coming into his house.

4 Which of these responses:

a) mentions what Pinter 'does'?

b) refers to the key focus – 'tension'?

c) provides evidence to support the points made?

d) includes an alternative interpretation for one of the character's behaviour?

5 Based on this assessment, which one of the two responses evaluates Pinter's skills more successfully? (Check against the features of an effective personal response on page 218.)

Chapter 5 . Lesson 9

There are two further key skills which one of the responses demonstrates.

These are:

Skill	Example	Effect
probing, thoughtful language	The writer of the response uses words such as **'seems'**, **'almost'**, **'could be'**.	These words or phrases allow you to consider ideas as if you are thinking aloud, rather than committing to a fixed view.
interpretative comments	**'like** a child' **'as if** she is nervous… worried that…'	Using a comparison or an analogy helps the writer of the response explore what the character is like or develop a point.

Modal verbs such as 'could', 'might', 'may' are all useful if you want to think through possible interpretations.

6 Write a further comment about Edward. You could comment on:

- how he speaks back to Flora
- what he says about the old man's smell.

As part of this, draw a comparison between Edward and something/one else, and use a verb or phrase to probe or explore an idea. Use these prompts:

> Edward is like a………………………………………………….in his behaviour towards Flora.
>
> It……………..as if………………………………………………

7 Now read the script again, and make notes about other aspects that could create tension.

For example:

- What is mysterious or strange about the match-seller (according to what we are told)?
- What do we learn about where the three characters are as this dialogue happens?
- What might the audience be aware of, or be able to see that the characters can't?
- What does Edward say about the weather the previous week?

Think carefully about each of these points and the idea of interpretation.

Lesson 5.9 Evaluating the dramatic effectiveness of plays

You need to ask yourself:

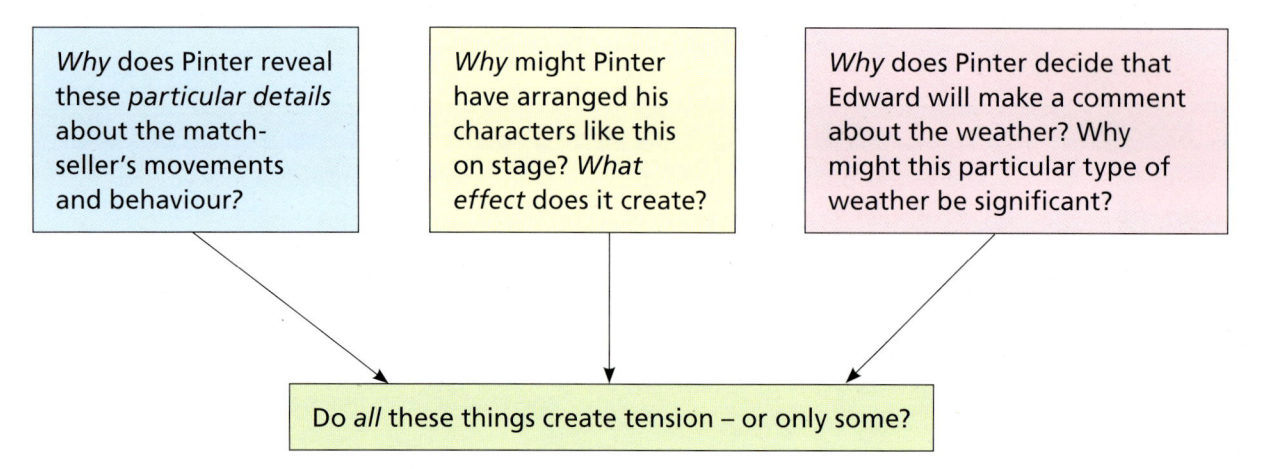

- *Why* does Pinter reveal these *particular details* about the match-seller's movements and behaviour?
- *Why* might Pinter have arranged his characters like this on stage? *What effect* does it create?
- *Why* does Pinter decide that Edward will make a comment about the weather? Why might this particular type of weather be significant?

Do *all* these things create tension – or only some?

Remember – there is no set answer to this. You cannot see inside Pinter's mind, but you can try out ideas.

Apply the skills

8 Now, write a full response to the original task:

> To what extent does Pinter make you feel tension at this moment in the play?

Checklist for success

- ✔ Stick to the key focus of task – Pinter's creation of tension.
- ✔ Comment on any aspects in the text that might show this.
- ✔ Support any comments you make with evidence from the text.
- ✔ Explore more than one possibility where it is appropriate.

Check your progress:

▲ I can make a reasonably developed and relevant personal response to a play and how it works.

▲ I can make a sustained, perceptive, convincing and relevant personal response to a play and how it works.

Extension: Evaluating key points and moments

Chapter 5 . Lesson 10

How do I explain the effectiveness of a particular moment in a play?

Start thinking

In Lessons 5.3 and 5.9, you looked at the structure of plays, and in particular, how a new scene can reveal a character, set up a contrast, or introduce new ideas. But what about the end of plays? What do you expect them to do?

Here, two students are talking about what makes the ending of William Shakespeare's *The Taming of the Shrew* memorable or satisfying. (The play ends with Katherina giving a speech pledging obedience to her husband.)

> I found the end very satisfying as it tied up all the loose ends. All the main characters are 'married off'. It was clever how Shakespeare presents this scene of married bliss.

> No, I don't agree. I think it was satisfying in a different way: we are completely unprepared for Katherina to give such a speech after her earlier behaviour. And it makes us think – Shakespeare left it deliberately *open to interpretation.* He wanted us to question whether Katherina really was 'tamed'.

1. What do you think the students mean from the phrases they use?

2. Is there a set formula that makes a play's ending 'satisfying, dramatic' or 'memorable'? If so, what would be the criteria? Think about these ideas:
   - that characters surprise you with what they do or say
   - that characters are shown to be 'true' to how they have been portrayed through the play
   - that events surprise you
   - that secrets, questions or plot-lines are 'tied up' or resolved
   - that the end raises new questions or sheds further light on key themes or ideas.

Explore the skills

'Satisfying' or 'memorable' does not have to mean shocking. As an audience, we might want to see or experience the following:

- the **natural fulfilment of actions** taken by a character for good or bad. A character makes a decision at the start of the play – or seems to have particular views – and by the end the consequences of those views or actions come full circle. For example, in Marlowe's *Dr Faustus*, the title character makes a pact with the devil in which he gains earthly power. At the end of the play he faces the reality of that pact – eternal damnation.

- **reconciliation or separation**: relationships that were in conflict are resolved or broken off forever. For example, in *The Crucible*, Proctor and his wife are hardly speaking; by the end of the play, the terrible events bring them together through mutual respect and love.

Endings can be memorable because they are *emotionally* satisfying. The Greeks referred to this as **catharsis**: the idea, particularly in tragedies, that audiences were taken on a rollercoaster ride of emotions as shown in the story – sadness, anger, fear, desire, despair… so that by the end of the play, they themselves were purged or cleansed of these powerful feelings.

3 What particular emotions do you think the play you are studying brings out? Can you identify any particularly powerful phrases, lines or speeches which represent or provoke these emotions?

Develop the skills

When you are exploring the dramatic effectiveness of the end of a play, there are therefore *three* stages you must go through:

Firstly, say *in what way* it is satisfying, memorable, significant or dramatic. → Secondly, explain *the effect* – which may be an emotional one. → Thirdly, explain *how it achieves this effect (or effects)*. Is it simply the events that take place (someone dies, marries or leaves)? Is it the use of language or gesture? Or something else?

4 Read the following plot summary and extract from Shakespeare's play *King Lear*.

224 Chapter 5 Studying drama

Think about:

- what we are shown happening – what is significant about it in the context of the play?
- the emotions this might inspire in the audience – what does it make us feel?
- how this is achieved through the language or events.

King Lear begins with the king, an old man, testing his daughters to say who loves him best – for which they will be rewarded. Two of the daughters flatter him; the third, Cordelia, who is truthful, does not. She is banished from the kingdom. The play then descends into civil war and Lear loses his throne to his evil daughters. He is finally reconciled with Cordelia, but at the end of the play she is murdered by Lear's enemies. He brings her body on to the stage, hoping she is still alive…

LEAR   And my poor fool is hanged. No, no, no life?
Why should a dog, a horse, a rat have life,
And thou no breath at all? Thou'lt come no more,
Never, never, never, never, never.
Pray you, undo this button.
Thank you, sir.
Do you see this? Look on her! Look. her lips!
Look there. Look there.
He dies.

EDGAR   He faints. My lord, my lord!

KENT   Break, heart; I prithee break.

William Shakespeare, from *King Lear*

5 In what way is this scene memorable or satisfying?

Write a paragraph explaining:

- how the scene brings the main character 'full circle' (you could consider how tragedies often begin with characters making a terrible error or feature protagonists who have a fatal flaw in their personality)
- how the emotional impact is created (you could consider Lear's actions, what he says to and about Cordelia, and the manner in which he says it).

Apply the skills

6 Consider the play you are studying. Make detailed notes on how the final scene – it can be the whole scene or the last 2–3 pages of it – could be described as 'satisfying' 'memorable' or 'significant'.

Use the grid below:

Feature	In what way	Key lines	Effect
resolves problems, mysteries or reveals secrets			(for example, satisfies our need for the truth to be shared)
character rewarded or reconciled			(for example, creates sense of joy/happiness?)
character punished/dies or learns hard lesson			(for example, creates emotional impact?)
embeds or further explores themes or key ideas (i.e. vanity is dangerous)			

7 When you have finished, write a response to this task:

> Explore the ways in which the author of the play you are studying makes the final scene (or the very last section of it) so memorable.

Remember: 'memorable' is a term you can explain in different ways, according to how you think the author has created impact on the audience.

Checklist for success

- ✔ Consider the shape and action of the play as a whole and how it leads up to this point.
- ✔ Consider emotional, thematic and dramatic impact.

Check your progress:

▲ I can make a reasonably developed personal response to a play, commenting on how a writer creates key moments.

▲ I can make a sustained, perceptive, convincing and relevant personal response to a play and how a writer achieves key effects.

Chapter 5 . Lesson 10

Planning and writing a critical essay

How should I respond to a discursive-style question on a play I have studied?

Understand the task

You may opt to write a discursive or critical essay on one of your drama set texts.

The question may be worded in a number of ways, but it will always ask you to think about **the ways in which** a writer creates a **particular** effect, for example, the feelings the playwright makes you have about a character in the play or how a key idea or theme is developed. You will need to explore the writer's methods (their use of language, structure, form, genre or staging).

Read this example question on William Shakespeare's *A Midsummer Night's Dream*.

> To what extent do you think that Shakespeare has created a play full of 'hateful fantasies' (Oberon)?

Step 1

The first thing to do is to highlight the key elements in the question you need to address.

Key element in question	What you have to do
'hateful fantasies'	*Understand* and *interpret* this phrase: it means horrible, cruel dreams or pretences.
Shakespeare has created	You are being asked *to consider the methods Shakespeare uses to create this impact.*
'the play'	This is not about Oberon. You must focus on the text *as a whole*. Do not simply focus on one scene or character.
'To what extent'	You are being asked to consider how true the statement is and give a balanced response.

Lesson 5.10 Planning and writing a critical essay

1. Looking at the question on the previous page, which of these explanations best describe what you need to do?

   A I must look at one particular relationship and see if it fits the key idea mentioned.

   B I need to consider a key theme or idea and how relevant it is to the play as a whole.

   C I have to say whether I like or dislike the play as a whole and why.

   D I must look at a key scene from the play and analyse whether it involves this theme.

For the next stage, you will need to be familiar with the overall plot of *A Midsummer Night's Dream* and, as a minimum, have read Act 2 Scene 1; Act 3 Scene 2; and the start of Act 4 Scene 1.

2. Now, go through the same process with the play you are studying. 'Decode' each of the following questions in the same way.

   a) Explore two moments in the play where the playwright vividly creates suspense for the audience.

   b) What do you find particularly memorable about the writer's portrayal of *[add name of character]* in the play?

Gather your ideas and evidence

Step 2

You must now generate ideas and gather evidence in order to construct an effective response to the task, whatever viewpoint you have.

Remember:

- You are not being asked to re tell the events of the play.
- Focus on several key scenes or moments of the play in detail, making links that bring in your wider knowledge of the play and its context.
- You must closely explore how the *language and structure* of key parts of the play demonstrate that it is about 'hateful fantasies'.

Here are some scenes you could choose to explore:

- Egeus suggesting Lysander has 'bewitched' Hermia (1, i)
- Hermia having a terrible dream (2, ii)

Chapter 5 . Lesson 11

- Puck using the magic potion on both Lysander and Demetrius who fall in love with Helena – she is convinced they are mocking her (3, ii)
- Hermia feeling betrayed by Helena; they argue bitterly (3, ii)
- Lysander and Demetrius also arguing and fighting as a result of the effects of the potion (3, ii)
- Titania being disgusted by the knowledge she fell in love with a half-man, half-donkey (4, i)

3 Which other scenes in the play contain 'fantasies' (hateful or otherwise)? Would any of these provide an alternative viewpoint – that some of the fantasies are not 'hateful'?

4 You now need to add evidence to support your ideas. Here are three quotations from the play. Can you link them to the points above?

| HELENA: | O spite! O hell! I see you all are bent |
| | To set against me for your merriment. |

| TITANIA (*to Oberon*): | How came these things to pass? |
| | O, how mine eyes do loathe his **visage** now! |

HERMIA (*awaking*):	[....]
	Ay me, for pity! what a dream was here!
	Lysander, look how I do quake with fear.
	Methought a serpent eat my heart away...

5 Now find your own quotations from the play which show:
- Oberon's thoughts about punishing Titania
- Bottom looking ridiculous and frightening away his friends.

Plan your response

Step 3

Once you have chosen key scenes to explore in detail, you can organise your ideas into a balanced argument.

There are several ways to do this.

Lesson 5.11 Planning and writing a critical essay   229

Method A

Focus on *parts of the play* that you believe show 'hateful fantasies'.

> Consider how **one part** presents a 'hateful fantasy'. Build one or more **language/structure/form** analysis paragraphs around this point, making links to broader ideas.

↓

> Then move on to the **next part** of the play that presents a 'hateful fantasy'. Build a further **language/structure/form** analysis paragraph around this point, making links to broader ideas. (For example, you might balance your point by considering how the fantasy leads to a positive outcome.)

↓

> Continue until you have covered several parts in detail, making sure you explore aspects of **language, structure and form** that demonstrate the theme in action.

Method B

Focus on *ways* that 'hateful fantasies' are presented.

> Consider how the **structure** contributes to the theme across your chosen parts. Write an analysis paragraph including **several parts of the play** to make your point.

→

> Next, consider how **language choices** contribute to the strength of 'hateful fantasy' as a key idea across the parts you chose. Write a number of analysis paragraphs exploring different techniques, including **several parts** to make your points.

You can also write your essay in another way of your own.

Whatever approach you take, you will need to develop an **overview** of the argument or discussion. In other words: you have a **general perspective** on the **whole play and the writer's treatment of the key idea from the question**. You are able to **maintain your focus** to develop this overall viewpoint throughout your essay.

6 The following is the beginning of a plan based on the different points in the play which show 'hateful fantasies'. Copy the table and select three further examples from the list on pages 228–229 to add to the plan. Where there is contrasting evidence (that it is not 'hateful'), you could mention this too.

Chapter 5 . Lesson 11

Paragraph 1	Introduction – explain what 'hateful fantasies' means and briefly mention some of the cruel things that happen.
Paragraph 2	Explain why Oberon's treatment of Titania is cruel.
Paragraph 3	
Paragraph 4	
Paragraph 5	
Paragraph 6	Conclusion – restate my overall view but don't list all my points again.

Write your response

Once you have your overall outline, you must bring together a response that:

- shows detailed knowledge of the plot, setting, characters and themes
- demonstrates deeper appreciation of themes, key ideas, contexts and the writer's intentions or motivation
- shows knowledge of the writer's methods – language choices, form, structure, staging
- engages with the play, and responds thoughtfully and personally to its ideas and characters.

Look at this sample paragraph, based on the second paragraph in the plan above.

> The cruelty of magic is at the heart of the play as it is Oberon's spiteful plan for revenge on his Queen, Titania, which has a domino-effect on the other characters. At the end of Act 2 Scene 1 he says, 'with the juice of this I'll streak her eyes,/And make her full of hateful fantasies'. However, it is not only her who suffers, but the lovers too. The adjective 'hateful' is interesting because it is not clear whether it means she will hate what she experiences or the fantasies will make her look bad. This reflects on a more general unpleasantness in the play when women seem punished for being independent – like Hermia with her father. Yet how does Hermia really suffer? By the end of the play she has the man she wants.

- counterpoint starts to show consideration of another viewpoint
- knowledge of and quotations from the text
- close analysis of language that explores main idea
- links to deeper understanding of character, themes and context

Lesson 5.11 Planning and writing a critical essay 231

7 Write your own analytical paragraph, taking a further point from the plan. Use the quotation by Helena from page 229 when she believes Lysander and Demetrius are pretending to be in love with her.

> ### Checklist for success
> ✔ Start with a topic sentence:
>   *Another time when magic creates cruelty is when…*
> ✔ Add the relevant quotation.
> ✔ Analyse its effect.
> ✔ Add further comments if you can, linking it to other points in the play.

8 Now, write the whole essay in response to the task:

> To what extent do you think that Shakespeare has created a play full of 'hateful fantasies' (Oberon)?

Chapter 5 Studying drama

Chapter 5 . Lesson 12

Evaluating your critical essay

How should I evaluate my response?

> To what extent do you think that Shakespeare has created a play full of 'hateful fantasies' (Oberon)?

Evaluate your response

Before you evaluate how well you have done, check the table on page 244. It will help you decide if your work falls broadly into the first or second category – or outside them.

1. Go through your own response and write annotations around it, like the example paragraph in the previous lesson.

2. Read the following response, thinking about what has been done well and what advice might need to be given to the writer to make more progress.

My essay is about 'hateful fantasies' and how many there are of them in the play. The first 'hateful fantasy' is when Hermia wakes up and finds out that Lysander has run off – 'Ay me for pity! What a dream was here!'. This is at the end of Act 2 Scene 2. When she says 'What a dream!' it means she had a nightmare, and she then goes on to say that a snake ate her heart. It is really cruel that the potion made Lysander abandon her in a cold, dark forest at night. I think that Hermia gets a rough deal because her father also treats her in a hateful way. It must seem like a bad dream that her father cannot accept the man she loves but fathers had control over their daughters so it is not that surprising.

   Another very cruel event is the way Helena is treated. She has not done anything wrong except to love Demetrius and he has been very nasty to her.

- reasonable response to the task, developing a personal view
- knowledge of text, but not expressed very fluently
- some comment on the writer's use of language, but missed opportunity to comment on the symbolism of the serpent
- developing response but expression still limited
- knowledge of context but doesn't really lead to much exploration of the theme

Lesson 5.12 Evaluating your critical essay 233

He told her earlier, 'I am sick when I do look on thee' (Act 2 Scene 1) so how is she supposed to feel when Demetrius and Lysander both tell her they adore her later? It might sound nice but actually she finds it very disturbing: 'Can you not hate me, as I know you do, But you must join in souls to mock me too?' She is saying they have teamed up to make fun of her.

I also think that Oberon treats Titania in a very unpleasant way. Yes, they are not humans, but why does he punish her just because of a child she took as a servant? Titania is forced to kiss Bottom who has become an animal – 'And kiss thy fair large ears, my gentle joy' (Act 4 Scene 1). The fact she is kissing his 'large ears' makes her look ridiculous and even Oberon takes pity on her in the end.

So, yes I think the play is full of 'hateful fantasies.' It ends with the lovers all together but I can't forget the way people suffered.

Annotations:
- some knowledge of whole text linking two different parts
- inference used to build argument
- starting to explore deeper meanings about structure/genre but undeveloped

Comment:
The response shows a reasonably developed understanding of the text and task, and includes a number of relevant quotations. There is some exploration of language and some links are made between different parts of the play. However, there is no balance in the response which might have explored alternative views.

3 How could this sample response be improved? Using the table on page 244, think about what advice you might give the writer of the response to improve their work.

4 Now read a second response to the same question. Think about what has been done that is an improvement on the first response.

Although this is superficially a comedy, Shakespeare's introduction of a number of disturbing, even cruel episodes and ideas initially leaves a bitter taste in the mouth. The 'hateful fantasies' which Oberon intends to bring to Titania's dreams in fact emerge much earlier, in Egeus's own treatment of his daughter. He believes Lysander has 'bewitched' Hermia with 'feigning voice' in Act 1 Scene 1. Not only does this introduce ideas about pretence and disguise, it also suggests that Egeus is the one 'bewitched' – otherwise what could account for him saying he demands the right to 'dispose of her' as he wishes, or for her to be killed, if she refuses? This patriarchal society is not surprisingly one that Hermia wishes to escape.

Annotations:
- clear argument and focus on task
- good range of references relevant to task
- confident response making inference from text
- fluent reference to context but linked to task

234 Chapter 5 Studying drama

Chapter 5 . Lesson 12

However, the forest in which she plans to meet Lysander becomes yet another place of 'hateful fantasy'. Her true love is himself 'bewitched' by the magic potion intended for Demetrius and Hermia is left alone in the wood, dreaming of a 'serpent' that eats at her heart. The symbolic serpent reminds the audience of the Garden of Eden in which Eve was tempted to eat the apple from the tree. It sounds as if Hermia, like Eve, is being punished for desiring something she should not have. The 'hateful fantasy' that afflicts Hermia, is also applied to Helena too. She has already suffered the indignity of knowing that Demetrius, who once loved her 'dissolved', when Hermia showed him some affection (Act 1 Scene 1). The verb 'dissolved' suggests that Demetrius is a vacant, empty man who is inconstant and weak. But worse is to come. First he tells her he is 'sick' when he looks at her and will abandon her to the 'mercy of wild beasts'. (Act 2 Scene 2) Then, he miraculously seems to fall in love with her. It is no surprise that she does not believe his adoring words, and it seems rather unbelievable that by the end of the play, they are presented as a happy couple– after all, it is only the magic which keeps them together: one wonders how this relationship may develop (or not) after the play ends?

Yet it is difficult to sustain the idea that 'hateful' fantasy is the only force in the play. Bottom's dream is a wonderful one. His Garden of Eden is Titania's bower filled with 'purple grapes', 'green figs' and fans made from the wings of 'painted butterflies' (Act 3 Scene 1). This is surely paradise.

It is difficult to forget the unpleasant tricks Oberon plays, but it would be too strong to say that 'hateful fantasies' entirely dominate.

— fluent link made to later part of text

— confident contextual interpretation showing real engagement with task

— integrated range of references; confident analysis

— character overview with thoughtful response

— thoughtful exploration of ambiguous relationship

— confident expression of alternative ideas

— clear summative final paragraph which returns to the key focus

Comment:
This is a sustained personal response to the task and text which demonstrates a confident critical understanding, with fluent use of references. The analysis is detailed and more profound issues are explored as appropriate.

5 What advice might this student need to make even more progress? Use the table on page 244 to guide your ideas.

Lesson 5.12 Evaluating your critical essay   235

Chapter 5 . Lesson 13

Planning and writing a passage-based essay

How do I plan a response to a passage-based question on a play?

Understand the task

During your course, you may be asked to respond to a passage-based question.

The question may be worded in a number of ways, but will always ask you to think about **the ways** a writer creates or reveals a character's feelings or explores a key idea in the given extract. Therefore, you need to explore **the writer's methods**. For example, follow these steps:

Step 1

Read the given extract carefully.

Read this extract from *The Ash Girl*, a retelling of the Cinderella story, by Timberlake Wertenbaker.

Silence. A movement towards darkness.

    Ashgirl remains alone.

    A shadow falls suddenly across the walls. Sadness enters, moves and tests the room for a dominant place.

SADNESS   The sudden hush of dusk is a good time.

    Animals fall silent, ready for the night, and humans feel alone…

    (*Whispers.*) Ashgirl …

    Behind a curtain, sometimes in the corner, I am the shadow cast against the wall.

    Ashgirl…

    It's not even a sound, it's a ripple in the air, a chill in the light, a voice they hear and do not hear.

    Ashgirl…

    Ashgirl stops working for a moment.

    Young girls are easiest, but I can seep into boys too, anyone… I'm the icicle in the heart, the one who makes the world so dark you wish you weren't in it. Sadness… Stretch out your hand to touch something: all you feel is an invisible layer of cold ash covering all.

	Call for help: I'll muffle your voice. Dream of relief: I'll shrink your thoughts to dust. Don't even try to move…
	Ashgirl…
ASHGIRL	I'll sew through the night and make these dresses memorable.
SADNESS	No one will thank you.
ASHGIRL	The dresses will dance at the ball.
SADNESS	But… never you… you stay alone.
	Ashgirl droops for a moment.
SADNESS	I probe, I test, study the defences and slide through the crack. An unquieted doubt, a fear, the unguarded thought…
	(*to Ashgirl*) No one cares what you do, no one cares for you…
ASHGIRL	My father was proud of my sewing, even more proud of my writing.
SADNESS	He abandoned you, no one's there for you. Ashgirl, listen…
	Owl appears at the window.
OWL	Ashgirl?
ASHGIRL	Owl!
SADNESS	I hate owls!
OWL	Who were you talking to? I heard a voice I didn't like.
ASHGIRL	I may have been talking to myself.
OWL	There's a disturbance in the air…
SADNESS	You listened to me, Ashgirl. I found the breach. I won't let you go now.

Sadness moves away.

Timberlake Wertenbaker, from *The Ash Girl*

2 Read the task and identify the key aspects the question wants you to focus on.
For example, read this example question on the extract above:

> How does Wertenbaker make this scene so moving and emotional?

Look at the highlighting. For this question, the key focuses are:

a) the emotion this scene makes the audience feel

b) *how* the writer makes it like this through her use of language, structure and dramatic techniques in general.

Gather your ideas and evidence

Step 2

The next step is to plan what to include in your response.

Remember:

- You are not being asked to re-tell the story. Focus on several parts of the extract in detail, not forgetting the beginning and end.
- You must closely explore how the language and dramatic structure of key parts of the extract make the audience feel sad or emotional.

Here are some parts you could choose to explore:

A. the stage directions at the start of the scene

B. the things Sadness says and what they evoke

C. how Ashgirl acts and responds

3 What other elements of the scene could you also comment on? Which parts are the most interesting to explore?

Plan your response

Step 3

Once you have chosen key parts to explore in detail, you can organise your ideas into an argument. There are several ways to do this:

a) Focus on *parts of the extract* that convey a moving or emotional mood.

- Consider how **the start of the extract** conveys a downbeat mood.
  Build one or more **language/dramatic structure/form** analysis paragraphs around this point, making links to broader ideas.
- Then move on to the **next part** of the extract, that in which 'Sadness' speaks and explains her methods. Build a further **language/dramatic structure/form** analysis paragraph around this point, making links to broader ideas.
- Continue until you have covered several parts in detail **including the end**, making sure you explore aspects of **language, dramatic structure and form** that convey the sad and emotional tone of the scene.

b) Focus on *ways* that convey a moving or emotional mood:

- Consider how the **structure of the extract** introduces a sad tone, and builds sympathy for Ash Girl, and how this changes when Owl appears. Write an analysis paragraph including **several parts of the extract** to make your points.
- Next, consider how **imagery and figurative language** convey the sad tone across your chosen parts. Write an analysis paragraph including **several parts of the extract** to make your points.
- Next, consider how **other language choices or character dialogue** convey the emotive tone. Write an analysis paragraph including **several parts of the extract** to make your points.

You can also write your essay in another way of your own.

Chapter 5 . Lesson 13

Step 4

Decide your approach now.

4 The final step is to plan your paragraphs, thinking about how to address the required skills.

> ### Checklist for success
> Paragraphs should:
> - ✔ show a clear focus on the question (here, how the scene is made moving and emotional)
> - ✔ give a clearly argued viewpoint
> - ✔ support ideas with clear knowledge of the text and range of relevant quotations
> - ✔ clearly explain how language/form/structure choices create sadness or an emotive mood; explore interpretations
> - ✔ make links to deeper ideas about themes or setting/context where relevant.

5 Read the annotated paragraph:

> The writer creates a sad, downbeat tone from the opening to the scene. The stage directions 'Silence' and a 'movement towards darkness' (probably a lighting direction) both set the scene for the entrance of 'Sadness'. The nouns 'Silence' and 'darkness' create a sense of loneliness – 'Darkness' is both literal and metaphorical, suggesting depressed feelings as well as lack of light, and this is emphasised by the stage direction which states that Ash Girl 'remains alone'. 'The shadow' which falls across the wall as 'Sadness' enters could suggest a ghostly figure who invades the stage and brings feelings of gloom. The audience can't help but wonder if the shadowy figure will damage Ash Girl in some way, and this creates a further emotional connection with her.

Annotations:
- clearly reasoned argument; strong focus on the question
- knowledge of and quotations from the text
- close analysis of language that creates the core mood/tone
- links to deeper understanding of character, themes and context

6 How has the answer covered the objectives? What do you notice about their paragraph structure?

Write your response

7 Now plan and write your response to the following task in 45 minutes:

> How does Wertenbaker make this scene so moving and emotional?

Lesson 5.13 Planning and writing a passage-based essay 239

Chapter 5 . Lesson 14

Evaluating your passage-based essay

How should I evaluate my response?

Before you evaluate how well you have done, check the table on page 244. It will help you decide if your work falls broadly into the first or second category – or outside them.

1 Go through your own response and write annotations around it, like the example paragraph in the previous lesson.

2 Read the following response, thinking about what has been done well and what advice might need to be given to the writer in order to make more progress.

Response A

The writer makes this scene moving and emotional in lots of ways, and one of the main ways is through the description of 'Sadness'. The way this character moves and speaks creates a gloomy and unpleasant tone which is bound to make you feel sorry for poor Ash Girl. — focus on task

For a start, Sadness is described as a 'shadow.' This is not a very nice thing and makes you think of a death, Grim Reaper type character. This makes it seem like Ash Girl is in danger so you want to protect her. Also, it says, Sadness 'tests the room for a dominant place'. The word 'dominant' means having power so this also adds to us feeling anxious for Ash Girl. What will Sadness do or make Ash Girl do?

— relevant evidence drawn from extract
— attempt to analyse language but rather stilted expression
— attempt at interpretation but undeveloped

Another important thing is the way they speak to each other. It is very tense and it is like Sadness is really trying to hurt Ash Girl. When Ash Girl says she will make dresses all night long, Sadness says 'No one will thank you'. This suggests it will all be for nothing – she might as well not have bothered because her sisters and her mother don't care. This really stresses how awful the situation is for Ash Girl.

— further support for point
— beginning to develop point and explain effect

240   Chapter 5 Studying drama

It is the same in lots of other fairy tales when a poor girl is deprived of love and kindness. — contextual reference but doesn't really add to analysis

I also think the way Sadness describes herself and what she does to girls and boys really makes the audience sympathise with Ash Girl. She makes herself sound like something that really goes deep into people, 'I'm the icicle in the heart, the one who makes the world so dark you wish you weren't in it.' — point with supporting evidence

The 'icicle in the heart' is a powerful metaphor which suggests a stabbing power. it , makes you wonder if depression will destroy Ash Girl even though you know the story is supposed to end happily. — language analysis but could be linked to wider points / better attempt at interpretation linked to context

To sum up, I think making 'Sadness' a character makes the scene even more emotional. This is because sadness is really a threat to Ash Girl. The way she talks and moves creates a gloomy, sad tone and makes you feel lots of sympathy for Ash Girl. — ending reiterates main argument without adding anything

Comment:
There are some reasonably developed points made here with relevant use of quotations. There are attempts to analyse in detail, and in places to interpret language but these remain rather undeveloped.

3 How could this sample response be improved? Using the table on page 244, think about what advice you might give the writer of the response to improve their work.

4 Now read a second response to the same question. Think about what is an improvement on the first response.

Lesson 5.14 Evaluating your passage-based essay   241

Response B

The writer's use of both dramatic structure and powerful language are key factors in creating a moving and emotional mood in this scene, which is only lifted by the appearance of Owl as a counterpoint to Sadness at the end. — *long, single sentence paragraph establishes overview*

The imagery used by Wertenbaker is particularly powerful. 'Sadness' describes the impact of her presence on stage, and on people as a 'shadow cast against the wall' and a 'chill in the light.' — *clear point made with supporting evidence*

The imagery here conveys a sense of impending doom, a gathering darkness and the word 'chill' suggests iciness – as if happy feelings are frozen or smothered. Later, this is linked to the metaphorical 'icicle in the heart', a sensory description which conveys the sharp pain of loneliness or sadness which can penetrate deep into your whole being. Such descriptions cast a very gloomy mood over the stage. — *detailed and developed analysis of language* / *excellent wider link indicating knowledge of text*

This threatening mood is further stressed by Sadness's anticipation of any sort of comfort felt by someone who might be lonely or depressed. The statement and reply structure hammers home the message that there is no way out: 'Call for help: I'll muffle your voice.' Again, this idea of smothering silence is emphasised. For the audience who know Ash Girl is already isolated and alone, this can only create more sympathy for her plight. — *new language point linked to speech structure* / *sustained focus on task*

A similar structure can be perceived when Ash Girl finally finds her voice and attempts to stress her right to be heard and recognised. When she says she'll sew all night long and 'make these dresses memorable', 'Sadness' replies bluntly, 'No one will thank you'. The use of the second person 'you' in this dialogue almost makes Sadness seem like a 'bad angel' on her shoulder, telling her to give up. — *develops comment on language structure* / *detailed language analysis with deeper interpretation*

Chapter 5 . Lesson 14

> This personification of sadness continues with the verbs she uses to describe her actions – 'I probe, I test... slide through the crack...'. In this way, the writer makes us believe she is getting through to Ash Girl and we begin to feel dread that sadness will win over hope. **The idea that people in fairy stories live 'happily ever after' seems a distant dream to the audience at this point.**
>
> **When Sadness really twists the knife by reminding Ash Girl that her father 'abandoned' her and 'no one's there for you...' the scene really reaches its emotional height,** or should that be 'depth' as surely Ash Girl has been brought to the brink of despair? Fortunately, the writer finally relents and lifts the mood. Owl appears – someone is there for her after all. **In these ways, the writer has taken the audience on an emotional journey – mostly plunging downwards into darkness, but at the end finally beginning to see the light.**

- contextual comment linked clearly to dramatic effect
- comment on overall dramatic structure of scene
- final overview of scene's effect on audience

Comment:
This response shows sustained personal engagement with the task and extract. A wide range of skills displayed by the writer are analysed in depth, with very well-chosen references and links made across the extract. There is evidence of interpretation and deeper insights and context is handled sensitively and relevantly.

5 What advice might the writer of this response need to make even more progress? Use the table on page 244 to guide your ideas.

Lesson 5.14 Evaluating your passage-based essay

What are the features of a *reasonably developed, relevant* personal response?

Knowledge	- You show how you know the text **well** by making reference to it and/or by quoting from it. - You make points that are **relevant** (close textual reference and/or quotation) to the task set.
Understanding	- You show a **sound** understanding of the text, reading beyond the surface to explore implicit meanings. - You **develop your ideas** on themes, characterisation or ideas.
Language and effects	- You write about **some** of the ways in which the writer uses **language, structure and form**. - You make **some exploration** of the **effects of the writer's choices** and how these effects are created.
Personal response	- You make your own honest and **considered** response to the text, appropriate to the task. - You show **some development of your own ideas** about the text and task.

What are the features of a response showing *sustained personal and evaluative engagement* with task and text?

Knowledge	- You show a **detailed** grasp of the text as a whole and a **deep** understanding of the task. - You support your **original** ideas with **carefully selected, well-integrated reference** to the text.
Understanding	- You show a **sophisticated understanding** of the implicit meaning of the ideas, characterisation and themes in the text. - You show your ability to **analyse, evaluate and interpret** the text in an **original** and **perceptive** way.
Language and effects	- You examine **in depth** the way the writer uses **language, structure and form** and you explore different **interpretations.** - You show the ability to make a **close analysis** of extracts from the text and (where appropriate to the question) respond to the writer's effects in the text as a whole.
Personal response	- You make a **convincing** response, showing deep interest, understanding and an involvement with both text and task. - You have your own individual **ideas and judgements** about the text and express them with **confidence and enthusiasm.**

Preparing for coursework 6

This chapter guides you through the process of developing your coursework. This chapter will be relevant if you are taking the coursework route for your IGCSE® Literature in English.

You will agree with your teacher which texts you would like to use for your coursework and what your coursework assignments should be. You will need to submit two assignments.

There are two types of task that you can submit for your coursework:

- critical tasks – a conventional essay type response
- empathic tasks – a creative response that responds to and reflects the way an author has created the world of the text.

The first half of this chapter helps you to prepare to write a critical coursework essay. You will work through the process of preparing, planning, writing and editing a coursework assignment, in this case, using two poems. The framework outlined here can be applied to other texts and can support you as you prepare to write your own critical assignment on poetry – or prose or drama.

The second half of this chapter helps you to prepare to write an empathic piece of coursework. Again, you will work through a process of preparing, planning, writing and editing that can be applied to your chosen coursework text.

6.1 Preparing for a critical coursework essay

6.2 Planning a critical coursework essay

6.3 Writing a critical coursework essay

6.4 Planning and preparing an empathic response

6.5 Writing an empathic response

6.6 Evaluating your work: coursework-style responses

Chapter 6 . Lesson 1

Preparing for a critical coursework essay

How do I generate ideas for my coursework essay?

The purpose of Lessons 6.1, 6.2 and 6.3 is to provide you with a framework to support the process of preparing, planning, writing and editing your coursework essay. You can use this process with any poetry texts.

Start thinking

The first stage of working on a poem or text is to read and gather together your first ideas, to get to know the text and begin to find out what interests you about it.

Read through (to yourself) these two poems:

Woman Work

I've got the children to tend
The clothes to mend
The floor to mop
The food to shop
Then the chicken to fry
The baby to dry
I got company to feed
The garden to weed
I've got shirts to press
The tots to dress
The can to be cut
I gotta clean up this hut
Then see about the sick
And the cotton to pick.

Shine on me, sunshine
Rain on me, rain
Fall softly, dewdrops
And cool my brow again.

Storm, blow me from here
With your fiercest wind
Let me float across the sky
'Til I can rest again.

Fall gently, snowflakes
Cover me with white
Cold icy kisses and
Let me rest tonight.

Sun, rain, curving sky
Mountain, oceans, leaf and stone
Star shine, moon glow
You're all that I can call my own.

Maya Angelou

246 Chapter 6 Preparing for coursework

I Hear America Singing

I hear America singing, the varied carols I hear,

Those of mechanics, each one singing his as it should be blithe and strong,

The carpenter singing his as he measures his plank or beam,

The mason singing his as he makes ready for work, or leaves off work,

The boatman singing what belongs to him in his boat, the deckhand singing on the steamboat deck,

The shoemaker singing as he sits on his bench, the hatter singing as he stands,

The wood-cutter's song, the ploughboy's on his way in the morning, or at noon intermission or at sundown,

The delicious singing of the mother, or of the young wife at work, or of the girl sewing or washing,

Each singing what belongs to him or her and to none else,

The day what belongs to the day—at night the party of young fellows, robust, friendly,

Singing with open mouths their strong melodious songs.

Walt Whitman

1 Try the following tasks to help to familiarise yourself with the poems:

   a) Read the poems aloud. What new things do you notice about the poems when you do this?

   b) Make some notes to answer the questions: *What happens in the poem?* and *What's it about?*

   c) Look up the meanings of any words in the poems that you don't fully understand. Remember that writers sometimes use words literally and sometimes figuratively.

   d) Make a drawing of what is being described in each of the poems, developing it and adding detail as you read through the stanzas. Remember to include details about the imagery being used. You could include labels too.

Explore the skills

Next, think about getting to know the two poems better.

Look at the way in which the following excerpt from 'Woman Work' has been annotated.

Shine on me, sunshine	— sun symbolises life and hope
Rain on me, rain	— the speaker is not afraid of challenges
Fall softly, dewdrops	— this has the tone of an appeal
And cool my brow again.	— nature is shown to have healing powers

Another good way for you to develop your understanding of the poem is to ask yourself some questions and annotate as you read:

Storm, blow me from here	— What is the 'storm' being referred to here?
With your fiercest wind	— Why is the speaker making this unusual request?
Let me float across the sky	— Is this a literal appeal or is it referring to something metaphorical?
'Til I can rest again.	— Why does the persona need this rest so badly?

2 a) Try answering the annotated questions above.

   b) Now annotate the rest of 'Woman Work' and the whole of 'I Hear America Singing' with similar questions of your own.

248　Chapter 6 Preparing for coursework

Chapter 6 . Lesson 1

3 Use the table to complete some notes about what happens in each of the poems, what they are about and what you find interesting.

	'Woman Work'	'I Hear America Singing'
What happens in the poem?		
What is the setting?		
Who is speaking? And from what perspective?		
What seem to be the themes of the poem?		
What is the tone/mood?		
Are there any changes or developments in the poem?		
What appeals to you about the poem?		
What, if anything, do you find puzzling or uncomfortable in the poem?		

> I think 'Woman Work' is about the difficulties faced by homemakers.

> I think 'I Hear America Singing' celebrates the pleasures of labour.

> The second part of 'Woman Work' presents a big change in the poem.

> In the last line of 'I Hear America Singing' there is a shift to describing leisure time.

4 Are the meanings of the poems ambiguous in any way? Make some notes.

Develop the skills

You've now explored some of the possible meanings of the poems – their themes, the feelings they express and what they describe. This next stage allows you to develop a more detailed understanding of *how* these meanings are created through poetic techniques.

Poets use many techniques to convey their ideas in a poem.

Lesson 6.1 Preparing for a critical coursework essay   **249**

These can include:

- voice and perspective – who is speaking in the poem or narrating its events?
- word choice – straightforward literal meaning
- figurative language and linguistic devices
- imagery, similes and metaphors
- poetic techniques – alliteration, assonance, sibilance, listing, monosyllables, caesura, enjambment, and so on
- use of tense and time – sometimes poets switch between the past, present and future
- rhythm
- rhyme
- form.

Remember, it is always important to do more than just list a poet's use of techniques. You need to state what the effect that technique or language choice has on the reader, and how the feature contributes to the meaning of the poem.

5 Read back through the two poems and complete the following table.

	'Woman Work'	'I Hear America Singing'
voice/perspective		
language choices		
use of tense and time		
rhythm		
rhyme		
form		
structural choices		

Apply the skills

6 Imagine your poetry coursework is going to be about these two poems. You do not have to compare the poems, but you will need to give a **personal response** to them. For each poem, make a list of anything you personally find interesting, inspiring, puzzling or even uncomfortable.

Chapter 6 . Lesson 2

Planning a critical coursework essay

How can I plan my critical coursework essay effectively?

The purpose of Lessons 6.1, 6.2 and 6.3 is to provide you with a framework to support the process of preparing, planning, writing and editing your coursework piece. You can follow this process with any poetry texts.

Start thinking

The next stage of preparing for your coursework is to choose and understand your title. For this coursework you are going to write a critical response piece.

1. In your coursework, you will need to show that you understand how the writers of the poems use language to communicate ideas and to convey meanings and feelings. With this in mind, decide which of the following are strong coursework essay titles:

   a) How do the poets vividly convey their thoughts and feelings about these working people?

   b) Describe the events being presented in these poems and show what you think might happen next in each case.

   c) What makes the poets' portrayal of these characters and events particularly striking to you?

As you start planning, it could be that you decide to change the focus of your title if you find that another approach will suit you better. Stay open to this idea. You are quite entitled to do it!

Explore the skills

Assume that the final title for your practice piece is going to be:

> **How do the poets vividly convey their thoughts and feelings about these working people?**
>
> Remember to consider the poets' use of language, structure and form in your answer.

2 It is very important to plan before writing a piece of coursework. Have a look at these different ways of planning, and decide which ones suit you best for this task:

- listing 
- brainstorm 
- flow chart 
- storyboard 
- bullet points 
- continuous writing

At this stage, you don't need to think too hard about the order of the ideas in your final piece. That can come later.

Now that you have explored the poems and your personal response to them and have begun putting together some ideas, you are ready to approach the detailed planning stage. Try building an extended spider diagram.

3 a) First, write down the main ideas about each of the poems that you would like to include in your essay.

b) Find a quotation to support each idea and add it to the diagram.

c) Extend the spider's arm by explaining the technique and the effect of each quotation.

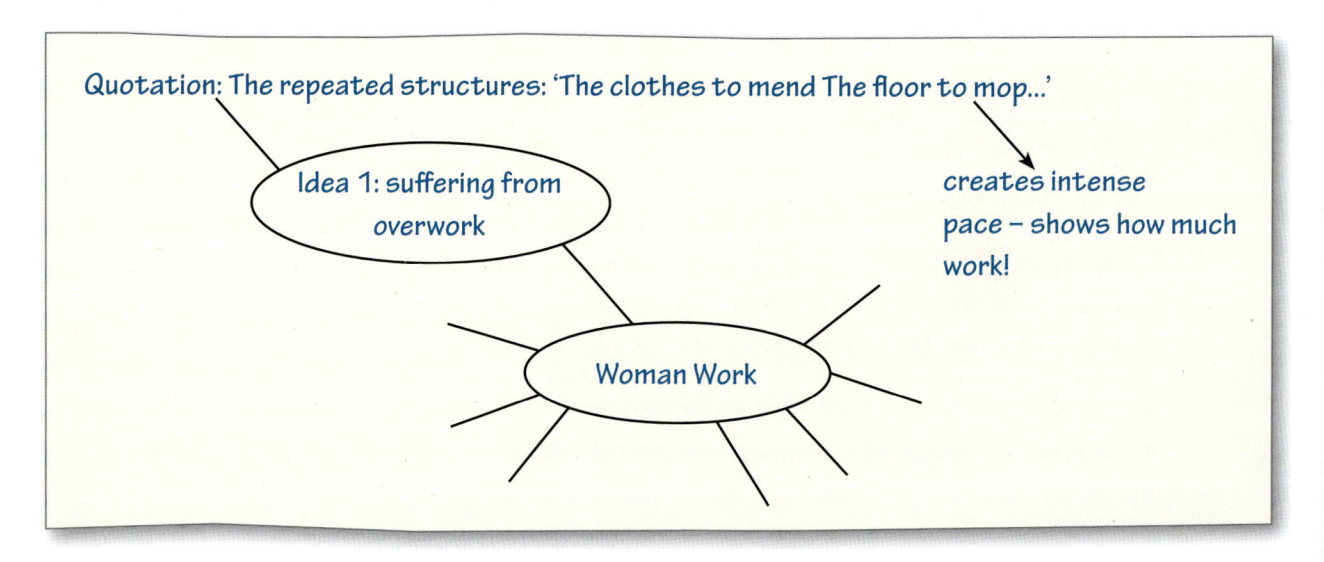

Quotation: The repeated structures: 'The clothes to mend The floor to mop...'

Idea 1: suffering from overwork

creates intense pace – shows how much work!

Woman Work

252 Chapter 6 Preparing for coursework

Chapter 6 . Lesson 2

Remember there are many other methods of planning your work and you might want to consider some of these instead.

4 a) You could also use the grids below to make a list of seven quotations from each of the poems which you might include in your coursework essay. Choose your quotations to show a range of different poetic techniques. Remember that the best quotations are often fairly short.

'Woman Work'	Quotation	Technique and its effect
1	'I've got the children to tend…'	Colloquial tone draws the reader in and makes them empathise with the woman's experiences.
2		
3		

'I Hear America Singing'	Quotation	Technique and its effect
1	'I hear America singing…'	Repetition of line creates effect of emphasising the pleasure gained from work by the speaker in the poem.
2		
3		

b) Try adding these points to the spider diagrams you completed earlier.

Develop the skills

5 Now that you have generated and developed your ideas, you can reorganise your points into a linear bullet-point plan that sequences your ideas into a logical order. You could reflect the following structure:

- **Introduction:** You will need to introduce the poems and the focus of your essay ('thoughts and feelings about working people' and 'language'). It would be helpful if you could link the two poems in some way.
- **First body paragraph:** Interpretation of 'Woman Work' – for example: *The narrator in the poem is overworked but still manages to dream about a better future.*
- **Second body paragraph:** Interpretation of 'Woman Work'

Lesson 6.2 Planning a critical coursework essay

- **Third body paragraph:** Interpretation of 'Woman Work'
- **Fifth body paragraph:** Interpretation of 'I Hear America Singing'
- **Sixth body paragraph:** Interpretation of 'I Hear America Singing'
- **Seventh body paragraph:** Interpretation of 'I Hear America Singing'
- **Conclusion:** You should try to make some sort of connection between the two poems, perhaps giving a sense of overview.

Write down the points you would like to make under each bullet-point heading. Don't worry at this stage about writing in full sentences or linking your points together.

Apply the skills

6. If you want to aim even higher, then you might want to consider linking the points you are making about each poem by comparing them. You are not required to do this but it will make your performance more sophisticated and could help you to write an even more impressive coursework piece. In this case your plan might look like this:

- **Introduction:** Focus on the terms in the question ('working people' and 'language') and remember to link the two poems in some way.
- Aim to write four or five paragraphs during which you develop ideas about the terms in the question while referring to both the set poems at the same time.
- **Conclusion:** You should finish by making connections between the two poems (referring to your title) and by evaluating the poems as a pair. You will need to provide a sense of overview and come to a conclusion about what each of the poets is doing and showing. For example: *Purposeful, masculine work is celebrated by Whitman, whereas Angelou shows us the relentless labour women suffer...*

   You could also end on a new idea or an explanation of a personal response. For example*: I was more engaged by the Angelou poem as it seemed to reflect the modern world I live in...*

Writing a critical coursework essay

Chapter 6 . Lesson 3

How can I write an effective piece of critical coursework about poetry texts?

The purpose of Lessons 6.1, 6.2 and 6.3 is to provide you with a framework to support the process of preparing, planning, writing and editing your coursework piece. You can use this process with any poetry texts.

Start thinking

This section focuses on writing a coursework essay about the poems 'Woman Work' by Maya Angelou and 'I Hear America Singing' by Walt Whitman.

The title of the piece is:

> **How do the poets vividly convey their thoughts and feelings about these working people?**
>
> Remember to consider the poets' use of language, structure and form in your answer.

Always highlight the key terms in the question you are answering to help you focus on them. It can be helpful to reference those key terms in every new paragraph you write.

You should start your essay with an introduction.

It needs to include:

- a reference to the poems you will be covering
- reference to the key terms in the question
- an indication of how you are going to approach the question
- (if possible) links between your chosen poems.

1 **a)** Check the following introductory paragraph against this checklist.

> In both 'Woman Work' by Maya Angelou and 'I Hear America Singing' by Walt Whitman, striking linguistic effects are used by the poets to highlight different working conditions (and the people involved with them). Using a variety of techniques, the poets at times employ similar – but also sometimes strikingly different – methods to present the lives of working people in the United States of America.

b) Do you think this is an effective introduction? What could be added or made clearer?

Explore the skills

Once you have written your introduction, you need to write your main body paragraphs. You'll probably have a further four, five or six paragraphs (depending on the overall length of your coursework piece) before you arrive at your final conclusion.

- Introduction
- Body paragraph 1 – focus on one aspect of your interpretation of 'Woman Work' in relation to the question, supported with textual analysis
- Body paragraph 2 – focus on another aspect of your interpretation of 'Woman Work' in relation to the question, supported with textual analysis
- Optional body paragraph 3 – focus on a different aspect of your interpretation of 'Woman Work' in relation to the question, supported with textual analysis
- Body paragraph 4 – focus on one aspect of 'I Hear America Singing' in relation to the question supported with textual analysis
- Body paragraph 5 – focus on another aspect of 'I Hear America Singing' in relation to the question supported with textual analysis
- Optional body paragraph 6 – focus on a different aspect of 'I Hear America Singing' in relation to the question supported with textual analysis
- Conclusion

2 **a)** Read the following paragraph and identify where it:
- links to the essay title/topic sentence
- includes reference to text/features
- analyses the effect on meaning of the feature identified.

> In contrast, at the start of the second section of 'Woman Work', the move to a different metrical pattern and rhyme scheme ('Shine on me, sunshine/Rain on me, rain') suggests a shift in the mood of the persona. This suggests that the apparently negative mindset of the persona at the start of the poem can be challenged when she remembers more positive aspects of her daily experience and is able to put the challenges life brings into context when they are seen as part of the more fulfilling experiences of being alive.

b) Use one of the ideas you developed in Lesson 6.2, Question 3 to write a paragraph of your own.

As you are trying to develop an argument in your critical essay rather than just listing ideas, you will need to start each paragraph with a connective.

| Therefore | As a result of this | Subsequently |
| However | Moreover | In fact | In this way |

3 **a)** Identify the connective in the response paragraph above.

b) Can you think of any other useful connectives?

If you are feeling confident, and choose to use a plan that compares your poems through every paragraph, you will need to use connectives within your paragraphs to make your meaning clear.

A sophisticated plan that compares poems throughout, might look like this:

> Introduction
> Paragraph 1: First poem and second poem
> Paragraph 2: First poem and second poem
> Paragraph 3: First poem and second poem
> ….
> Conclusion

Lesson 6.3 Writing a critical coursework essay

If you choose to plan this way, then not only do you need to keep returning to the key points in the question and develop an argument using connectives, but you also need to keep comparing the two poems all the way through your essay.

4 **a)** Identify the comparison connective in this paragraph.

> Whereas in 'Woman Work' there is a clear sense of the suffering felt by the woman ('Let me rest tonight'), in 'I Hear America Singing' joy is expressed at their labours by the male protagonists ('Singing with open mouths').

b) If you are feeling confident, write a sentence comparing aspects of the two poems that uses the connective 'whereas'.

Develop the skills

Remember that you are writing a serious, academic essay for this coursework piece.

You will not be expressing your ideas using the everyday **colloquial** (chatty) tone you might use if you were discussing these poems with your friends. Aim for a formal tone.

Here is an example of the expected style:

> Clearly the persona in 'Woman Work' is suffering from her labours and, in the second half of the poem, she makes an extensive appeal ('Let me…') to the elements to sustain her.

Key term

colloquial: informal, chatty language

5 Using this example, try re-writing the following comments in a style more suitable and precise for a piece of IGCSE coursework:

- The woman in 'Woman Work' is having a bad time of it.
- Loads of different men are working hard in 'I Hear America Singing'.
- There's plenty of listing going on in both poems.

Chapter 6 . Lesson 3

> **Apply the skills**

The final paragraph of your coursework piece should be a conclusion. Your conclusion should include:

- reference to both the poems you have been discussing
- a summary of the main findings of your essay
- an interesting final idea to make an impression at the end of your essay.

It's a good idea to start this final paragraph with a standard formulation like: *In conclusion…*

6 Identify the features listed above in this conclusion.

> In *conclusion*, both 'Woman Work' and 'I Hear America Singing' address aspects of working life for ordinary individuals in the United States. Although the challenges of manual labour are never far from the surface of both poems (and at times these can threaten to overwhelm any more optimistic considerations) it is nevertheless the case that the positive features of working life – and of broader existence itself – emerge triumphant in either case. In this way, we are reminded of the power of poetry to offer solace and consolation.

7 a) Read through the essay plan you developed in Lesson 6.2 and decide what you would like to say in your conclusion.

b) Now write your final paragraph. You could try writing two different conclusions, then choose the one you think is most successful.

Writing and drafting

When you have had a good go at writing the first version of your essay, you will have a first draft. This is not the finished piece but – instead – a chance for you to read through, remove anything that doesn't work well, add some new ideas, re-order the information, and check carefully for the following:

- an appropriately formal tone
- a clear focus on the requirements of the title
- effective use of quotations and detailed analysis of the effects of writers' choices.

Remember: the coursework isn't finished until you hand it in!

Chapter 6 . Lesson 4

Planning and preparing an empathic response

How can I work with my drama set text to prepare an empathic coursework piece?

The purpose of Lessons 6.4 and 6.5 is to provide you with a framework to support the process of preparing, planning, writing and editing your empathic coursework piece. You can use this process with any drama text.

Start thinking

Empathy is the ability to understand somebody else's ideas and feelings. For your empathic response, you are going to show that you can 'get under the skin' of one of the characters in a text you have studied, at a key moment in the play or novel, and write as if you are that person, using their voice. You will need to show that you know the text and the character you are writing about well. This is a chance for you to be creative!

This process will be exemplified here by a task on the character of Shylock in Shakespeare's play *The Merchant of Venice*. You can choose a character from a play you know well and follow the same process.

> **Key term**
>
> **empathic:** showing understanding of another person's thoughts and feelings

1. First of all, choose a character from the play you are working on. Make a list of everything you know about the character.

    Consider:
    - appearance/direct description of the character
    - how they move and how they speak
    - their status
    - how they interact with other characters
    - any language or imagery associated with them
    - plot events they feature in
    - what effect they have on the action of the play
    - key moments (for example, important individual speeches, important exchanges with other characters)
    - themes they are associated with
    - how they change and develop through the play.

Chapter 6 . Lesson 4

For Shylock in a Merchant of Venice you might begin:

- **Shylock has a daughter called Jessica.**
- **He is a moneylender.**

2 a) Now find ten key quotations for your character. These could be lines spoken by the character themselves or by another character about them. For example, for Shylock you might begin:

- **'I am a Jew. Hath not a Jew eyes?' (Act 3 Scene 1)**

b) Explain what each quotation reveals about the character.

Explore the skills

Now you're going to look more closely at the demands of an empathic piece. Assuming you are writing about *The Merchant of Venice*, the question you are going to answer for your empathic practice piece is as follows:

> You are Shylock. You have arrived at the courtroom (Act IV, scene i). Write your thoughts.

It is important to use a title like this that focuses on a key moment and allows you to represent the thoughts of the character as you understand them.

Remember that you can adapt this to any other character in any other play.

3 First of all, remind yourself of the action that precedes this scene. You could show this as a storyboard, using five pictures to show the plot.

4 Now reread the opening of Act IV, scene i and remind yourself of what is happening in the courtroom scene. Shylock is in court to demand a pound of Antonio's flesh because the merchant has failed to repay the 3000 ducats owed to the moneylender. Check that you are clear about:

a) when and where this action takes place

b) what immediately precedes it. What do you know about Shylock's feelings towards Antonio by this moment in the play?

c) who is present.

Lesson 6.4 Planning and preparing an empathic response   261

Have a look at this speech from Act IV, scene i in particular – where Shylock tries to explain to the Duke (who will be the judge) exactly why he does not like Antonio:

I have possess'd your grace of what I purpose;	Shylock speaks boldly to the Duke – revealing misplaced confidence/arrogance
And by our holy Sabbath have I sworn	he thinks of the matter in legal terms – revealing that he thinks he is unquestionably right
To have the due and forfeit of my bond:	
If you deny it, let the danger light	the alliteration emphasises how strongly he feels about the subject as he almost spits his words out
Upon your charter and your city's freedom.	
You'll ask me, why I rather choose to have	plans ahead with arguments – good at scheming
A weight of carrion flesh than to receive	
Three thousand ducats: I'll not answer that:	money is on his mind – more concerned with personal gain than with justice or humanity
But, say, it is my humour: is it answer'd?	
What if my house be troubled with a rat	
And I be pleased to give ten thousand ducats	
To have it baned? What, are you answer'd yet?	the use of repeated questions reveals how subtle, persistent and cunning Shylock can be in his approach
Some men there are love not a gaping pig;	
Some, that are mad if they behold a cat;	
And others, when the bagpipe sings i' the nose,	
Cannot contain their urine: for affection,	
Mistress of passion, sways it to the mood	
Of what it likes or loathes. Now, for your answer:	
As there is no firm reason to be render'd,	
Why he cannot abide a gaping pig;	
Why he, a harmless necessary cat;	
Why he, a woollen bagpipe; but of force	
Must yield to such inevitable shame	
As to offend, himself being offended;	
So can I give no reason, nor I will not,	remember why Shylock hates Antonio: he has spat on him, called him a dog, scorned, mocked and humiliated him; his daughter Jessica has run off with his friend; Antonio lends money without charging interest
More than a lodged hate and a certain loathing	
I bear Antonio, that I follow thus	
A losing suit against him. Are you answer'd?	

William Shakespeare, from *The Merchant of Venice*

5 Work through Act IV scene i closely, drawing careful inferences about Shylock's thoughts and feelings. Read the annotations above on this speech, then continue this process of inference for the whole scene.

Develop the skills

Next you need to collect and analyse examples of language from the scene. You will need to use similar language and techniques in your own empathic writing.

6 Read the annotations around the highlighted phrases, then continue this process of identifying and analysing features of Shylock's speech throughout the whole scene.

For example, a semantic field of visceral, disgusting or animal language is highlighted above. Is this perhaps an appeal to the baser instincts of his audience? Does it perhaps reflect Shylock's own anger?

Next answer these questions about the effect of the language used in the scene.

7 a) What is surprising about the tone Shylock chooses to use when he is addressing the Duke? How does this fit with the language of the law and the language of money?

b) How does Shakespeare use language to make us both admire and despise Shylock at the same time?

c) Why does Shylock use quite so many questions in this speech? Does the repeated questioning reflect impatience, bullying, manipulation – or something else?

Apply the skills

By now, you will be developing a real understanding of what is going on in Shylock's mind.

8 Read through the inferences you have made in Questions 5, 6 and 7, then organise them into groups.

You might to choose headings such as:

- How Shylock feels as the case comes to court
- His thoughts about Antonio and the money
- His thoughts and feelings about Jessica's elopement
- How he feels his religion has been insulted
- His thoughts about revenge and why it is so important to him
- How he looks ahead to the possible conclusion of the trial.

You can make a list of different categories for the character you have chosen to write about if you are working on a different text.

Chapter 6 . Lesson 5

Writing an empathic response

How can I write an effective piece of empathic coursework about a drama text?

The purpose of Lessons 6.4 and 6.5 is to provide you with a framework to support the process of preparing, planning, writing and editing your empathic coursework piece. You can use this process with any drama text.

Start thinking

You are now going to pull together the empathic observations you made in Lesson 6.4 and create a voice for your empathic coursework piece. The title of the piece is going to be:

> You are Shylock. You have arrived at the courtroom (Act IV, scene i). Write your thoughts.

But remember that you can use this process and adapt this title for a character in a different play, poem or novel.

1 Highlight the key terms in the title of the coursework piece you will be writing.

Checklist for success

Remember a good answer:

- ✔ adopts an appropriate task and responds well to its terms
- ✔ stays in, and understands, the moment that has been chosen
- ✔ is rooted in the detail of the text, integrating textual reference to support and develop a character's voice (This can be direct quotation, but doesn't have to be. It can be a textual echo or approximation.)
- ✔ uses a convincing voice.

Chapter 6 . Lesson 5

Explore the skills

In Lesson 6.4, you worked through Act IV scene i, drawing out inferences to really understand what was going on in Shylock's mind.

Now think about the best way to organise your coursework piece.

Unlike a critical coursework essay, you do not need a formal introduction/main body/conclusion structure – but you will still need to divide your work into clear, focused paragraphs.

A good way to structure this piece would be:

- first to highlight briefly how Shylock feels about events that have already taken place and how these have led the characters to the courtroom. You could include Antonio's treatment of Shylock and Jessica's elopement

- then to describe Shylock's thoughts and feelings as the trial begins – this might include comments on Shylock's thoughts about Antonio and the money; how he feels his religion has been insulted; his thoughts about revenge and why it is so important to him.

2 Decide on how you want to organise your ideas, write out a skeleton plan, then add inferences and observations to each section.

Develop the skills

The next stage is to create a voice that will reflect Shylock's character, and his thoughts and feelings at this point in the play.

You are not required to use language with the same structure and vocabulary as Shakespeare's, though you can do this if you choose. You can use modern English if you like, but you need to think about how Shylock might express his ideas by drawing on the vocabulary and ideas in the original text.

3   a) Shylock is angry; he wants revenge. How could you show this in the language you choose for him?

      b) Write an angry, vengeful thought in the style of Shylock's voice.

4   a) What other emotions have you decided Shylock is feeling? (For example, hatred or a sense of injustice.)

      b) What techniques might you use to express these feelings?

5   Look back at the work you did in Lesson 6.4 on the language of Act IV scene i.

      a) What semantic fields did you identify?

      b) What imagery did you find?

      c) Did you find any characteristic structural features such as repetition or questions?

      d) What other features did you identify?

In your coursework practice piece, you are going to express some of the thoughts and ideas Shylock has in your own words. You will need to use these language features to help create a sense of Shylock's voice.

Apply the skills

Remember, to be successful, your coursework piece will need to:

- stay in and understand 'the moment' you are describing
- stay rooted in the detail of the text and integrate textual references to support the voice you are creating
- use a convincing voice.

Unlike your discursive coursework piece, you do not need such a formal structure. There is a creative element to the piece and you should feel free to express a range of thoughts in Shylock's mind as he flits from one set of ideas to another.

Remember that you can be creative but – in the end – this coursework piece is an opportunity for you to display your knowledge of the character of Shylock and you should make the most of this in your writing.

6   Compare the following two empathic responses. Which one do you think is more successful? Explain your answer with reference to the checklist above.

Chapter 6 . Lesson 5

a) Does each response stay 'in the moment' and convincingly represent Shylock's thoughts and feelings at that moment?

b) Highlight examples of well-chosen language. What does the language express? How does it relate to the original text?

c) Is Shylock's voice convincing?

Response A

> At last I have a chance to stand up in front of all the most important people in Venice and demand fair treatment. The Duke himself is here to pass judgement and I have as much right as any Christian in this city to have access to a just legal system. I was never keen to lend the money to Bassanio in the first place – especially considering the way Antonio has abused me and my religion in the past. He even spat on me on at least one occasion! Oh dear – I wonder where my daughter Jessica is right now. That lawyer does look strangely familiar…

Response B

> Now I have him on the hip. My chance to feed my ancient grudge has come. I have been called a dog and – if that is the case – then you better beware my fangs. I am determined to have my bond because there is a certain loathing I bear Antonio and now is my chance to gain my revenge just as any Christian in this city of Venice is entitled to the same before the law applied by the Duke. Vengeance is mine! At last I will show this city that a Jew has feelings and emotions just like any other human beings.

Chapter 6 . Lesson 6

Evaluating your work: coursework-style responses

How can I evaluate and improve my coursework response?

Critical essay

> **Texts:** 'Woman Work' by Maya Angelou and 'I Hear America Singing' by Walt Whitman
>
> **Title:** How do the poets vividly convey their thoughts and feelings about these working people?
>
> Remember to consider the poets' use of language, structure and form in your answer.

Before you evaluate how well you have done, check the table on page 275. It will help you decide if your work falls broadly into the first or second category – or outside them.

1. Go through your own response and write annotations around it.

2. Read the following response, thinking about what the writer of the response has done well and what advice they might need to make more progress.

Response 1: extracts from a critical writing coursework response

> Both 'Woman Work' by Maya Angelou and 'I Hear America Singing' by Walt Whitman are about different experiences of work. The former uses language to show a woman doing some work and the latter is mainly about men working although there is also some mention of women in that poem at one point as well.
> 'Woman Work' begins with an extensive list (listing technique) of what one woman has to do in a day of work. She uses the first person to describe it all the way through. It is easy to feel sorry for the woman because the amount of work she is required to get through in a day is very large.

- a clear start focused on linguistic approaches
- some effective comparison, although this is not a requirement of the task
- some good response to the writer's use of language in recognising listing technique
- use of appropriate terminology
- reasonably developed personal response

The poet uses language to suggest she is a poor woman without much joy in her life and the rhyming effect used ('sick' and 'pick') adds to the effect of the monotony of these seemingly never-ending tasks. The litany of tasks she is required to cover conveys the demands on her as a working woman. — *detailed observation about linguistic effects*

The second half of the poem uses different techniques of language as it becomes a kind of prayer to the elements in the natural world (like rain, storm and snow) – 'Let me rest tonight'. It's almost as if the woman feels lonely in her hard work because at the end of the poem she says 'You're all that I can call my own' as if she has nobody to help her. — *thorough use of supporting evidence from the text – using quotation*

*****

'I Hear America Singing' is different because it is mainly men who are being described and I think they sound positive about their work. The structure of the poem on the page makes you feel how positive they are. Whitman says 'I hear America singing' (with the word 'singing' frequently repeated — *literary analysis* to show that it is a long-lasting effect) and the long lines copy the happy sound of a song. The women all appear at the — *linguistic structure* end of the poem and that might be suggesting about them — *contextual observation contributes to the analysis but is not necessary* being second class citizens. It is important to remember that at the time the poem was written (the nineteenth century), there was a major difference between the way that men and women were treated in the society.

*****

In conclusion, in 'Woman Work' by Maya Angelou and 'I Hear — *a clear conclusion* America Singing' by Walt Whitman, we see the poets expressing their views about work. They use a variety of linguistic techniques to suggest what the experience of work is like for the different personas being described. Even though they are writing at different times, from different standpoints, and with slightly different conclusions, it seems that poetry provides a good way to describe this experience — *some stylish expression of ideas* which we all go through at one point or another in our lives.

Comment:
This answer is reasonably developed, relevant and presents some personal response. There is some understanding of the deeper implications of both poems. Some response is made to both writers' use of language and this is backed up with some use of supporting evidence.

3 How could this sample response be improved? Using the table on page 275 and the annotations on the sample response, think about what advice you might give the writer of the response to improve their work. Write your advice in three or more bullet points.

4 Now read a second response to the same question. Think about what is an improvement on the first response.

Response 2

Both 'Woman Work' by Maya Angelou and 'I Hear America Singing' by Walt Whitman approach the key American theme of manual labour from particular (and contrasting) perspectives. In reading these poems – from different centuries – we are reminded that the idea of the American Dream has always taken inspiration from the dignity of work and from the limitless possibilities towards which labour can lead the ambitious man or woman. The poems use language in significantly contrasting ways to explore these ideas. The different tone achieved in each poem (broadly negative in one case; positive in the other) seems to suggest considerably different viewpoints. Clearly work can bring fulfilment in some cases ('strong melodious songs') but can only heighten suffering ('Let me rest') in others. An exploration of gender arguably provides the most fruitful approach to the poems. Clearly the first person persona in 'Woman Work' is female and Angelou is possibly reminding the reader of the historical limitations placed on women in society who were often required to channel their efforts and resources into domestic tasks. The list of activities requiring attention from the narrator (as presented in the first stanza) is overwhelming. It is only in the contrasting second half of the poem (with its four separate stanzas employing an entirely different tone) that the protagonist is allowed to express some of her personal hopes for the future in a litany of prayers full of imagery of the natural world ('sunshine'; 'rain'; 'storm'; 'snowflakes') where both the imperative and personification are employed to good effect ('Shine on me, sunshine'). By contrast, in the work by Whitman a much more optimistic world view is created through the poet's employment of the first person ('I hear...'), exclamations ('robust, friendly'), and a semantic field

Annotations:
- strong comparative approach established from the start – although this is not necessarily a requirement of the task
- relevant contextual information – again an extra rather than a necessity
- focus on linguistic techniques
- incorporates well-selected reference to the poems
- a specific and sophisticated critical line of approach
- appropriate use of technical language
- sophisticated and appropriate expression of ideas
- detailed response to the way the writer achieves effects
- effort is made to keep the two poems 'in play' throughout the essay

Chapter 6 . Lesson 6

of optimism ('the delicious singing of the mother'). The short — **specific linguistic techniques identified**
lines of Angelou are in contrast to Whitman's flowing clauses
and prolific use of enjambment which suggests an outpouring
of joy and positivity. The regularity in Angelou's stanzas is
replaced by an almost free-verse quality as the poet 'sings' his
joy at the very act of being alive. — **use of appropriate technical terminology**

*****

In conclusion, it is clear that both poets are very effective at
using the various linguistic techniques at their disposal to
illustrate the respective (yet related) ideas which they are
portraying in these poems. From Whitman's long effusions of
joy to Angelou's cramped utterances of suffering we experience – — **linguistic analysis**
as the reader – a variety of responses to the world of work as
cleverly portrayed via the respective use of language by each
poet. The contrast between the way in which the two poems
explore work is a reminder of the ever-present contradictions
within the American dream itself.

Comment:

This is a sustained response showing personal and evaluative engagement with task and text. It is a sophisticated and literary response to the question. The writer of the response sustains personal engagement with the task – and with both the poems – throughout the essay. There are signs of individuality, insight and flair throughout this sensitive and skilful answer.

5 What advice might the writer of this response need to make even more progress? Use the table on page 275 to guide your ideas.

Empathic writing

Text: *The Merchant of Venice* by William Shakespeare
Title: You are Shylock. You have arrived at the courtroom (Act IV, scene i). Write your thoughts.

Before you evaluate how well you have done, check the empathic writing descriptors on page 275. They will help you decide if your work falls broadly into the first or second category – or outside them.

1 Go through your own response and write annotations around it.

2 Read the following response, thinking about what the writer has done well and what advice they might need to make more progress.

Empathic response 1: extracts from an empathic writing coursework response

> My time in court has arrived! The journey here has been a long one. So much is taking place in this changing city at the moment and it is difficult to keep up in a world where so much is happening. This is the moment for Shylock to be in the limelight though.
>
> *****
>
> But at last I have the chance to stand up in front of all the most important people in Venice and be treated fairly. The Duke himself is here to judge me and I have as much right as any Christian in this city to have access to a good legal system. I was never keen to lend the money to Antonio in the first place, especially when you think about the way he has insulted me personally – and my religion – in the past. He even spat on me once! Why should Jewish people be treated any differently from Christians – or even from Moors? We have exactly the same feelings as any other human being: stick a pin in us and we are bound to bleed just like our Christian neighbour.
>
> *****
>
> My ultimate aim from all of this is to gain a pound of Antonio's flesh. Although I seem to be a villain I also have some positive characteristics – although it's true that in some ways I could be said to love money more than my own daughter. Oh dear. That reminds me – I wonder where my daughter Jessica is at the moment? I am really concerned about her following her recent eloping. The lawyer is now entering the court and the first thought to enter my head is this: 'Can such a young, effeminate-looking man be a sensible person for a lost soul like Antonio to put his trust in?' Surely this will be playing straight into my hands. Revenge is what I want and revenge I will get. And if Antonio bleeds to death when that pound of flesh is cut from his body then it will be nobody's fault but his own.
>
> *****
>
> And now hush descends in the court. How could I possibly lose? I am looking forward to the hours ahead.

Annotations:
- introductory statement – 'in the moment'
- factually correct outline of the situation for this moment
- reference to the original play
- textual reference
- specific allusion to an earlier line in the play
- textual reference
- some attempt to express the complexity of the character
- some subtlety
- some sense of a conclusion – structure

272 Chapter 6 Preparing for coursework

Chapter 6 . Lesson 6

> *Comment:*
> The response uses expression that suits the character at the chosen moment. Voice is sustained effectively at times. There is a good understanding of the moment and the response uses detail from the text to support a sense of voice. Some of the deeper implications of the text are understood and suitable features of expression are often used to present the character of Shylock. There is good use of supporting evidence from the play.
> **The task:** this is a good empathic task. The character and the moment for the empathic response are given, followed by the instruction 'Write your thoughts'.

3 How could this sample response be improved? Using the empathic writing level descriptors on page 276 and the annotations on the sample response, think about what advice you might give the writer of the response to improve their work. Write your advice in three or more bullet points.

4 Now read a second response to the same task. Think about what the writer has done that is an improvement on the first response.

Empathic response 2: extracts from an empathic writing coursework response

> Here I stand in court – at last!
> This is my moment of triumph so long awaited – and before the Duke of Venice himself! It gives me great pleasure to survey the whole of Venetian society in its greatest pomp standing before me and me alone!
> I stand in this court a victim not only personally but also representing the centuries of oppression my race has suffered. No more shall members of the merchant class like Antonio be able to accuse me and treat me like an inferior dog or other animal. How dare anybody spit on me! I am a human being like anybody else – I bleed; I cry; I have feelings. I am a Jew. Well – don't Jews have eyes like any other human being? Why cannot people appreciate that Jews are like anybody else on this earth? Indeed we are God's chosen people.
> *****

Annotations:
- 'in the moment' is established
- awareness of context which helps contribute towards the authenticity of the voice
- reference to events and language in the play to create Shylock's voice (animal imagery)
- linguistic reference that is typical of Shylock: the venom here is typical of his 'voice'
- link to the 'If you prick us…' speech but now 'in the moment' and matching Shylock's voice elsewhere in the play

Lesson 6.6 Evaluating your work: coursework-style responses

> Now it is my turn to gain revenge and cannot you see why this is indeed justified? This is no place to talk of humility when revenge itself is on the menu. I will have that pound of flesh and the victory will be mine. No more shall people take advantage of me. Why – even my own daughter has been disrespectful to me with her recent elopement to the extent that I am unsure whether I miss her or my stolen ducats more.
>
> *****
>
> Now on to my moment in the limelight – although the undoubted feminine qualities of that young lawyer are somewhat disconcerting. How could anything but good for me come of this moment? – with Antonio and Bassanio the undoubted losers. This is no place to talk of mercy.

- reference to specific event/language – appropriate to Shylock's voice in its concern for Jessica but also for money
- reference to an event later in the scene – but remaining in the moment

Comment:

Sustained engagement with the voice and character at the chosen moment. Remains 'in the moment' throughout. This is a sophisticated and well-expressed response, which reveals a clear understanding of the moment. There is clear personal engagement with the play and the voice of Shylock throughout is highly convincing. There is excellent response to Shakespeare's language and to the events in the rest of the play.

This is a good empathic task. The character and the moment for the empathic response are given, followed by the instruction 'Write your thoughts'.

5 What advice might the writer of this response need to make even more progress? Use the empathic writing level descriptors on page 276 to guide your ideas.

Chapter 6 . Lesson 6

Critical coursework assignment

What are the features of a *reasonably developed, relevant* personal response?

Knowledge	- You show how you know the text well by making reference to it and/or by quoting from it. - You make points that are **relevant** to the task set.
Understanding	- You show a **sound** understanding of the text, reading beyond the surface to explore implicit meanings. - You **develop your ideas** on themes, characterisation or ideas.
Language and effects	- You write about **some** of the ways in which the writer uses language, structure and form. - You make **some exploration** of the effects of the writer's choices and how these effects are created.
Personal response	- You make your own honest and **considered** response to the text. - You show **some development of your own ideas** about the text and task.

What are the features of a response showing *sustained personal and evaluative engagement* with task and text?

Knowledge	- You show a **detailed** grasp of the text as a whole and a **deep** understanding of the task. - You support your **original** ideas with **carefully selected**, well-integrated reference to the text.
Understanding	- You show a sophisticated understanding of the implicit meaning of the ideas, characterisation and themes in the text. - You show your ability to **analyse, evaluate and interpret** the text showing **individuality and insight**.
Language and effects	- You examine **in depth** the way the writer uses **language, structure and form** and you explore different **interpretations**. - You show the ability to make a **close analysis** of extracts from the text and (where appropriate to the question) respond to the writer's effects in the text as a whole.
Personal response	- You make a **convincing** response, showing deep interest, understanding and an involvement with both text and task. - You have your own individual **ideas and judgements** about the text and express them with **confidence and enthusiasm**.

Lesson 6.6 Evaluating your work: coursework-style responses

Empathic Coursework assignment

What are the features of a response showing suitable expression?

- The language chosen and the voice created are appropriate to the character.
- You show a knowledge of what the character knows, thinks and feels at that moment in the text.

What are the features of a response showing sustained engagement?

- You create a convincing voice for the character, reflecting characteristic modes of speech or using textual echoes.
- You show perceptive and original insight into what the character knows, thinks and feels at that moment in the text.

Glossary of key terms

abstract: the opposite of concrete; something that cannot be seen, like an emotion

achronological: events are told in a different order from the order they occur in time

adjectives: words that describe a noun

adversary: enemy or rival

alliteration: repeated consonant sounds at the start of a sequence of words

ambiguous: open to more than one interpretation

analepsis or flashback: the story cuts backwards in time to an event which happened earlier

anaphora: the deliberate repetition of the first part of a sentence for effect

antagonist: a character who opposes the hero or heroine

archaic language: words no longer in everyday use, and which give the impression of coming from a historical time period

assonance: the repetition of vowel sounds in a sequence of words with different consonant beginnings

atmosphere: the mood of a text

autobiography: someone's life story told from their own point of view

biased: taking a particular side

Bildungsroman: German term meaning 'education or growth novel'

caesura: a pause at or near the middle of a poetic line

central themes: key ideas or themes that occur throughout a text

chronological: events are told in the order they occur in time

cliffhanger: an ending which leaves the reader in suspense

colloquial: informal, chatty language

connotations: the associations brought to mind by a word or phrase

context: background to a text that aids in understanding the text

conventions: the usual rules or expectations of a text type

diction: the speaker's style of expression and the wording or phrasing they use

empathic: showing understanding of another person's thoughts and feelings

empathises: able to put yourself in the shoes of someone else and understand their situation

enjambment: a continuation of a phrase beyond the end of a line of poetry

epigraph: a short phrase at the beginning of a text that summarises the content or themes

epitaph: a phrase written in memory of a person who has died

exclamations: phrases or sentences which indicate surprise, shock or anger

extended metaphor: an image which is extended across a piece of writing

fiction: text dealing with imagined scenarios, imagined characters and events

first person: the narrator is within the story, giving their own point of view

first person plural: voicing the collective thoughts of several narrators

flashbacks: when a character suddenly goes back in time to earlier events

'flat' character: minor characters may be straightforward and 'flat' in that the reader never really gets to see their thought processes or empathises with them in the same way as a main character

flaw: a character weakness, such as pride

foreshadow: hint at events which will come later in the plot

form: the type of poem, which may follow rules about a set number of lines a set rhyme scheme and a set metre or rhythm for each line

free indirect style: a third person narrative where the narrator adopts the voice of a character, seeming to merge first person subjectivity with third person narration

genre: category or type of story

Gothic literature: a popular form of storytelling which came to prominence in the 17th century. It is a very broad genre but often includes supernatural or dream-like happenings; a villain who seeks to destroy or corrupt an innocent, younger person; gloomy, remote settings such as castles or ruins in mountainous areas or forests

hybrid: a text combining conventions of two or more genres

hyperbole: exaggeration for effect

imagery: vivid pictures created by words and phrases
infer: work out from clues
instigate: to bring about or set something in motion
interact: how people behave towards each other
ironic: when words and their apparent meanings are deliberately the opposite of the situation or intended meaning
literal: the usual, basic meaning of a word or image
metaphor: a stronger form of comparison that states that something really *is* something else
metaphorical: symbolic or figurative meaning of a word or image
minor character: a character who may influence a story but is not the main focus
minor sentences: phrases that stand for a whole sentence but omit an element, such as the subject
monologues: any long speech made by a character
mood: the feeling or atmosphere of a piece of writing
motif: recurring image or idea
motivations: reasons for a character's behaviour
multi-dimensional characters: characters who have a range of aspects to them – perhaps surprising ones (for example, an apparent villain who we learn is a carer for his old mother)
multiple narrators: many narrators providing a range of perspectives on the same event
narration: the telling, or manner of telling, of a story
narrators: people telling stories
non-fiction: text dealing with the real world, concerning real people and events
non-metrical: without a regular rhythm
omniscient narrator: all-seeing – the narrator knows everything about the character and the story
onomatopoeia: the sound of the word matches its meaning
oxymoron: combination of opposing ideas, for example, 'white blackness'
pastoral: of the countryside
pathetic fallacy: when human emotion is attributed to a natural scene, often the weather
person: point of view from which communication is delivered
personification: the attribution of human characteristics to things, abstract ideas
plosive: repetition or grouping of /b/ /p/ /t/ /d/ sounds
prolepsis or flash-forward: the story cuts forward in time to an event which will happen later
props: objects which are used by actors (for example, a cup or a letter)
protagonist: the leading character in a drama
puns: usually playing on two meanings of the same word or two words with the same sound to create humour. For example: 'I know the best *plaice* to buy fish'

quest: a journey in search of something or someone
reading: a way of interpreting a text
repetition: repeated words or phrases for impact or rhythmic effect
secondary theme: a less important theme or idea that is either explored in less depth, or is only relevant to certain parts of the text
second person: often found in advertising and poetry, this directly addresses the reader
semantic field: a set of words or phrases that can be grouped by their meaning, linked to a particular subject: for example, 'battle', 'helmet', 'gun', 'enemy' are from the semantic field of war
set: the objects – such as walls or furniture – which create the background for a play
sibilance: when words near each other begin with the same letter
simile: comparison made between two different objects, people, and so on, using the word 'like' or 'as'
soliloquies: longer speeches made by a character when they are on their own, which reveal their thoughts
speaker: the person in a poem who 'speaks' or describes the events
staging: the set, props, lighting and design that create the space in which a play takes place
statements: sentences in which a main idea or event is declared
status: level of power
stock characters: characters with very recognisable features or roles in stories (in fairy tales, these might be the evil stepmother or the handsome prince)
subjective: a personal view
sub-plot: a secondary plot, running alongside the main plot
superlative: adjective expressing the highest degree, for example, best, most
suspense: anxious or fearful expectation
symbols: when an image or description represents a wider or more general idea, such as spring flowers representing new life
syntax: word order
theme: a key idea running through a text
third person limited: the narrator is outside the story. However, their scope is more limited, following just one character
third person omniscient: the narrator is outside the story. They seem omniscient (all-knowing), observing multiple characters and events
tone: the voice, attitude or feeling created by the writer's language choices
viewpoints: the positions from which stories are told

Acknowledgements

The publishers gratefully acknowledge the permission granted to reproduce copyright material in this book. Every effort has been made to trace copyright holders and to obtain their permission for the use of copyright material. The publishers will gladly receive any information enabling them to rectify any error or omission at the first opportunity. The publishers would like to thank the following for permission to reproduce copyright material:

An extract on p.11 from The Piano Teacher by Janice Y. K. Lee, copyright © Janice Y. K. Lee, 2009. Reprinted by permission of HarperCollins Publishers Ltd and Viking Books, an imprint of Penguin Publishing Group, a division of Penguin Random House LLC. All rights reserved; Extracts on pp.14, 15 from Spilled Water by Sally Grindley, Bloomsbury Publishing Plc., copyright © Sally Grindley, 2005. Reproduced with permission; Poetry on p.17 'Yusman Ali, Charcoal Seller' by Ian Macdonald from Jaffo the Calypsonian, Peepal Tree Press, 1994. Reproduced with permission; Extracts on pp.19, 21 from 'The Homecoming' by Laila Lalami, published in Hope and Other Dangerous Pursuits, Algonquin, 2005; An extract on p.20 from 'The Werewolf' from The Bloody Chamber by Angela Carter, published by Gollancz, 1979, copyright © Angela Carter. Reproduced by permission of the author's estate c/o Rogers, Coleridge & White Ltd., 20 Powis Mews, London W11 1JN; Poetry on p.20 'The Closed School' by Raymond Wilson published in To be a Ghost, Penguin Books 1993, p.61, copyright © Raymond Wilson, 1991. Reproduced by permission of Penguin Books Ltd; An extract on p.29 from The Narrow Road to the Deep North by Richard Flanagan, published by Chatto & Windus and Vintage, copyright © Richard Flanagan, 2013. Reproduced by permission of The Random House Group Ltd; Alfred A. Knopf, an imprint of the Knopf Doubleday Publishing Group, a division of Penguin Random House LLC and Penguin Random House Australia. All rights reserved; An extract on p.30 from 'The Bed Sitting Room' by Maureen Ismay, from Watchers and Seekers', ed. Rhonda Cobham and Merle Collins, Cambridge University Press, p.40. First published in 1987 by The Women's Press Ltd, First published in this edition by Cambridge University Press 1990. Collection copyright © Rhonda Cobham and Merle Collins, 1987, Introduction copyright © Rhonda Cobham and Merle Collins, 1989. Supplementary material © Cambridge University Press, 1990. The copyright in each of the poems in this volume remains with the original copyright holder. No part of any work in this collection may be reproduced without permission first being obtained from the copyright holder; An extract on p.31 from 'The Coalminer's Scarf' by Russell Celyn Jones, published in Time Out Book of New York Short Stories, ed. Nicholas Royle, p.5, Penguin. Reproduced by permission of the author; Extracts on pp.39, 40 from The Wasp Factory by Iain Banks published by Abacus, copyright © Iain Banks, 1984. Used with permission from Little, Brown Book Group Ltd and Simon & Schuster, Inc. All rights reserved; Extracts on pp.42-43 from 'Everyday Use' by Alice Walker from The Complete Stories, The Women's Press, 1994. Reproduced by permission of The Joy Harris Literary Agent, Inc. for the author and Houghton Mifflin Harcourt; Poetry on pp.44-45 'Nettles' by Vernon Scannell, published in New and Collected Poems 1950-1993, Robson Books Ltd. Reproduced by permission of the Estate of Vernon Scannell; Poetry on pp.46, 47-48 'The Manhunt' by Simon Armitage, published in The Not Dead, Pomona Press, pp.78-80, copyright © Simon Armitage, 2007. Reproduced by permission of Faber & Faber Ltd and David Godwin Associates Ltd; Poetry on p.54 'Between Walls' by William Carlos Williams, from The Collected Poems: Volume I, 1909-1939, copyright © New Directions Publishing Corp, 1938. Reprinted by permission of New Directions Publishing Corp and Carcanet Press Limited; An extract on p.64 from Brighton Rock by Graham Greene, Vintage Classics, copyright Graham Greene, 1938. Reproduced by permission of David Higham Associates Ltd; Extracts on p.66 from Adverbs by Daniel Handler, HarperCollins, copyright © Daniel Handler, 2006. Reprinted by permission of HarperCollins Publishers Ltd and Charlotte Sheedy Literary Agency, Inc.; Extracts on pp.67, 68 from Keep The Aspidistra Flying by George Orwell, Secker and Penguin Books, 2000, copyright © Eric Blair, 1936; the Estate of the late Sonia Brownwell Orwell, 1956; © renewed 1984; This edition © 1987, 1999. Reproduced by permission of The Random House Group Ltd; Penguin Books Limited; Houghton Mifflin Harcourt Publishing Company and Bill Hamilton as the Literary Executor of the Estate of the Late Sonia Brownell Orwell. All rights reserved; Extract on p.68 from 'The Flowers' by Alice Walker from The Complete Stories, The Women's Press, 1994. Reproduced by permission of The Joy Harris Literary Agent, Inc. for the author and Houghton Mifflin Harcourt; Extracts on pp.75, 76 from As I Lay Dying by William Faulkner, published by Vintage 2004, copyright © William Faulkner, 1930, © renewed 1957/1958. Reproduced by permission of Curtis Brown, London on behalf of the Estate of the author; W. W. Norton & Company, Inc.; and Random House, an imprint and division of Penguin Random House LLC. All rights reserved; An extract on p.77 from The Bluest Eye by Toni Morrison, published by Chatto & Windus, copyright © Toni Morrison, 1970, 1979, © renewed 1998. Reproduced by permission of The Random House Group Ltd and Alfred A. Knopf, an imprint of the Knopf Doubleday Publishing Group, a division of Penguin Random House LLC. All rights reserved; An extract on p.81 from The Thing Around Your Neck by Chimamanda Ngozi Adichie, HarperCollins, 2009, p.116, copyright © Chimamanda Ngozi Adichie, 2009. Reprinted by permission of HarperCollins Publishers Ltd; The Wylie Agency (UK) Limited and Penguin Random House Canada Limited; An extract on p.81 from Paddy Clarke Ha Ha Ha by Roddy Doyle published by Secker, copyright © Roddy Doyle, 1993. Reproduced by permission of The Random House Group Ltd and Viking Books, an imprint of Penguin Publishing Group, a division of Penguin Random House LLC. All rights reserved; Extracts on pp.82, 99 from Things Fall Apart by Chinua Achebe, William Heinemann, 1958, Penguin Classics, 2001, copyright © Chinua Achebe, 1958. Reproduced permission of Penguin Books Ltd and of The Wylie Agency (UK) Limited; Extracts on pp.82, 83 from The Poisonwood Bible by Barbara Kingsolver, Faber and Faber 1999, copyright © Barbara Kingsolver, 1998. Reproduced by permission of Faber & Faber Limited and HarperCollins Publishers; Extract on p.91 from The Siege of Krishnapur by J.G. Farrell, published by Wiedenfeld & Nicolson, 1973, copyright © J. G. Farrell, 1973. Reproduced by permission of the author's estate c/o Rogers, Coleridge & White Ltd., 20 Powis Mews, London, W11 1JN and The Orion Publishing Group, London; An extract on p.96 from Mom & Me & Mom by Maya Angelou, published by Virago, copyright © Maya Angelou, 2013. Reproduced by permission of Little, Brown Book Group Ltd and Random House, an imprint and division of Penguin Random House LLC. All rights reserved; Poetry on p.129 'This is just to say' by William Carlos Williams, published in The Collected Poems: Volume I, 1909-1939, copyright © New Directions Publishing Corp, 1938. Reprinted by permission of New Directions Publishing Corp and Carcanet Press Limited; Poetry on p.136 'The Fist' by Derek Walcott published in Collected Poems: 1948-1984, Farrar, Straus & Giroux, copyright © Derek Walcott, 1986. Reproduced by permission of Faber & Faber Limited and Farrar, Straus & Giroux Publishers;

Poetry on p.139 'Sleep Training' by Siân Hughes, published in The Missing, Salt Publishing, 2009. Reproduced by permission of the author Siân Hughes; Poetry on p.141 'What lips my lips have kissed, and where, and why' by Edna St. Vincent Millay, published in Collected Poems, copyright © Edna St. Vincent Millay and Norma Millay Ellis, 1923, 1951. Reprinted with the permission of The Permissions Company, Inc., on behalf of Holly Peppe, Literary Executor, The Millay Society, www.millay.org; Poetry on p.142 'I(a' by E. E. Cummings, published in Complete Poems: 1904-1962, ed. George J. Firmage, copyright © the Trustees for the E. E. Cummings Trust, 1958, 1986, 1991. Used by permission of Liveright Publishing Corporation; Poetry on p.143 'Quick Draw' by Carol Ann Duffy, published in Rapture, Macmillan. Reproduced by permission of Macmillan Publishers; Poetry on pp.153-154 'Mrs Faust' by Carol Ann Duffy, published in The World's Wife, Picador, 1999, copyright © Carol Ann Duffy. Reproduced by permission of the author c/o Rogers, Coleridge & White Ltd., 20 Powis Mews, London, W11 1JN; Poetry on p.157 'We real cool' by Gwendolyn Brooks, published in The Essential Gwendolyn Brooks, American Poets Project, Library of America. Reprinted by consent of Brooks Permissions; Poetry on pp.160-161 "Stopping by Woods on a Snowy Evening" by Robert Frost published in The Poetry of Robert Frosh, ed. Edward Connery Lathem, copyright © Henry Holt and Company, 1923, 1969, © Robert Frost, 1951. Reprinted by permission of The Random House Group Ltd and Henry Holt and Company. All rights reserved; Poetry on p.165 'Blessing' by Imtiaz Dharker, published in Postcards from god, Bloodaxe Books, 1997 p.45. Reproduced with permission from Bloodaxe Books, www.bloodaxebooks.com; Poetry on p.181 'Harmonium' by Simon Armitage, published in Book of Matches, Faber & Faber, 2001 and The Unaccompanied Poems, Knopf, 2017 copyright © Simon Armitage. Reproduced by permission of Faber & Faber Limited and Alfred A. Knopf, an imprint of the Knopf Doubleday Publishing Group, a division of Penguin Random House LLC. All rights reserved; Extracts on pp.200, 201, 240-241 from The Ash Girl by Timberlake Wertenbaker, Faber & Faber, 2000, copyright © Timberlake Wertenbaker, 2000. Reproduced by permission of Faber & Faber Limited; An extract on p.203 from *Collins Drama – Treasure Island* by Ken Ludwig adapted from the novel by Robert Louis Stevenson, copyright © Ken Ludwig, 2007. Reprinted by permission of HarperCollins Publishers Ltd; An extract on p.209 from Beauty and the Beast by Laurence Boswell, Nick Hern Books, pp.46-47. Reproduced by permission of Nick Hern Books; An extract on p.211 from Humble Boy by Charlotte Jones, Faber & Faber, 2000, p.1. Reproduced by permission of Faber & Faber Limited and United Agents; An extract on pp.212-213 from 'Scene One' from 'Ti-jean and His Brothers' from Dream on Monkey Mountain by Derek Walcott, copyright © Derek Walcott, 1970. Reproduced by permission of Farrar, Straus & Giroux; Extracts on pp.214, 215-216 from Private Peaceful by Michael Morpurgo, adapted by Simon Reade, copyright © Michael Morpurgo, 2003. Stage adaptation, copyright © Simon Reade, 2004, 2012. Reproduced by permission of Berlin Associates Ltd; Extracts on pp.219, 220 from 'Making History' from Plays 2 by Brian Friel, copyright © Brian Friel, 1999. By Brian Friel. Reproduced by permission of Faber & Faber Ltd and Farrar, Straus & Giroux; An extract on p.220 from Waiting for Godot by Samuel Beckett, copyright © Grove Press, Inc., 1954, © renewed 1982 by Samuel Beckett. Reproduced by permission of Faber & Faber Ltd and Grove/Atlantic, Inc. Any third party use of this material, outside of this publication, is prohibited; An extract on p.223 from 'A slight ache' from Complete Works, Vol 1 by Harold Pinter, Methuen, 1976, copyright © H. Pinter Ltd, 1962, 1964. Reproduced by permission of Faber & Faber Ltd and Grove/Atlantic, Inc. Any third party use of this material, outside of this publication, is prohibited; and Poetry on pp.250-251, 252 "Woman Work" by Maya Angelou, published in And Still I Rise: A Book of Poems, copyright © Maya Angelou, 1978. Reproduced by permission of Little, Brown Book Group Ltd and Random House, an imprint and division of Penguin Random House LLC. All rights reserved.

The publishers would like to thank the following for permission to use reproduce pictures in these pages:

Key: t = top, b = bottom, l = left, r = right, c = centre

p 12 AF archive, p 14 Thomas Cockrem, p 16l Everett Collection Inc, p 16r Mim Friday/all Alamy Stock Photo; p 9 Cebas, p 11 jannoon028, p 13 Bruno Passigatti/all Shutterstock; p 19 Best_photo_studio, p 21 Morocko, p 22 Jaydon Hartman/all Shutterstock; p 24l sjbooks, p 24cl gbimages, p 24cr sjbooks, p 24r sjbooks, p 27b Lebrecht Music and Arts Photo Library/all Alamy Stock Photo; p 29 Bogdan Sonjachnyj, p 28 Michael Warwick, p 26 Carlos Amarillo/all Shutterstock; p 30 ableimages, p 34 Chronicle/all Alamy Stock Photo; p 36 RosnaniMusa, p 39, p 41 Tatiana Grozetskaya, p 42 Foxtography, p 44 Lungu Denis, p 46 horkins, p 50 Matt Gibson/all Shutterstock; p 52t Chronicle of World History/Alamy Stock Photo; p 52b NaomiTurtle/Shutterstock; p 86 David Bagnall Photo, p 87 thislife pictures/all Alamy Stock Photo; p 88l Mitar Vidakovic, p 88c Martin Spurny, p 88r Supriyo Chatterji, p 91 AlokVerma/all Shutterstock, p 93 Everett Collection Inc, p 94 ClassicStock, p 96 Paul Fearn/all Alamy Stock Photo; p 57 SERGEI PRIMAKOV, p 58l alberto clemares exposito/all Shutterstock; p 58cl Lukeson / Alamy Stock Photo; p 58cr Robert Hoetink, p 58l Lucky Business, p 60 Korionov; pp 60-61 Iakov Kalinin/all Shutterstock, p 62, p 63 Trinity Mirror/Mirrorpix/Alamy Stock Photo; p 64 Fotos593, p 66 Jupiterimages, p 68l Algol, p 68r Creaturart Images, p 72t kurhan, p 72b Lindasj22/all Shutterstock; p 76 PSC-Photography/Alamy Stock Photo; p 79 africa924, p 80 Jack.Q/all Shutterstock; p 82 Photo 12/Alamy Stock Photo; p 98 chronicler, p 105 Zamurovic Photography, pp 110-111 Smileus, p 115 Vyntage Visuals, p 121 Aaltair, p 158 Robsonphoto, p 161 Victorian Traditions, p 163 AJP, p 172 pixelparticle, p 179 Antoine Beyeler, p 126b Zeljko Radojko, p 129 nienora, p 130 Laborant, p 132 Ed Waldrop, p 134 Improvisor/all Shutterstock, p 136 Granger Historical Picture Archive/Alamy Stock Photo; p 139 Fokin Oleg, p 140 Inna Reznik, p 142 Nando Machado, p 142 Platslee, p 142 Luigi Trevisi, p 143 Songquan Deng, p 144 Nataliia Sokolovska/all Shutterstock; p 146 Chronicle, p 148 Granger Historical Picture Archive/all Alamy Stock Photo; p 150 Tadija Savic/Shutterstock; p 154 John Baran/Alamy Stock Photo; p 155 Kucher Serhii/Shutterstock, p 224 Geraint Lewis, p 225 Geraint Lewis/all Alamy Stock Photo; p 190, p 191 Heritage Image Partnership Ltd, p 192 Geraint Lewis, p 195 Everett Collection Inc/all Alamy Stock Photo; p 198 Donald Cooper/Photostage, p 199 Johan Persson/ArenaPAL, p 200 Petr Jilek/Shutterstock, p 202 Johan Persson/ArenaPAL, p 204 Johan Persson/ArenaPAL; p 208 Nenad Basic/Shutterstock; p 211 Moviestore collection Ltd, p 213 Geraint Lewis/all Alamy Stock Photo; p 214 Zorro 12, p 215 Matthew J Thomas/all Shutterstock; p 217 Vibrant Pictures/Alamy Stock Photo; p 218 dwphotos, p 221 Dark Moon Pictures, p 228 Sergey Petrov, p 236 Stacyann 105, p 241 Alex Cherepanov, p 243 welburnstuart/all Shutterstock; p 246 Big Cheese Photo LLC/Alamy Stock Photo; p 247 Donna Beeler, p 248 nature photos, p 252tl ankudi, p 252tc By ESB Professional, p 252tr Samarets, p 252bl Mila Basenko, p 252bc IconBunny, p 252br Jane Kelly, p 254 Bildagentur Zoonar GmbH, p 255 Uber Images, p 256 Everett Historical/all Shutterstock, p 258, p 261 Entertainment Pictures/Alamy Stock Photo, p 263 cristapper/Shutterstock, p 265 Everett Collection Inc/Alamy Stock Photo; p 7 PUSCAU DANIEL, p 33 Tatiana Grozetskaya, p 57 connel, p 127 Zeljko Radojko/all Shutterstock; p 191 jeremy sutton-hibbert/Alamy Stock Photo, p 249 By wavebreakmedia/Shutterstock